HOLONOMICS

Praise for Holonomics

Fritjof Capra, author of *The Hidden Connections,* coauthor of *The Systems View of Life*

"The authors of this remarkable book have distilled the essence of the ideas and values taught at Schumacher College, a unique transformative learning centre based on systemic thinking and grounded in deep ecology, and they show how these teachings can be applied with many case studies of enlightened businesses. *Holonomics* is a powerful antidote to the fragmentation and materialistic orientation of today's dominant culture."

Margaret J. Wheatley, author of *Leadership and the New Science*

"The central question of our time is 'How can we live divided no more?' This wonderful book provides the science, the philosophy and the business practices that lead us to an answer. The Robinsons present the concepts and thinkers who first awakened a new sense of excitement and possibility in me many years ago. What a gift to have these monumental, mind-changing ideas woven together skilfully in one book. If you absorb their perspectives, you can't help but have your mind changed – for the benefit of both people and planet."

H. Thomas Johnson, Professor of Sustainability Thinking, Portland State University, and co-author of *Profit Beyond Measure*

"In *Holonomics: Business Where People and Planet Matter*, Simon and Maria Robinson draw from works by several holistic thinkers, most notably the late Henri Bortoft, to present a powerful mode of thinking that promises to deliver a new and life-enhancing approach to human economic activity. I urge all economists, elected public officials, and people in business to connect with the timely and important message the Robinsons convey to us in *Holonomics*."

HOLONOMICS

BUSINESS WHERE PEOPLE AND PLANET MATTER

SIMON ROBINSON AND
MARIA MORAES ROBINSON

Floris Books

In memory of Henri Bortoft
1938–2012

Published in 2014 by Floris Books
© 2014 Simon Robinson & Maria Moraes Robinson

Simon Robinson and Maria Moraes Robinson have asserted
their rights under the Copyright, Designs and Patent Act 1988
to be identified as the Authors of this Work

 This book is also available
as an eBook

British Library CIP Data available
ISBN 978-178250-061-2
Printed in Great Britain
by Bell & Bain, Glasgow

Contents

Acknowledgements

Holonomics came about after many requests for recommended texts from our students at Sustentare Business School who were looking to explore more deeply the themes of complexity, sustainability, strategy, innovation, leadership and change management. Our aim was to capture in a single volume the philosophy and teachings from Schumacher College, and particularly the unique Masters degree in Holistic Science – a radical rethinking of our ecological, social and economic systems, taught by some of the most cutting-edge and influential thinkers, practitioners and scientists around the world. In structuring the book into three parts – *The Dynamics of Seeing, The Dynamics of Nature* and *The Dynamics of Business* – we then wished to show how these teachings could be implemented in a practical manner in business, governmental and other organisations based on our many years of experience in industry, in both the private and public sectors.

We would like to thank our friends, colleagues and students at Schumacher College and at Sustentare Business School who have provided such rich discussions and dialogue, exploring the many themes in our book. We are especially grateful to Satish Kumar, Fritjof Capra, Margaret Wheatley, Ingrid Stefanovic, H. Thomas Johnson, Wilmar Cidral, Giles Hutchins, Alan Moore, Stephan Harding, Philip Franses and Margaret Colquhoun for their advice, guidance, conversations and support for our work.

A very special thank you to the late Henri Bortoft whose profound insights on the nature of wholeness run throughout *Holonomics*.

We thank Luís Norberto Pascoal and Sergio Chaia for the time they gave to us, and for providing us with such open, inspirational and personal accounts of their stories during our interviews.

Thank you to Christopher Moore, our editor at Floris Books, who has provided continual support and advice throughout the writing of our book, and who helped guide us to its final form.

We sincerely thank Michael Pruett for the huge amount of work he offered us in the creation and rendering of the many illustrations in *Holonomics*.

We would like to thank Professor John Bonner for offering us personal permission to use still shots from his original slime mould films, to Stephen Morris for allowing us permission to reuse his photograph of the BZ reaction, and to Isabelle Stengers for her permission to reuse the bifurcation diagram from *Order Out of Chaos*.

We thank Kati Radziszewska from the International Fund for Animal Welfare for her assistance in granting us permission to use the Northwest Atlantic food web figure and Karen Stambrovskis from Pion Ltd. for her assistance in granting us permission to use the Hidden Man figure.

We thank Dimitris Antoniadis for granting us permission to reproduce tables and quote his work from his PhD research, and the team at Nervous System for permission to reuse still shots from their video *Hyphae — growth process diagram in 2D*.

We are extremely grateful to Jonathan Robinson (father of Simon) for the time he gave both proofreading and providing many helpful comments during the process of editing.

We would like to thank our parents and our many friends who have offered inspiration and encouragement, including Marcello Pimentel, David Seamon, Roberta Simonetti, Daniela Carvalho, Emma Kidd, Cristina Morini, Ricardo Torres and Julio Bin.

A special thank you to the late Alexandros Anastas Maraslis, organiser of the Sathya Sai Programme of Human Values in Education, co-ordinator Valéria Ferreira de Paula, and all our friends from the Sri Sathya Sai Educational Institute in Brazil.

A final and heartfelt thank you to educator Sri Sathya Sai Baba for inspiring and providing the educational program in human values, a truly authentic foundation for our lives.

Simon Robinson and Maria Moraes Robinson
São Paulo, Brazil, November 2013

Foreword:
A Declaration of Wholeness

This book is a declaration of wholeness. Holonomics represents a complete system of living, working and interacting.

In the modern world we are used to thinking in compartments and divisions. Our universities all over the world are notoriously organised into departments. The faculty of sciences does not connect with the faculty of the arts. The Department of Theology has nothing to do with the School of Business. The study of literature or poetry is far from the study of politics. And the classes in economics are held in total disregard for ecology. As a result, society suffers from this complete disconnection and disorientation.

In *Holonomics* Simon and Maria Robinson have made a great contribution in healing this disease of division and separation. The authors show that every discipline is connected to every other discipline.

Simon and Maria were students at Schumacher College. I am happy to say that the college benefited as much from their profound search for holistic knowledge and their experience of the business world as they benefited from the radical approach to learning at the college.

We believe that not only are economy and ecology two sides of the same coin and sciences are perfectly in harmony with the arts, ethics and business, but learning and living are also not to be divided; theory and practice should be a continuum. Our body itself is a perfect example of this wholeness. We have all the faculties of a university in our one body. With my brain I think, analyse and evaluate, with my heart I feel, intuit and appreciate, with my hands I make, create and produce. With my senses I learn to see, speak, listen, taste and touch. Intellect, intuition and action are intrinsic to my existence. If that is me – my whole self and my whole being – then why should I be compartmentalised during the course of study?

This is why at Schumacher College students participate in gardening, cooking, meditation, arts and crafts while they pursue their studies for a degree in outdoor classrooms as well as indoor classrooms.

This holistic approach to learning and living is as old as the hills and as fresh as the morning dew. We learn from the wisdom of old masters like Spinoza and Goethe as well as new masters like James Lovelock, Ilya Prigogine and Henri Bortoft. Simon and Maria bring all these approaches together and show how thoughts and theories of complexity, chaos and emergence are fundamentally relevant to the economy, to business and to life.

The days of compartmentalisation are passing. We are at the dawn of a new age where we must look for unity in diversity, the big picture in small parts, macrocosm in microcosm, large vision in little details and holonomics in economics.

We can enter this new age of wholeness by the act of deep seeing, by expanding our consciousness, and by transforming our perceptions. This book is a handy tool to accomplish such metamorphosis, a manual to move from a linear model to a cyclical system of business.

I am delighted that two students of Schumacher College have come up with such a comprehensive understanding and explanation of a new world view, or a new paradigm which is urgently needed in our time. When the world is faced with dilemmas and dichotomies, we need Holonomics so that we can avoid disorder and build a sustainable and fulfilling future which is full of creative possibilities.

This book contains many examples, case studies and practical applications of projects which show that collaboration can override competition, happiness can be derived without endless pursuit of material accumulation, and the Buddhist wisdom is as relevant to our time as it was two and a half thousand years ago.

This book is a manifesto for mindful living. It will help the reader to make a shift from a static state to a dynamic state of business.

Satish Kumar
Founder of Schumacher College
Editor-in-Chief, *Resurgence & Ecologist*

Authors' Preface

The introduction of a new idea is often framed with the observation that we cannot solve our existing problems with the same level of consciousness that created them. The subsequent call to action is frequently accompanied by an appeal to change our paradigms, and at other times a call to change our mental models. It is very easy to say these things, yet much more difficult to understand and more difficult still, to put into practice.

Holonomics is not a new idea *per se;* it is a new way of seeing, one which is able to comprehend the wholeness of economic systems. This way of seeing is not a 'dogmatic annunciation' but a 'creative conception' of economics which understands the deeply interwoven relationship with our planet's ecosystem.

Hence our coining of a new definition for the word 'holonomics', which can be thought of as the combination of the words 'whole' and 'economics'. If we look at the Greek origins of these words we find three components; ὅλος (holos – all, whole, entire, total), οἶκος (oikos – house) and νόμος (nomos – custom or law). Economics can be thought of as the understanding of the laws and customs of our home *(oikos + nomos)*. We cannot have a limited view of our home, for home is a living planet of finite resources. Our understanding of economics has to encompass an understanding of the wholeness of nature and business systems in all their complexity, and this can only come from holonomic thinking.

Holonomics introduces the reader to a dynamic way of seeing and thinking about systems. It is a way of seeing which expands our mode of consciousness from the analytical to the intuitive;

one that not only is able to understand the parts of a system, but at a deeper, intuitive level of perception, is also able to understand the relationships and processes within that system – not from the perspective of a whole which is superior to the parts, but from one which is able to encounter the whole through the way in which it comes to presence in the parts. ('Intuition' as we use the word should not be confused with 'feeling' as it is used in everyday language, but as a higher level of cognition to that of our intellectual minds).

This mode of consciousness sees each part in a system as an expression of the whole, the whole of which can only be the whole because of the parts, and the parts of which can only be parts because of the whole. It is a mode of consciousness which, while acknowledging the importance of the analytical-logical-symbolic aspect of our minds, fully embraces intuition, feeling and sensing so as to enable us to encounter and comprehend systems in their entirety.

This mode of consciousness can be found in western philosophy from Plato onwards, although its articulation varies from the scientific writings of Johann Wolfgang von Goethe, the phenomenological school of philosophy founded by Edmund Husserl, and the philosophical hermeneutics of Hans-Georg Gadamer and Ludwig Wittgenstein. The late physicist and philosopher Henri Bortoft described the way of seeing which resulted from this expanded awareness as 'the dynamics of seeing'.

Henri, along with mathematician and visionary biologist Brian Goodwin, Satish Kumar, a peace and environmental activist, and ecologist Stephan Harding, plus inspiration from a number leading thinkers and scientists such as James Lovelock, Fritjof Capra and Rupert Sheldrake, encapsulated the dynamic way of seeing in a unique Masters programme which they termed 'Holistic Science' and launched in 1998 at Schumacher College, Devon in the UK.

The foundations of Holistic Science covered Henri's philosophy of 'wholeness', Gaia Theory, Complexity Science and Chaos Theory, plus additional modules on economics, ecology, and sustainability, and enabled students to explore a science not just of quantities, but also of qualities. Both authors of this book are alumni of Schumacher College, with Simon graduating in Holistic Science in 2010 and Maria participating in the course 'The Economics of Happiness'. In *Holonomics* we have aimed to capture the essence of Holistic Science and the philosophy of Schumacher College, in order to lead the reader's thinking into the dynamic way of seeing, that they may truly be able to comprehend the world and reality in a new light, perceiving new relationships in the systems in which they participate, and so inspiring new insights and solutions to the many entangled and complex economic, business, social and ecological problems that we are now facing across the globe.

While Henri was writing his final book, the name he almost settled on was *The Dynamics of Being.* It was at the last moment that he had the inspiration to call it *Taking Appearance Seriously,* a name which is a philosophical play on the word 'appearance', which can be read as either a noun – the outward appearance of an object – or as a verb – the appearing of an object. We named the three parts of *Holonomics* as *The Dynamics of Seeing, The Dynamics of Nature,* and *The Dynamics of Business* in honour of the profound insights of Henri, and they are written in a manner that will lead the reader towards their own understanding and experience of the dynamics of being. We have such great affection for Henri, as do so many of his students, colleagues and friends who knew him, that we have taken the liberty in referring to him by his first name, as opposed to the more formal 'Bortoft', a break in convention which we hope the reader will forgive.

Part One of this book is devoted to leading the reader into the dynamics of seeing. These four chapters introduce the reader to the work of Henri who passed away in 2012, just a few months after the publication of *Taking Appearance Seriously: The Dynamic Way of Seeing in Goethe and European Thought.* This last book built on his previous two works *Goethe's Scientific Consciousness* (1986) and *The Wholeness of Nature: Goethe's Way of Science* (1996).

Henri taught Simon at Schumacher College in 2009. He was a truly remarkable teacher, a philosopher who dedicated his life to the study of authenticity and wholeness, and who, as our fellow student Ben put it, 'took words to places I thought they couldn't go'. Henri had a deliciously witty sense of humour, which he would put to great use in his classes in a way that, more often than not, would either leave students spellbound or perplexed, bewildered and unsettled. Henri's teachings were less about the transmission of facts which could be easily integrated into one's existing body of knowledge, and more about shifting the student's mode of consciousness. This is by no means easy to grasp in the first instance, especially if one has grown up with the western scientific mechanistic paradigm – a Cartesian conception of reality.

The rewards to those who have a genuine desire to experience the dynamics of seeing cannot, however, be underestimated. The greatest asset that businesses have in this post-industrial era of the knowledge economy is the intelligence of its workforce, and the competitive advantage which comes from the creativity not only of the leadership, but also of the whole organisation. *Holonomics,* through the dynamics of seeing, will enable the reader to understand the exciting and emerging new business models of a new economics with what one of our students described as 'an entirely new window on the world'.

In Part Two of *Holonomics* we examine Complexity Science, Chaos Theory and Systems Thinking, starting with non-linear chemical reactions and amoebas, and ending with an analysis of Gaia Theory – our biosphere as a whole. We explore the concepts of emergence, bifurcation, self-organisation and feedback loops from the perspective which Philip Franses, lecturer in Complexity at Schumacher College, terms 'Transition Science'. Philip and Satish Kumar are introducing Holistic Science to people via a way of learning which they call 'Process and Pilgrimage'. To truly comprehend the deep insights from complexity science and quantum theory, we have to let go of our Cartesian fixed frameworks of reality. Pilgrimage is about both the inner journey as well as the outer journey, and so Franses and Kumar take their students on journeys of transformation, where students are no longer fixed or rigid in their thinking, but are fluid and flexible, and are able to evolve their consciousness, just as life is always evolving.

One of the key insights from Part Two is the manner in which the dynamic way of seeing can prevent systems thinking from falling into the trap of what Henri called 'dogmatic annunciation'. To be able to perceive authentic wholes – whole systems – we need more than just our analytical mode of consciousness. When we describe systems in this mode of consciousness, we attempt to bring together the parts of a system artificially, in a counterfeit manner, imagining that the whole is superior to the sum of the parts. In Henri's language, we force the parts to belong *together*. But in organic systems, the parts only have an existence and meaning because of their relationship to the whole, a whole which can only be experienced in the way in which it comes to presence in the parts. We therefore need a higher intuitive mode of consciousness to experience the *belonging* together of the parts in what we now perceive as an authentic whole.

When we develop systems models, we need to avoid this 'dogmatic annunciation' whereby we are convinced that we now have the truth, and we move to a more fluid and dynamic mode of consciousness, whereby our models are seen as 'constructive conceptions'. These models are not the truth, but have a sufficient level of truth to be able to move our thinking and understanding forward. Science comes to be understood as 'Transition Science', since the scientist is no longer an outside observer immersed in abstract models, but becomes transformed from within as he or she experiences genuine encounters with the phenomena that they are studying.

Having explored the notion of a more expansive holonomic vision, Part Three turns to business and economics, and asks how this new mode of consciousness and seeing can be applied in practice. The case studies which we cite – PUMA SE's environmental profit and loss accounting, Robert Kaplan and

David Norton's Balanced Scorecard methodology, Visa Inc.'s chaordic structure, Kyocera's amoeba management system, Gore Associates' lattice organisation, Genie Internet's agile structure, Toyota's dynamic way of seeing, and DPaschoal's business ecosystem – all represent key aspects of holonomic thinking, demonstrating how a change in our mode of consciousness can directly impact on financial results while at the same time facilitating a shift to authentic and long-term sustainability.

We end Part Three with an exploration of mindful leadership and the importance of human values, and we ask the question: 'Is being happy an impossible dream?' Having examined mechanistic thinking, which focuses on objects, and systems thinking which focuses on relationships, we arrive at a complete understanding of holonomic thinking, where the wholeness of systems can be encountered and profound meaning comes into vision.

Ultimately, then, we are asking the reader to undertake a restructuring of their consciousness in order for them to be able to see a complex system whole. Our aim is to help the reader to be able to see both the *intrinsic* as well as *extrinsic* dimensions of complex systems. Once a person is able to see authentic wholes and the processes, dynamics and meaning of living systems, they reach a deeper understanding of the world, one in which economics is no longer seen as separate from ecology. It is a new world of holonomics – business where people and planet matter.

PART I

The Dynamics of Seeing: The Transition to Holonomic Thinking

1. Holonomic Thinking

What is Holonomics?

Do you remember your first mobile phone? In 1993 Nokia launched their 2110 handset to great critical acclaim. Although a simple phone with text messaging and no internet capabilities, it is a design classic, with its oval and graphical (albeit text) display and context-sensitive menus integrating harmoniously and intuitively into the innovative soft keys. At the time it was inconceivable that anyone could knock Nokia off its dominant perch, but Apple achieved this with its iPhone, which now generates more revenue than Microsoft's entire product range.[1]

Although functionally simple compared to phones of today, we can say that the Nokia 2110 was complicated, because if you had an adequate level of expert knowledge, it could be fully understood. While the last twenty years have seen a huge amount of technological progress, the Apple iPhone can still be thought of as complicated, since it too is a piece of technology which although requiring a wider range of expert knowledge, can still be fully understood.

Now think about a plant. If you have one to hand, take a close look at it. With some plants you can take a small piece of say a stem or leaf from which, if you then plant in a new location, an entire new plant will grow. But take one piece out of your phone's circuitry and it will fail. There is something fundamentally different about the organisation of a plant, whereby the whole is contained within the parts. The thinking that has got us from

the 2110 to the iPhone is not the same type of thinking that
we need to understand a complex, dynamic and organic living
plant. Many people in business are now discovering that the
same organisational principles that are required to understand
the plant can now be used to understand their own organisations,
which are also complex living dynamic systems, and not just fixed
hierarchical structures. To truly understand an organic system we
need 'holonomic thinking'.

The term 'holonomic' was first introduced in 1894 by German
physicist Heinrich Rudolf Hertz (1857–94).[2] The term is derived
from the Greek ὅλος meaning 'whole', 'entire' and νόμ-ος meaning
'law'. The term 'holonomics' as used by us takes inspiration from
the word 'holon', coined by Arthur Koestler in his 1967 work *The
Ghost in the Machine*. Our use of the term 'holonomics' represents
a way of understanding economics from a perspective which
is able to comprehend complete systems – living, working and
interacting.

To help us understand what he means by 'holon', Koestler
introduces us to two watchmakers in a story created by Herbert
Simon, one of the founding fathers of both artificial intelligence
and complexity science.[3] Both watchmakers made watches of
around one thousand parts each, and even though watches from
both makers were in high demand, one maker had to close
while the other prospered. The key difference was how they
manufactured their watches. One would construct his watches
one bit at a time, and every time he was interrupted or made a
mistake, he would have to start all over again. The other, though,
created subassemblies of ten parts, and these could then be built
into larger subassemblies, before the units were brought together
forming the final watch. Any interruption or mistake would
therefore have very limited consequences. There has not been
enough time available for life to evolve in the manner of the failed
watches, Koestler argues, but complex life can evolve from more
simple life forms if it does so in a hierarchical manner.

Organic life is organised hierarchically, as is social life. But
if we look at what a part is in a hierarchy, it has an ambiguous

existence. As well as being a part of a greater whole, in which case we think of the part as being somehow incomplete, a part is also a whole in its own right. Just as our bodies are composed of cells, cells are whole systems in their own right too. To help us think about these 'sub-wholes', Koestler invoked the image of Janus, the double-faced Roman god, who could look in opposite directions at the same time. Hence he coined the term 'holon' to refer to parts which behave 'partly as wholes and wholly as parts'.[4]

Koestler identified a variety of hierarchies operating in human societies, including authoritarian 'control' hierarchies, 'geographical' hierarchies, 'distribution' hierarchies, and 'family-clan-caste' hierarchies. We confront hierarchies in all aspects of our lives, and would easily be able to identify many. Koestler did so in order to be able to compare a hierarchy with a 'holarchy of holons'. He felt that 'Behaviourism' (an extreme school of thought in Psychology) was too atomistic, and that 'Gestalt' psychology was wrong to conceive of wholes as absolutes. Both schools of thought failed to take into account the intermediate structures in between parts and wholes. Although Koestler's holon is not a widely used term, it is excellent in helping to broaden our discussion about systems, and the relationships between wholes and parts.

There are four current uses of the word 'holonomics'. The first use, which we have previously mentioned, is in physics and comes from classical mechanics, relating to mechanical systems ('holonomic systems'). The second use refers to a technical term in mathematics ('holonomic basis'), and the third use of the term (phrased as 'holonomicity') comes from robotics, and relates to the degrees of freedom a robot or controllable object such as a car has.

The final use of the word relates to 'holonomic brain theory', normally associated with Karl Pribram and David Bohm. Here the word 'holonomic' is relating more to 'hologram', where both theories of the brain and of subatomic particles were influenced and inspired by thinking about the holographic principle, where each part of a hologram contains the whole.

In the business world we occasionally see words derived from 'holos', one example being 'Holacracy', a social technology for structuring, governing, and running an organisation developed by HolacracyOne. In *Beyond Business Process Reengineering: Towards the Holonic Enterprise,* Patrick McHugh, Giorgio Merli and William Wheeler use Koestler's terminology in their description of 'holonic networks' which they define as 'a set of companies that acts integratedly and organically'.[5] Holonic networks are virtual business organisations made up of a number of equal partners – holons – who all contribute unique core competencies. The theory is that holonic networks, being non-hierarchical, self-regulating, self-learning, evolutionary and open, allow business systems to continually 'de-invent and reinvent themselves as they face increasingly ambiguous markets'.[6]

As authors, we decided to call our book *Holonomics* in order to be able to discuss what we call 'holonomic thinking', a profound way of thinking about mental models, systems models, and business and economic models. At the heart of all strategic business thinking is the desire to understand new business models. Much of this new thinking is influenced by paradigms and frameworks which are still based on a Taylorian, linear and Newtonian world view. A newer world view, taking inspiration from complexity science, is challenging the assumption that what has worked in the past will still continue to now work in the modern hyper-connected and complex world that we are living in, suggesting that we are now experiencing a turning point in society, where a new form of thinking is required. Many new business models have their basis in the organic and dynamic organisational models found in nature, and that is why, before we can discuss these new business models, we first have to examine systems models and systems thinking.

While science as a discipline is transforming itself greatly, based on dramatically new ways of thinking, the business world has been slow to adapt and to exploit the new sciences. The reason is fundamental. Before we can acquire new ways of thinking, we have to understand the limitations and traps within our current ways of thinking, and this requires us to examine our mental models of our world view. If the introduction of new ideas is done without understanding either the systemic nature of organisations or people's current ways of thinking, then new paradigms or frameworks will be forced into the old ways of thinking and ultimately will not be successful.

In Part One of this book we will be focusing on the concept of 'wholeness' and the relationship between the parts and the whole. Systems theory has been attempting to provide methodologies and frameworks to answer this question, starting with the cybernetic approach pioneered in the early part of the twentieth century, which then evolved in its attempt to understand the notion of 'control'. This gradually evolved into what is now known as 'systems thinking'. It is important, though, to note that this term – systems thinking – covers an extremely diverse range of theories, frameworks and world views, and as such it should perhaps be seen only as a general umbrella term.

Complexity in Business

In 2010, IBM published a study *Capitalizing on Complexity* based on face-to-face conversations with more than 1,500 chief executive officers worldwide.[7] The four main findings were as follows:

⇣ Today's complexity was only expected to rise, and more than half of the CEOs doubted their ability to manage it.
⇣ Creativity was the most important leadership quality.
⇣ The most successful organisations co-created products and services with customers, and integrated customers into core processes.
⇣ Better performers managed complexity on behalf of their organisations, customers and partners.

Interestingly, IBM referred to what they called the 'complexity gap'. While 79% of CEOs expected a high degree of complexity over the next five years, only 49% felt prepared for it. IBM used the term 'standouts' for those companies best able to handle complexity. The three main factors which led to the success of these companies in a complex environment were:

> Embodying creative leadership.
> Reinventing customer relationships.
> Building operational dexterity.

A similar recent study by KPMG also examined complexity in business and came to the same conclusion – that complexity was the overriding issue for CEOs and businesses today.[8] This study asked business leaders how they had attempted to manage complexity in the last two years, and how they were expecting to deal with complexity in the future. In both cases, the three most popular strategies were:

> Improve information management.
> Reorganise all or part of the business.
> Significantly change the approach to human resources.

In many ways this is not a surprising observation. The world has moved from the industrial age to the information age, and much of the complexity arises from the greater involvement of people in business processes, as opposed to pure manufacturing. When working with business executives, it is always interesting to ask the questions: 'What is complexity?' and 'What comes into your mind when you think of the word "complexity"?' Both of us (the authors) teach holonomic thinking to MBA and postgraduate students at Sustentare Business School in Joinville, Brazil. Our students are always asked to fill in a pre-course questionnaire which probes their conceptual understanding of complexity, and their replies are always highly revealing:

> Complexity can be understood as a situation that involves many variables to achieve a common goal.

Complexity for me means that we need to put into practice our creativity in solving problems; simplification of processes that will optimise the outcome of the organisation. Words that I relate complexity to are: bureaucracy, slow, problems.

Complexity is a very broad definition in my opinion. Complexity is a set of factors that make a goal, regardless of its nature, extremely challenging. In plain language, complexity means to me something running hard but which can be highly enjoyable at the end. Words associated with complexity: fear, difficulty, challenge, opportunity.

I define complexity as something complex, involving a higher level of knowledge for better understanding. To me that word relates to the difficulty involved in assimilating a given activity, so I associate complexity with difficulty.

I define complexity as something that requires a great effort to be understood or interpreted. I do not see complexity in a bad light. On the contrary, I think complexity relates to something that is not divided into small parts. Every structure or complex problem follows logical, separate elements, where we need to identify the logic that will simplify it considerably.

Typical answers in relation to words and phrases our students associate with complexity include:

- ⩔ Something complicated.
- ⩔ Many parts.
- ⩔ Lots of relationships.
- ⩔ Many people involved.
- ⩔ An unknown relationship between cause and effect.
- ⩔ Unpredictable.
- ⩔ Chaotic.

In general, the majority of responses are seen to have potentially negative components, so that complex problems are seen as complicated and difficult. What we have noticed is that people in business are rarely influenced by the language of scientific complexity theory, which when studied leads to a very different understanding from those answers above. In the scientific conception of complexity, we begin to realise that complex systems often demonstrate resilience and stability, and through dynamic and non-linear relationships between the parts of the system, can exhibit both chaotic behaviour on one level, but ordered behaviour at a higher level. These concepts may seem strange if you have not studied complex systems before, and of course they will be examined more fully in Part Two.

David Baccarini, Associate Professor in Project Management at Curtin University, defines project complexity as 'consisting of many varied interrelated parts which can be operationalised in terms of differentiation and interdependency'.[9] In this definition, 'differentiation' refers to the number of varied elements, for example tasks, specialists and components; and 'interdependence' (or 'connectivity') refers to the degree of interrelatedness between these elements. If a project team has a framework for defining complexity, then it is in a position to be able to manage that complexity. Baccarini suggests that there are a number of dimensions which should be taken into account when classifying the complexity faced in large construction projects and which often result in the temporary creation of multi-organisational structures. These are: depth of hierarchical organisation, number of organisational units, task structure, technological complexity and organisational interdependencies.

Research from the construction industry suggests that there is still a considerable failure even to define complexity, with only 10% of those surveyed responding that their organisations do define it. From a related analysis of 31 in-depth interviews, only 41% of project managers replied that they were using any formal tools to define and manage complexity, and the majority of those related to risk assessment tools and techniques.[10] Figures 1.1 and 1.2 show the perceived sources of this complexity.[11]

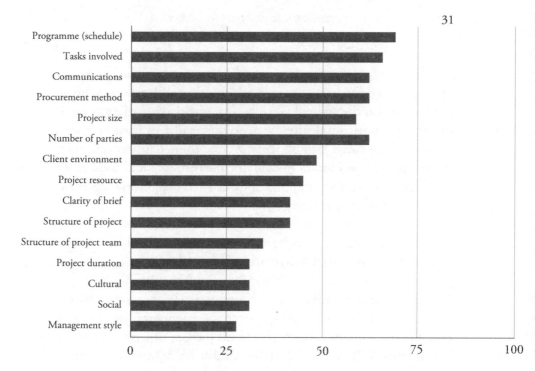

Figure 1.1. Responses regarding the identification of complexity in projects at company level.

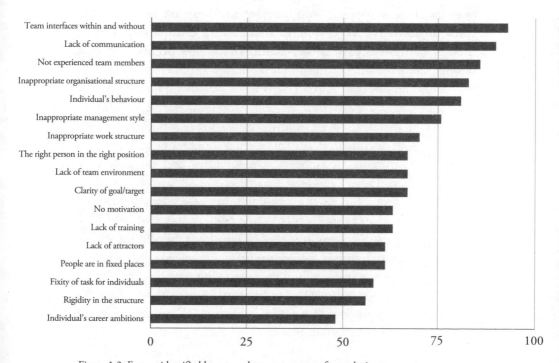

Figure 1.2. Factors identified by respondents as a source of complexity.

Dimitris Antoniadis, one of the analysts who carried out this research, believes that most research in organisational complexity has focused on the individual elements, rather than attempting to understand how complexity can arise from the myriad interactions between these parts. He also suggests that there has been a general failure to pay attention to the socio-organisational aspects of complex interactions, and the impact of these on management style and project structuring.[12]

The Transition to Holonomic Thinking

In order to understand the many new varieties of business model being created and why they work, we have to study systems models, and the ones which this book focuses on come from the natural world. However, to understand these organic and natural systems, we have to move from a 'mechanistic' way of thinking, whereby we think of the world as functioning like clockwork, engines and computers, into an 'organic' way of thinking. To think organically, we first have to radically change our mental models of the world in order to be able to *see* organic systems whole.

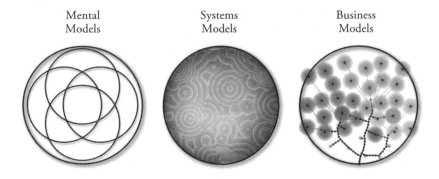

Figure 1.3. The three components of holonomic thinking.

Holonomic thinking, therefore, consists of three components: mental models, systems models and business models (Figure 1.3). The concept 'mental model' refers to the structures, paradigms, frameworks, concepts, ideas, assumptions and beliefs that we hold about the world and about reality. We can think of many outmoded mental models of reality in science, such as the Earth being flat, the Earth being at the centre of the universe, and more recently, continents always being static. When Alfred Wegener (1880–1930) suggested in 1912 that the world's continents were once one single land mass, he was roundly ridiculed, in an often hostile manner, since how could an entire continent possibly move? The first edition of *The Origin of Continents and Oceans,* outlining Wegener's theory, was published in 1915 but would not be widely accepted until the 1950s with the theory of plate tectonics.

Venkat Ramaswamy and Francis Gouillart offer an interesting example of how mental models can restrict our creativity in business by comparing the move into retail outlets of Sony and Apple.[13] Sony has a far greater catalogue of products across a wider range of categories than Apple, and yet Apple has become a dominant retail force, with Sony receiving much criticism of its failure to engage customers emotionally. The difference is the mental models of the retailers, with one seeing the shop as a retail outlet, and the other, Apple, focusing on the retail environment as an opportunity to create a customer experience, where customers can play with the products as if they had already taken those products home with them.

Peter Senge has made a huge contribution to our understanding of systems in relation to learning in organisations. He defines 'systems thinking' as a discipline for seeing 'wholes', a set of general principles derived from the physical sciences, engineering, and management, and a set of tools and techniques originating in cybernetics and engineering theory.[14] In systems thinking, therefore, there is a movement from focusing on the nature of the parts of a problem to seeing the structures which underlie complex situations. The essence of systems thinking is therefore twofold:

1. Seeing interrelationships rather than linear cause and effect.
2. Seeing processes of change rather than snapshots.

Senge points out that while business strategies may well benefit from insights from systems thinking, these ideas never get put into practice, or, if they do, the results may fail to meet the expectations of what are brilliant ideas. The reason is that there is a conflict between systemic insights and our deeply ingrained mental models.[15] The ability to shift into systems thinking is a potentially vast source of competitive advantage for businesses, argues Senge, but, in order to truly master this discipline, organisations need to become learning organisations, necessitating the mastery of building shared visions, mental models, team learning and personal mastery.

In our daily lives we rarely think about how our mental models affect our *seeing*. The word 'seeing' is highlighted here because it is not being used it in a commonsense way. 'Naive empiricism' is very closely aligned to our everyday view of the world. In this world view, there is an external world consisting of separate objects (Figure 1.4). Through light and our eyes and nervous system, we are able to perceive images of this external world and thus know things about it, such as how fast objects fall due to gravity, their weights, and what things are made of.

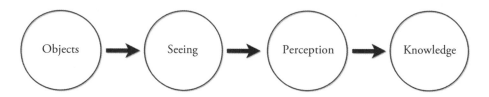

Figure 1.4. An 'everyday' view of the world.

It is only when we consciously move our attention from objects, or *what is seen,* to the *act of seeing* that we discover that our mental models have a major impact on how we see. If we come to accept this, then we can see how studying dynamic systems provides us with a new source of mental models, which then opens up to us a new way of seeing the world. Here then, is the first challenge – to move from 'mechanistic thinking' to 'systems thinking' (Figure 1.5). The trap here is that many people who are systems thinkers are still thinking in mechanistic terms. They still see the world in terms of fragmentation, parts and objects, even though they claim to be thinking in terms of 'wholes'.

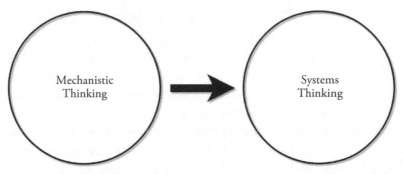

Figure 1.5. The first challenge to our way of thinking

In Figure 1.6 there is a dotted line which represents a wall, a barrier beyond which many systems thinkers do not go. It represents their inability to break out of their mechanistic world views; it is 'the point of liminality'. Liminality can be thought of as a human type of singularity point in a black hole, a halfway point in transition, where existing structures have broken down but new ones have not yet been built. The word comes from Victor Turner's anthropological work on rites of passage and rituals.[16]

In indigenous cultures, Turner identified three stages in a ritual process. The first is 'separation', where a youngster is taken from their familiar surroundings, their family, friends, and village, with a view to taking them out of all known cultural and social norms. The second phase is the 'liminal state', which has no attributes of either past or coming states. In the final phase of the rites of passage, the initiate achieves a new form of awareness, coming out of the ambiguous state to achieve a new sense of wholeness.

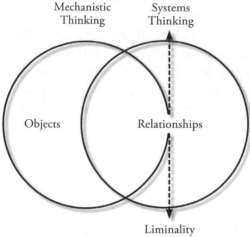

Figure 1.6. The 'point of liminality'.

In first world countries – advanced technological countries – we have lost these ancient rites of passage, and unless we have gone through them, we cannot begin to understand the change of consciousness that they are designed to invoke. Instead, we may experience deep discomfort and frustration, and a lack of truly grasping the importance of what is being taught.

Unlike Figure 1.5, where mechanistic thinking is seen as separate from systems thinking, the intention is not for anyone to lose their mechanistic thinking. Holonomic thinking is a way of thinking in which our seeing and thinking is *expanded*. We do not move from one way of thinking to another way of thinking; we stay within the act of seeing, and go 'upstream' so that we are able to see the *act of seeing* itself (Figure 1.7). Most people are only

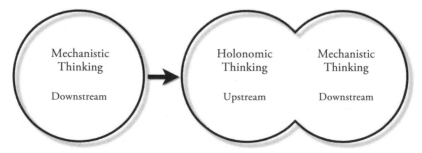

Figure 1.7. Expanding our seeing and thinking.

able to focus on what is seen, the objects. The following chapters in Part One examine 'seeing' in its entirety, so that we can begin to understand how and why we see objects as we do.

If we can somehow expand our way of seeing, we are then given a choice as to how we see a system (Figure 1.8). Do we see it in terms of its parts, which of course we often need to, or can we see the system 'whole'? This is not the same thing as seeing the whole system, where we simply try to increase the number of parts or dimensions that we wish to model, describe, or understand in order to get a better picture of the system.

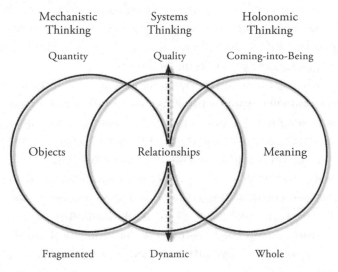

Figure 1.8. Choices as to how we see a system.

Ultimately, then, what we are describing is a movement in thinking – a restructuring of consciousness – to give us the ability to see a complex system whole. As is becoming clear in many scientific disciplines, true understanding can only be achieved through one's *intuition*, and not just via rational thinking. We also need to rethink what we mean by a 'whole'. The aim is to help you to be able to see both the *intrinsic* as well as *extrinsic* dimensions of complex systems. Only when you have been able to see 'authentic wholes' – the processes, dynamics and meaning of living systems – will you then yourself be transformed by the system, reaching a deeper understanding of both the world and your place in it.[17]

Throughout this book we will be examining case studies from businesses which have all been inspired by nature, having a deep reverence for nature, and a connection to nature, people and our planet; a reverence which does not just come through an intellectual understanding where nature is viewed as some kind of object separate from us. Although we have now moved from the industrial age into what is now referred to as the age of the knowledge economy, it is remarkable how little attention companies and organisations are giving to the process of thought, and how developing new ways of thinking can be a source of competitive advantage which can lead to new creative business models, processes, products and solutions.

Luckily, we do not have to undergo intense ritualistic initiations to attain this new way of thinking. We simply need to reacquaint ourselves with nature, and this book has many practical suggestions and exercises to show how this can be done. There is perhaps no more successful business consultant than nature, which has already developed solutions to the problems that we humans now face, in terms of constructing resilient and sustainable organisational structures which have survived for many millions of years. When we let nature be our teacher, and enter her non-linear world, we are shown the secrets of her business models, and that consultancy is priceless.

2. Knowing

Complexity and Consciousness

While business leaders identified complexity as the greatest challenge they face today, Otto Scharmer identifies leadership failure as the key issue of our times, with most organisations being unable to release themselves from the grip of 'pathologic patterns of destruction'.[1] Scharmer identifies three types of complexity which impact on the challenges of leaders: dynamic, social and emerging. 'Dynamic complexity' refers to the systemic nature of a system, where there are delays or distance between cause and effect. 'Social complexity' is a result of the different world views, mental models, attitudes and opinions of people, and this is very much reflected in the type of complex problems that business leaders in the KPMG study (see Chapter 1, Endnote 8) reported that they were trying to solve. Scharmer defines the third form of complexity – 'emergent complexity' – as being 'disruptive change'.[2] This is where:

1. The solution to the problem is unknown.
2. The problem statement itself is still unfolding.
3. It is not clear who the key stakeholders are.

Scharmer has developed a process to help leaders free themselves from being stuck in the patterns of their past experiences, in order to optimise their decision making and creativity. He calls this the 'U Process', by which leaders can learn to shift their attention in relation to the 'source' that they are operating from. One of the greatest problems that Scharmer identifies in people, organisations and societies is their blind spot, which refers to the fact that most are not aware of where they are operating from.

One of the key elements of the U Process is helping leaders to solve problems by helping them to see in a new way. This was famously articulated by Albert Einstein in 1946, when he was looking to raise money to help develop an awareness campaign regarding both the good and evil uses of nuclear power:

> A new type of thinking is essential if mankind is to survive and move toward higher levels.[3]

It seems almost trivial to say that in order to solve problems we need to change our thinking. In what ways can we change our thinking? If we are stuck in one way of thinking, how are we meant to be able to recognise new ways of thinking? Which new ways of thinking are likely to lead to improved results? Einstein's famous quotation has also been paraphrased by other people in a number of ways, one of them being: 'No problem can be solved from the same level of consciousness that created it'.

This last statement, while seemingly the same as Einstein's, introduces an interesting problem of interpretation. What exactly is meant by 'consciousness' and what is meant by a 'level' of consciousness? It is only in the last twenty to thirty years or so that science has begun to fully engage with the mystery of explaining how we as human beings can be sentient and have awareness of ourselves resulting from the interactions of unconscious matter, that is, the chemical and electrical activity in the neurones in our brains. The reason for this can be traced back to the paper published by John B. Watson in 1913 in which he proclaimed:

> The time has come when psychology must discard all reference to consciousness ... Its sole task is the prediction and control of behaviour; and introspection can form no part of its method.[4]

His motivation was to attack the practice of introspection, a practice decried as unscientific and an invalid method for developing insights into mental processes. Behaviourism became the dominant school of psychology in the US and Europe, greatly popularised by Burrhus Frederic Skinner (1904–1990). Behaviourism became dominant, despite its near farcical contortions in explaining scientific discovery and artistic behaviour without reference to mind or imagination. Complex human behaviour, including language, was reduced to stimulus-response theory, a position expertly dismantled by Arthur Koestler, who saw behaviourism as merely 'reducing behaviour to salivating and bar pressing', referring to the experiments which were mostly conducted with dogs and rats.[5]

Every year books are published on new business methodologies, many of which are extremely successful, such as 'triple bottom line', 'co-creation', and 'double-loop learning', to name just three. These methodologies refer to processes which people are normally able to take on board if they have the right attitude and motivation to understand them and how they can be deployed. But, as Richard LeVitt of Hewlett Packard told Scharmer, the next basis for competitive advantage that they are focusing on is 'how managers can improve their quality of thought and their *deep perception of customers* and the experiences customers should have with us'.[6]

Ecologist Stephan Harding refers to Carl Jung's four ways of knowing as 'the Jungian mandala',[7] and this can help us better explore what is meant by 'quality of thought'. Jung did not propose this as a psychological model (Figure 2.1). He used it more as a framework for viewing the dominant mode of thinking in people. In diagnosing his patients, Jung came to see the ways of knowing as opposites, with 'thinking' opposite 'feeling' and 'intuition' opposite 'sensing'. These are seen as opposites since, in order to help a patient return to a more balanced way of thinking, it would often be the opposite characteristic that would be the hardest for the patient to acquire.

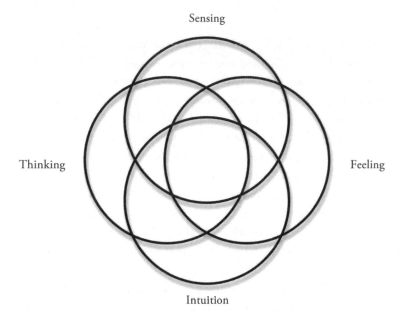

Figure 2.1. Jung's four ways of knowing.

'Thinking' in the mandala refers to a verbal, analytical, conceptual and abstract form of thinking, which dominates western societies. This way of knowing is dominant in the extreme, whereby the ability to manipulate abstract symbols is valued far above all other ways of knowing, to the point where scientists either explicitly reject or ignore the other ways of knowing as legitimate forms of enquiry. However, it is interesting to read a study of eminent mathematicians undertaken in 1945 by Jacques Hadamard. One of his interviewees was Einstein, who answered:

> The words or the language, as they are written or spoken, do not seem to play any role in my mechanism of thought. The psychical entities which seem to serve as elements in thought are certain signs and more or less clear images which can be "voluntarily" reproduced and combined ... The above mentioned elements are, in my case, of visual and some muscular type. Conventional words or other signs have to be sought for laboriously only in a secondary stage ... It seems to me that what you call full

consciousness is a limit case which can never be fully
accomplished because consciousness is a narrow thing.[8]

So for Einstein, a description of consciousness should not be limited
just to 'thinking'. The mandala can be used to explore both the
strengths and weaknesses of the different ways of 'knowing'. If we
start with 'thinking', from the perspective of the last ten thousand
years of humanity, it is quite astonishing just how accelerated the
more recent technological achievements of humanity have been,
seemingly almost logarithmic in development. However, these
achievements have been based on our ability to think in logical
and abstract terms. In many ways, this type of thinking divorces
us, or separates us, in our awareness from the sensual world,
seeing abstract categories rather than the things in themselves.

Perhaps the destruction of the world we see today is a result of
both this and our desensitising and lack of affinity with our fellow
humans, animals, plants and planet. In an extreme form of this
thinking, everything is separation – atomised, so to speak. We are
able to act the way we do, develop weapons of mass destruction
and wreak havoc on a global scale, because we have simply lost all
feeling, or sense of connection, to those whose lives we affect.

On the other dimension, 'intuition' is opposite 'sensing', our
knowing which comes from our senses. We will be examining
the concept of 'seeing' in more detail, as, quite literally, 'there
is more to seeing than meets the eye'. Our mental models, ideas
and concepts are more directly linked to the act of seeing than
we suppose. If we can train ourselves to develop our faculties of
perception, we can gain better insights into problems than if we
were to simply 'think' about them with mistaken ideas about what
it is that we are seeing.

A good example of this comes from Peter Senge, who, in the
mid 1980s joined a group of executives from the car industry in
Detroit who were travelling to Japan for their first factory visits.
When visiting a Toyota production line, the executives were not
able to see what it was – a new method of production for the
maximum personalisation of products with minimal stock held.

Their mental models were so restricting, so stuck in their ways of thinking, that they literally could not see this new production process and assumed that it was all a charade, a confidence trick put on for their benefit.[9]

It is interesting to read how Walter Isaacson, the biographer of Steve Jobs, describes him. He points out that, whereas Bill Gates was 'super smart', Steve Jobs was 'super ingenious'. The key differentiating factor was how Jobs was not an analyser of data nor a number-cruncher, and that his ingenuity and 'experiential wisdom' in part depended on his intuiting the relationships between different things.[10]

In many spheres of life we often hear calls for a 'paradigm shift' in order to find solutions to the many complex problems we face, be they economic, social or ecological. Fritjof Capra, building on the work of Thomas Kuhn's studies of scientific revolutions, defines a social paradigm as 'a constellation of concepts, values, perceptions, and practices shared by a community, which forms a particular vision of reality that is the basis of the way the community organises itself'.[11] The element of this definition is 'vision of reality'. What makes true communication in organisations so difficult at times is that, more often than not, they are unable to recognise that people's ideas and concepts are actually based on very different realities.

Communication skills are one of the most valuable sets of skills we can possess, and yet so few organisations devote any amount of significant resources to developing new ways of thinking by their employees. One powerful way to develop new ways of thinking is to study how scientists throughout history have managed to do so, since in science we can find genuine paradigm shifts, one such being the shift from a quantitative, mechanistic thinking to a more qualitative, organic way of comprehending, which we will now explore.

The Whole and the Parts

When we study the history of science, we find that, in each era, scientists and philosophers have struggled to take on board new conceptual ways of thinking. Eventually, though, these new ways of thinking are adopted, perhaps only after a previous generation of scientists in prominent positions have either retired or died, enabling a new generation of younger scientists, unencumbered with the old ways of thinking, to make their mark.

The business world, though, can still be seen to be stuck in a mechanistic clockwork world. When we study the history of science, by understanding the thinking processes of the scientists (and not just the actual science), we can gain a lot by learning how to develop powerful new ways of thinking. This is something that business leaders almost never do. While new ideas and methodologies are published each year, very few challenge us to really examine in a profound way our ways of thinking.

However, this is a double-edged sword, in that while science is in one way exemplary in its ability to think creatively and intuitively, when we study the history of science we find many surprising aspects. We begin to understand that the greatest influence on most of our thinking comes from ancient Greece, from Plato and Aristotle – or, rather, misconceptions by teachers and experts of what they thought Plato and Aristotle were teaching.[12] Science is never quite as objectively pure as perhaps its practitioners would like us to imagine, with the social and economic orders of the times impacting on the world view and mental models of the scientist. Science is often more like politics in terms of it being based on building consensus at the expense of truly gifted thinkers with new insights, and the need to stay within the prevailing *status quo* in order not to rock the boat that funds the scientific establishments.

But a surprising discovery when studying the history of science is the battle that philosopher scientists have had in understanding the relationship between the parts and the whole. One of the first accounts was written by Plato, in *Parmenides,* one of his final works. In this dialogue, Plato is attempting to solve some problems that he himself created in his earlier writings, having understood that many people had not comprehended his philosophy, which was now seen as dualistic. While some have questioned why Plato chose to critique his own thinking in this work, other people such as Hans-Georg Gadamer have seen it as Plato's attempt to help people understand where they misunderstood his concepts of the parts and the whole,[13] or in Plato's language, 'the One':

> The one itself, then, having been broken up into parts by being, is many and infinite?
>
> True.
>
> Then not only the one which has being is many, but the one itself distributed by being, must also be many?
>
> Certainly.
>
> Further, inasmuch as the parts are parts of a whole, the one, as a whole, will be limited; for are not the parts contained by the whole?
>
> Certainly.
>
> And that which contains, is a limit?
>
> Of course.
>
> Then the one if it has being is one and many, whole and parts, having limits and yet unlimited in number?
>
> Clearly.[14]

There are a number of ways of referring to a whole. Plato used the concept of 'the One'. The word 'holism' was coined by Jan Smuts, a South African philosopher, who became President of South Africa. He defined it as 'the fundamental factor operative towards the creation of wholes in the universe'.[15] For Smuts, both an animal or a plant could be taken as a type of whole, whose functioning could only be understood holistically, the whole being in the parts and the parts in the whole. Interestingly, Smuts had been influenced by Einstein, and although Einstein would later endorse Smuts' work in correspondence between them, the term was not generally adopted.[16]

The word 'holistic' was introduced in the early 1970s, in California, in the work of Roger Sperry, winner of a Nobel prize for his work in brain physiology and the processes involved in thinking. The term was popularised by his colleague Robert E. Ornstein, in his book *The Psychology of Consciousness*. While this was interesting, the work was perhaps hijacked by the New Age movement, where the right brain (emotion) was seen as holistic and feminine, and the left side (rationality) was analytical and male. The word 'holistic' was also absorbed into New Age philosophies relating to mind, body and spirit, and because of this it now has negative connotations for many in the scientific community.

While many neuroscientists have given up talking about the divided brain, psychiatrist Iain McGilchrist provides an important and revitalised analysis.[17] He has reviewed the evolution of the brain in birds, animals and humans, and feels that there is something extremely significant in the asymmetrical divisions in the brain, particularly in the corpus callosum, whose most important function could well be to keep the two sides of the brain separate.

McGilchrist argues that it is our frontal lobes which separate humans from birds and animals, the function of which is to inhibit the rest of the brain. This results in an ability to distance ourselves from the world, to take a step back from reality, thus enabling two things. On the one hand it can lead to Machiavellian thoughts and actions, where we can determine the thoughts and intentions of others, and so allow us to deceive. But, on the other hand, it can also lead us to empathise with others too, seeing them as people who might turn out to share the same interests, values and feelings as ourselves. We do need to manipulate the world, to be able to grasp, hold and use tools, but the trap for us is that this form of attention leads to a restricted view of reality, where we only utilise that information which is of use to us in the tasks we are carrying out.

The world as comprehended by the right hemisphere is entirely different. It sees things in context and understands implicit meaning, metaphor, body language, and emotional expression in the face. As McGilchrist puts it, the right hemisphere 'has a disposition for the living', unlike the left hemisphere, which is dependent on denotative language and abstraction, yielding clarity, and the power to manipulate things which are 'known, fixed, static, isolated, decontextualised, explicit, general in nature, but ultimately lifeless'.[18] The problem for humanity, as McGilchrist sees it, is that society has become dominated by the left hemisphere's mode of conceiving the world, and this has led to us living lives of great paradox, where, in our pursuit of happiness, we have become deeply unhappy. Our pursuit of freedom in western societies has led us to lives of intense intrusion and surveillance, lives dominated by obscure and complex rules and laws. We have information coming out of our ears, but we are less and less able to use it, having lost all sight of wisdom, awareness and knowledge of the whole.

Thus, in McGilchrist's view, we are victims of the feedback loops in the left hemisphere's way of thinking and knowing. It throws out any information that does not appear to fit into its world view. It can be likened to a corrupt military-industrial complex, controlling the media, which has shut out the voices and gentle animistic wisdom of our indigenous people from society. The left hemisphere is vocal, whereas the right hemisphere lacks a voice; and so our modern society, McGilchrist suggests, is a perfect reflection of the world according to the left hemisphere alone.[19]

Michael C. Jackson introduced the term 'creative holism' to refer to the use of different types of holistic thinking and practices in organisations. He classifies holistic approaches into four main types: those improving goal seeking and viability, those exploring purposes, those ensuring fairness, and those systems approaches for promoting diversity.[20] However, his definition of holism is not one that we will be adopting in this book. The reason is that Jackson places the whole before the parts, and suggests that organisations do not need to be broken down into parts in order to understand them:

> Holism puts the study of wholes before that of the parts. It does not try to break down organisations into parts in order to understand them and intervene in them. It concentrates its attention instead at the organisational level and on ensuring that the parts are functioning and are related properly together so that they *serve the purposes of the whole* (emphasis added).[21]

This is not holonomic thinking, where neither the whole nor the parts have primacy. Like Jackson, we will be exploring mental models and how they affect out thinking. Whereas Jackson's approach is to build on metaphors and paradigms, we will be suggesting that new paradigms may well hinder the intuitive understanding of organic systems. In a holonomic mode of thinking, problems are not only addressed via the thinking, analytical mind, but from a more holistic consciousness which fully utilises the Jungian mandala. In order to help understand and appreciate why, we have to examine what Henri Bortoft described as 'the unnoticed revolution', the biggest European philosophical movement of the twentieth century – phenomenology.

Phenomenology

Phenomenology is a philosophical movement the aim of which is to enquire into the nature of 'lived experience'. This definition immediately raises the problem of what is *lived experience,* since it can be interpreted both in the present tense – experience as it is lived in the now – or interpreted in the past tense, where the word 'lived' suggests experience which has already been lived. Phenomenology began with Edmund Husserl (1859–1938) at the very start of the twentieth century, and was then developed by Martin Heidegger (1889–1976), culminating in his work

Being and Time. It was also developed in France by existentialist philosopher Jean-Paul Sartre (1905–1980) and Maurice Merleau-Ponty (1908–1961), who was interested in the role the body played in cognition, perception and human experience.[22]

Phenomenology should not be confused with the previous century's introspection which was attempting to explain cognition and thinking. The main insight from phenomenology is that lived experience – our experience of life as it is lived in our consciousness – escapes from both our commonsense understanding of experience and scientific understandings of experience. Both of these are based in our deeply rooted mental models of the world, and the way in which we think about perception. As Francisco Varela said, 'The blind spot of contemporary science is experience'.[23]

The work of phenomenologist Henri Bortoft deserves a special mention. He is best known for his teachings on the scientific consciousness of Johann Wolfgang von Goethe,[24] and his concept of 'authentic wholeness' which Henri felt countered a form of 'counterfeit wholeness' found in General Systems Theory.[25] Henri built on these themes with his final work on phenomenology and hermeneutics, *Taking Appearance Seriously,* which was written in such a way as to lead the reader into what he termed 'the dynamic way of seeing'.[26] The importance of Henri's work on the dynamics of seeing in management and economics has been acknowledged by a number of authors such as Otto Scharmer in *Theory U,* by Peter Senge and colleagues in the book *Presence: Exploring Profound Change in People, Organisations and Society,* and by H. Thomas Johnson and Anders Bröms in *Profit Beyond Measure.* Henri's influence can also be found in the phenomenological approach to the environment and architecture in the work of Ingrid Stefanovic[27] and David Seamon.[28]

In the 1950s, Henri worked on the problem of wholeness in quantum physics as a PhD student under David Bohm at Birkbeck College, who first introduced Henri to new ways of thinking about wholeness. Henri also worked with J.G. Bennett, who in the 1960s created ISERG (Integral Science Research Group), of which Henri was a member. Much of this work consisted in developing the new discipline of systems theory, and in 1971 Bennett inaugurated the International Academy for Continuous Education, where Henri was invited to teach.

Having begun his career in quantum physics, Henri was now applying this new way of thinking in organisations, focusing on discovering new educational methods in business. It was Bohm's interest in the hologram that would inspire Henri's work on the perception of wholeness in organisations. The laser had been invented in the 1950s, so in the 1960s holograms were new. Although holograms today are manufactured using a different process, they were originally created using holographic plates. The key characteristic of these types of plate was that if they were broken into parts, the holographic image as seen by a person was still whole. For example, if the image was that of a horse, and the plate was broken in two, you would still be able to see the original and whole horse on both plates. This led Henri and a few other researchers to begin to contemplate the perceptions of organisations in a holographic manner, and not via that of the General Systems Theory, a methodology which Henri described as leading to concepts of 'counterfeit wholeness', an incorrect perception of what exactly the whole organisation is.

One of Henri's projects was to undertake an attitude survey in the company J. Lyons & Co., at the time a huge British food and restaurant chain, which in 1947 was the first company in the world to introduce computers, previously seen as tools only for scientists and not managers. Because of this prevalent view, they had been forced to create their own computer. The company now wanted to utilise computers as a management information tool across the entire company, and therefore Henri and his colleagues were asked to conduct an attitude survey to aid this project. Their key insight was based on their holographic thinking, seeing each person within the organisation as a part of the holographic plate, whereby, to some degree or other, the whole organisation 'came to presence' in each and every member of staff. That meant conducting surveys with people from every single department and level of the organisation, and then reporting the findings back in a matrix format.

In saying that the whole organisation 'comes to presence' in each person, we begin to realise that the concept of the whole organisation cannot be written down – it cannot be described in a diagram, and we can neither touch nor point to the whole organisation. It is not an object as we normally think of them, either solid or abstract. General Systems Theory views the organisation in terms of its separate parts. The analyst following this paradigm makes observations, and then describes the organisation in terms of a systems diagram, where the relationship between each of the parts is formalised as an external relationship as perceived by the analyst. But, for Henri, the analyst has not captured the whole organisation. What they have described is a 'counterfeit whole'. The reason for it being counterfeit is that what seems like a holistic methodology is in fact a subtle form of reductionism, and the system which has been described is counterfeit because the whole dominates the parts, a form of totalitarianism. The whole in this instance, because it has been articulated in a diagram, acts more like a 'super-part' to which all other parts are subordinate.

If we contemplate a hologram, we can begin to understand the relationship between the whole and the parts in a new way. In a hologram, neither the whole nor the parts dominate each other. You cannot analyse a hologram in either a bottom-up or a top-down manner. The whole is dependent on the parts in order to come to 'presence', and the parts depend on the whole in order to gain their identity as meaningful parts in a larger system.

However, you also need to consider another aspect of the hologram, which is the ability to be broken up into parts, but still remain whole. When we think of solid objects, our logic, or our commonsense way of thinking about the world, tells us that we cannot break up an object into parts, and it still remains whole. This is a contradiction. If we think about a photograph of a horse, which we were to then cut in two, we would end up with two pictures, each depicting half a horse, rather than a whole one. The trick with the hologram is that it is an aid that leads us to a new way of thinking; and when we think about the two holographic plates, and the fact that two images of horses can be seen on them, we realise that the images of the horses are one and the same.

So here we have an essential difference between Henri's understanding of the whole and the parts, and the General Systems Theory view of the parts and the whole. With the systems theory, you take a step back in order to see the whole, whereas for Henri, you can gain an intuition or feeling of the whole by going into the parts, such as looking into the attitudes and opinions of each and every employee and recognising that they are embodied or expressed in some way by some aspect of the whole organisation.

In terms of the Jungian mandala, we can see how the introduction of the hologram in the 1960s helped Henri and his colleagues to develop new mental models – new conceptual ways of thinking and insights – which came from a holistic mode of consciousness, one that is concerned more with relationships than discrete entities, as compared with the analytic, verbal and logical mode of consciousness, which favours a conception of reality based on solid objects.[29] They brought this new thinking into their ways of seeing the organisation, in this case holographically. Their research then gave them new insights that led to concrete recommendations and actions for the organisation, even though these were often based on intuitions and feelings for the organisation as a whole, which could not be easily expressed in language. So we can see here how we can begin to develop all four ways of knowing, so that they work together holistically, preventing us from getting stuck in just one way of knowing the world.

3. Seeing

Visual Perception

In 1910, French eye surgeons Moreau and LePrince performed an operation on an eight year old boy who had been blind from birth due to cataracts. They had restored his eyes to perfect functioning, and so, on removing the bandages from the boy's eyes, asked him what he could see. 'I don't know', the boy replied, even when shown a moving hand. Only when he could actually touch the hand could he then realise that it was moving.[1] Learning to see as an adult is not easy, and in many cases where 'sight' has been restored to an adult, the efforts involved in subsequently seeing can be so traumatising and difficult that adults who have had the necessary operations go through a psychological crisis, eventually neglecting their sight entirely. As Moreau wrote, 'To give back sight to a congenitally blind person is more the work of an educator than of a surgeon'.[2]

That the act of seeing is not merely an act of receiving sense data into our eyes is a fact that is missed by scientists who refer to themselves as 'empirical objectivists'. This is often referred to by others as 'naive empirical objectivism', and is the belief that reality only presents itself to us from the outside; the role of the perceiver is to remain objectively detached from phenomena being observed, phenomena which come to us through our senses.[3] In this book we will take a very different approach, one in which the perceiver takes a dynamic and active role in the act of seeing.

Before we consider alternative ways of understanding the act of seeing, we first need to briefly review the mainstream or most common way of thinking about visual perception, and that is in terms of physiology and cognitive psychology. The story starts with a consideration of light, a form of electromagnetic radiation which is reflected from different surfaces and structures before arriving at the eye. In our eyes, the light passes through the cornea and lens, before arriving at the retina at the back of the eye, which is covered in light-sensitive photoreceptors in the form of rods and cones.

In terms of optimal vision for a person, there are two factors to take into account. The first is the ability to focus the image in order to achieve minimal blurring of that image. The second factor relates to the efficiency with which the pattern of light can then be transformed into electrical activity. These factors are influenced by the density of packing of receptors (hence falcons have a much higher acuity of vision than humans), and the intensity of light falling on the retina. In having two types of receptor – rods and cones – human vision is able to adapt to both daylight and night-time or low light conditions, although we lose our colour vision at night.

Colour vision is explained by humans having three types of cone receptors, which contain different pigments leading to the absorption of different wavelengths of light. The image which is captured by the retina is not then sent to part of the brain for processing. The processing of information begins in the eye itself, which then sends information *about* the image to the brain. It is worth mentioning at this point Vicki Bruce, Patrick Green and Mark Georgeson's statement about what we know about the next steps in the process:

> The ultimate aim of this approach is to understand
> how information important to an animal is detected by
> networks of nerve cells and represented in the patterns
> of neural activity. For all but the simplest animals, this
> is a distant goal indeed, and our knowledge does not yet
> extend beyond the early stages of neural transformation of
> patterns of light.[4]

The most recent research is still not conclusive about exactly what form of processing occurs in the eye, although we can think of the eye as acting as a filter. The signals from the eye are then transmitted to the brain along visual pathways. Evidence suggests that there is at least more than one visual pathway in the brain, so that there is no single area of the brain processing information about the image. There is, however, still a debate as to whether there are just two separate pathways or a network of pathways, and on top of this there are a number of theoretical models to explain these findings. As Bruce *et al.* note, 'The relationship between most of our visual experience and the functioning of the brain remains largely unknown'.[5]

In looking at cognitive psychological theories of perception, we can therefore see that there is an attempt to understand how our brains are able to perceive the outside world of objects via representations of the world and via computational processes. This is by far the dominant paradigm. The whole problem of consciousness simply does not exist for cognitive psychologists, who refer to the concept of 'awareness', modelling the brain as a computer.

The insights from phenomenology which have led to a critique of modern cognitive psychology are not new. Henri Bortoft makes the point that the same movement in thinking – into lived experience – can also be found in the earlier scientific studies and methodology of Johann Wolfgang von Goethe (1749–1832).[6] This phrase 'movement of thinking' is central to Part One of this book. What it suggests is that we have the conscious ability to learn how to change into a new way of thinking and a new way of seeing, in order to enable us see more clearly and profoundly, which will lead to better observations, analysis and problem solving in our lives. So we will now turn to an examination of 'seeing' to help us better understand how we too can make this movement of thinking.

The Experience of Seeing

A wonderfully intriguing yet simple experiment carried out in Washington's L'Enfant Plaza metro station was designed to examine context, perception and priorities.[7] Joshua Bell, one of the finest classical musicians in the world, playing a $3.5 million violin handcrafted by Antonio Stradivari in 1713, would play six pieces of classical music incognito, to commuters in the subway. What would the reaction be, how much could he earn as an anonymous busker, and would anyone recognise him?

This experiment resulted in Bell earning a grand total of $32, which is a far cry from his concerts which sell out at $100 a seat. In the course of his performance, a total of 1,070 people walked past, of which just seven people stopped to take in the music and listen. The performance was videotaped, which made for uncomfortable viewing for journalist Gene Weingarten, who then asked the question whether Bell was not real to those who hurried past, not even glancing over to him, or whether it was the people who were not real, living a ghostly life with little conscious awareness of what was around them.[8]

This was obviously no scientific experiment, but it does beg this question: if one of the world's greatest living musicians cannot distract the public, who or what could? The public here were perhaps not a typical cross-section of society, since the metro station in question lies right in the heart of federal Washington, and so the majority of them would have been government workers. But it is tempting to see in this example, especially when you watch the video, just how much are we so lost in our heads, our thinking minds, that we fail to take in the beauty of our surroundings. Like the commuters walking past Bell, we should ask ourselves just how much of nature's great beauty and *livingness* passes us by. Do we really ever truly encounter nature, or are there aspects of nature that we miss? As Ilya Prigogine and Isabelle Stengers put it: 'Nature speaks with a thousand voices, and we have only begun to listen'.[9]

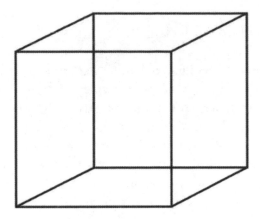

Figure 3.1. The Necker Cube.

Examining certain types of picture helps us to think about the act of seeing. It should be said that phenomenologists make great use of many types of ambiguous figures, since in these situations we can notice aspects of seeing that we would not do normally. The first picture to consider is very well known – the Necker Cube – consisting of twelve straight lines (Figure 3.1). Most people will see a three-dimensional cube, and perhaps with a little effort will be able to make it switch to another three-dimensional cube, as seen from a different perspective. From one angle it is as if we are looking at the cube from one of its sides, and from the other perspective it is as if we are looking at it from above. Many people tend to see one angle as the default, and have to make an effort to actively see the cube in the other perspective. Without this continued effort it seems to snap back to the original angle.

The interesting thing about this example is that it is almost as if we see the cube making the change. But what exactly is changing? If we think about the visual field, or the sensory field that meets our eyes, nothing has changed. So where exactly is the change? It is neither in the sensory field, and neither is it in our heads. From the perspective of phenomenology, the change is in the act of seeing itself. But what exactly does this mean? If we are to go upstream into the 'lived experience', we can catch seeing in the act. We have to go into 'the seeing of what is seen'.[10] 'Seeing'

Figure 3.2.

is an act of perception; it is not something that happens to us passively. We can explore this further by examining Figure 3.2. Stop reading at this point, and see if you can determine what the hidden image in the picture is.

You may be able to spot the hidden image in the figure immediately, or it may take you a few short moments. We have done this exercise with classes of between twenty and thirty students, and it is normal for two or three to put their hands up immediately to show that they have seen the image. Perhaps a minute later, a few more students will have managed to see it, and then following a few clues from us, more and more will see the shape. Every so often there are one or two students who simply cannot see what is there, and in that instance we show a photograph of the image to reveal exactly what is hidden. If you still cannot see the image, the answer is that it is the head of a giraffe. An additional question we ask our students after they have seen the giraffe is: 'Can you no longer see the giraffe?' We want to know if students can see the figure as they did before they spotted the giraffe. The answer is, inevitably, 'no'.

So what does it mean when you say that you are seeing a giraffe? Are you seeing an abstract figure, and then adding something on? Where is the giraffe? The answer Henri gives as a phenomenologist is not the same as the answer that a cognitive psychologist would give.[11] A cognitive psychologist could only answer this question in terms of mental representations in the brain. But Henri answers this by saying that 'the giraffe is in the seeing.' You are not attributing meaning; you are seeing meaning.[12] Another way of putting this is that you are having a direct experience of meaning.

Contemplating this figure allows us to better understand what Henri means when he discusses 'going back upstream into the act of seeing' (Figure 1.7). It can help us to understand that moment when objects appear to us which have always been there, or phenomena such as medical disorders. We have to stop focusing on the end objects, and move our attention to the way in which objects appear to us through the act of distinction (discussed in Chapter 4). When we look at the figure, we see a giraffe on the page, but the giraffe is not there; it is in the act of seeing. This suggests that in order to see a giraffe, we first have to have an idea of giraffe before we have the sensory experience. This goes counter not only to our commonsense notions of perception, but also to the philosophy of empiricism, which interprets experience to mean sensory experience. But if we now think about the phrase 'lived experience', we can begin to see how the phenomenological understanding of the phrase now differs, in that 'lived experience' is the seeing of 'meaning'. Could it be that pure empiricism has a fundamental flaw, in believing that our fundamental knowledge of the world comes directly through our senses?

Theory-Driven Seeing

There are many examples of theory-driven seeing in the history of science. If we go all the way back to Ptolemy, an astronomer born *c.* AD 90, we can see how the social order of his time greatly affected the science of that era. Here, the overriding mental model or world view was one where everything on Earth was said to be imperfect, and everything in the heavens was said to be perfect, so that the orbits of the planets, being in the heavens, were assumed

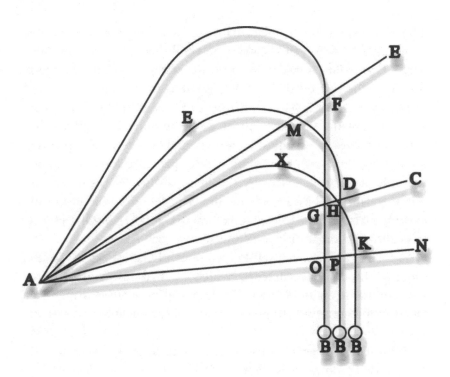

Figure 3.3. Trajectories of Albert of Saxony.

to be perfectly circular. When observations showed that this was not the case, Ptolemy created ever more elaborate mathematical models of cycles within cycles, so as to make the observations fit the order of celestial perfection.

Another striking theory of theory-driven 'seeing' is in medieval concepts of trajectories (Figure 3.3). Albert of Saxony (c. 1320–1390) conceived motion as consisting of three distinct phases – where a projectile such as a cannonball first travels in a straight line, then begins to lose its impetus, and then falls straight down, having lost all impetus. This idea of motion extended as far back as Aristotle, and is an example of a mental model being so strong as to affect what is actually seen. While we may laugh at this, Anne Prescott and Michael Mitchelmore have shown that there are still many misconceptions in school students today, with year 11 and year 12 Australian students drawing projectiles incorrectly.[13]

The sun was eventually placed in the centre of our universe by Copernicus (1473–1543), when he published *De revolutionibus orbium coelestium* (On the Revolutions of the Heavenly Spheres) shortly before his death in 1543. What is interesting about this discovery is that it is by no means obvious at all that the sun is at the centre of the universe. All of us commonly think about the sun as it moves across the sky and we rarely conceive of ourselves on Earth as moving around the sun. This, therefore, is a good example of scientific discovery not being a discovery of new facts out there in an objective world, but a new conceptualisation of existing facts, the creation of a new mental model, or what Henri has called the 'organising idea'.[14]

A final example is the well-known story of Galileo (1564–1642) looking through his telescope which he had just invented, to see mountains on the Moon. Reading Galileo's *Sidereus Nuncius* (1610) shows that, at first, he was not at all sure what he was seeing:

> Now let us review the observations made during the past two months, once more inviting the attention of all who are eager for true philosophy to the first steps of such important contemplations. Let us speak first of that surface of the moon which faces us. For greater clarity I distinguish two parts of this surface, a lighter and a darker; the lighter part seems to surround and to pervade the whole hemisphere, while the darker part discolours the moon's surface like a kind of cloud, and makes it appear covered with spots. Now those spots which are fairly dark and rather large are plain to everyone and have been seen throughout the ages; these I shall call the 'large' or 'ancient' spots, distinguishing them from others that are smaller in size but so numerous as to occur all over the lunar surface, and especially the lighter part. The latter spots had never been seen by anyone before me. From observations of these spots repeated many times I have been led to the opinion and conviction that the surface of the moon is not smooth, uniform, and precisely spherical

as a great number of philosophers believe it (and the other heavenly bodies) to be, but is uneven, rough, and full of cavities and prominences, being not unlike the face of the earth, relieved by chains of mountains and deep valleys.[15]

Galileo did not immediately see mountains on the Moon, at that very instant when he looked through the telescope for the very first time, and neither did others who also first looked. The discovery of the mountains on the Moon was, in fact, again a new organising idea, whereby Galileo was eventually able to give meaning to what he was perceiving. Once Galileo had described the Moon accurately, the mountains were there for everyone else to then see.

The Anatomy of Judgement

The Anatomy of Judgement was first published in 1960 and summarises Jane Abercrombie's research.[16] Abercrombie taught students how to think scientifically and objectively, based on the then recent branches of study in visual perception and group psychotherapy, helping them to develop their observational skills in order to be better able to obtain accurate information from specific situations. In her book she described her ten years' work with medical students, and how her unorthodox methods of teaching via free discussion groups led them to better understand the hidden assumptions and unconscious factors that influenced their decision-making when analysing radiographs (X-rays) of patients.

Abercrombie's background was zoology, and she had observed how, when dissecting an animal or looking into a microscope, university students would often not be able to distinguish between what was actually there and what they had been taught to expect, what 'ought' to be there. Her hypothesis was simple, in that she expected that people would be able to make better judgements if they could be taught to pay attention to the process of observing and thinking, and to become more aware of the factors that can influence our judgements. However, what is so interesting is that her book contains many extracts from conversations between her students, and these are extremely revealing in terms of the differences between students, their attitudes to the discussion groups, and just how uncomfortable many of them were.

Figure 3.4. The Hidden Man (after Porter 1954).

Abercrombie uses the term 'schemata' which she defines as the 'tools which help us to see, evaluate and respond'.[17] As well as referring to Porter's famous picture puzzle 'The Hidden Man' (Figure 3.4), in which a man is hidden using black and white shapes, she also refers to many other well known illusions to demonstrate the point that 'the relation between the inner and outer worlds – in this case, between the picture and what we see – is a complex one'.[18]

While Abercrombie cites many well known optical illusions, it is interesting to note her observations of how certain illusions can fail. A great example of her research relating to the 'distorted room' was created by Adelbert Ames. When viewed through a hole in a wall some distance from the room, it looks perfectly normal, and yet if two people stand at opposite sides, they appear dramatically different in size. We (the authors) have both had the opportunity to play in an Ames room in an art gallery in São Paulo, as did many other visitors to their great hilarity. Abercrombie notes how one woman saw all people as distorted apart from her husband, who she saw as normal and the room as distorted. Further research showed that this is true for many newly wedded couples. Her hypothesis is that for people who have recently wed, there is an anxiety that their spouse should remain the same. People, therefore, can be seen to interpret their sensory stimulus not only in part on experiences, but also on present and future needs.

The second part of Abercrombie's study describes how her course of free group discussions, which she facilitated, helped medical students to uncover their previously unrecognised assumptions or schemata, by testing them against those of their colleagues. These were all students between eighteen and twenty years old, and they were at that point in their lives where they were being forced to move out of their educational comfort zones from school, where the teacher was perceived as the authority who could impart objective and value-free facts to the students. Abercrombie noted how all of the students had a 'nineteenth century' schemata of science and the external world, whereby they assumed that they were passive receivers of information from the outside world through their senses.[19]

As it becomes clear when reading the transcripts from the discussions, many students felt uncomfortable to the point of fear, having to face the fact that their visual perceptions were so loaded with subjective aspects. These fears would more often than not translate into direct and explicit hostility towards Abercrombie. The actual discussions consisted of the following tasks:

- Observe the differences between the radiographs of two hands (one being that of a seven-year old and the other that of a 'normal' adult).
- Discuss the meaning of the word 'normal'.
- Discuss the process of classification and categorisation in science.
- Evaluate evidence.

When examining the difference between the two hands, students would often go beyond that which they could 'see' and would describe inferences, an inference being a conclusion that cannot be derived simply from the evidence available in the X-rays. Some students expressed these as 'facts', something undeniably true, whereas others would consciously describe their inference as a 'conclusion'. Students selected information from the X-rays and ignored that information which did not fit the ordained pattern expected, an example being the counting of the number of bones, where the actual images were ambiguous and where bones visually distinct from each other could not actually be seen. Students were therefore not able to keep alternative hypotheses open while they observed.

The second task that Abercrombie set her students was to read a short text by a technical author about anatomy, and to write down their own interpretations of what the author meant by the word 'normal'. This seemingly simple task showed just how much confusion there was amongst students in their understanding of this deceptively simple term. Abercrombie identified six different uses of the term ranging from informal to statistical definitions. It was not just the students who discovered confusion over this term, because Abercrombie noted the same confusions in biological scientific texts published by expert authors, not just around the word 'normal', but many others as well, such as 'primitive', 'fundamental', 'environmental' and 'inherited'.

An interesting example is also provided, whereby a doctor who is struggling to diagnose a patient asks him if his diet has been normal. The patient replies 'yes', but some days later the doctor learns that for three years the patient has only been eating bread, margarine and treacle. This then allows him to properly diagnose the patient as suffering from scurvy, which is a result of a deficiency in vitamin C. Here the doctor uses the term 'normal' to indicate suitability of diet, but the patient is using the term to indicate that there had been no change recently. While issues such as this can be overcome by being aware of the ambiguity of terms, other confusions can still remain due to the fact that the meanings of words such as 'normal' can overlap.

It is clear that many of the students found the format of free discussion far more useful in helping them to realise that the receipt of information involves the same kind of processes of selection and interpretation as does the receipt of information from a visual pattern; at the end of the course they were able to use language with greater effectiveness. In designing the free discussion groups the way she did, Abercrombie's objective could be seen not as imparting new knowledge or 'packets of facts', but to facilitate change in the students by helping them to reassess and rearrange what was already in their minds. This process, though, turned out to be not only an intellectual exercise. It is clear why Abercrombie also looked to group psychotherapeutic methodologies, since many students reacted with extremely negative emotions when their deep held convictions were challenged.

The task set for the students before they discussed classifications was to write a short essay on their thoughts on this subject. What was interesting here was that, while most students recognised the man-made arbitrary nature of most systems of classification, many of them also stated that there had to be an 'absolute' system of classification – one which 'does not depend on human convenience, which exists apart from man's conceptions, and is perfect, permanent and unchanging'.[20] Students expressed this in the following manner:

> ... in certain fields at any rate, there is a fundamental classification ... which always has existed and doesn't really depend on how you split it up, it's not purely a man-made thing.

> I think that in chemistry there is a fundamental order of things and ... perhaps in biology one might be discovered.

> I do insist that there must be an absolute classification, which is absolutely invariable, and is a product of the order of things.[21]

Abercrombie noted that these opinions were the 'nineteenth century view', where the emphasis in science is discovering an external and objective nature, which is distinct from our own subjective world of illusions, and where universal laws of nature are deductible by reason. These views on how the world 'must' be fixed and eternally stable appeared to strongly affect the ways in which students received information from their course, and, as we will see, how they would react emotionally.

A slightly cruel but interesting experiment by Jerome Bruner and Leo Postman from 1949 highlights just how much our perceptions can be affected by our conceptual way of seeing and just how passive it can sometimes be.[22] They showed to students participating in the experiment a series of playing cards which were projected on to a screen, each one for just a fraction of a second, but some of the cards did not in fact exist – for example, a black ten of hearts, or a red seven of spades. At a certain speed of viewing, the students were only seeing what they expected to see, and not what was actually there. When the speed of showing the cards was slowed down, they began to get slightly disturbed, but they could not articulate why. When the speed of projection was slowed down further, they began to see the actual fantasy cards, and many became extremely disturbed and upset. The effects of this experiment were so strong that some students even panicked as they thought that their minds were being interfered with.

This experiment shows just how directly we see categories, and in many ways this is a useful ability to have, stopping us from becoming overwhelmed by our sensory experience. While we may emphasise and value this mode of thinking in academia and business, for artists, such as a painter or sculptor, often the opposite case is true. Ronald Brady discusses this point in relation to the sculptor Constantin Brancusi's highly abstract work, *The Newborn*.[23] If you view this piece of work without any knowledge of his other works, it is incredibly difficult to perceive how Brancusi captured the first gesture of the cry of a baby. The point here is that it is important not to be caught up in a single mode of thinking, and that we can develop a deep awareness and experience of the different modes, so that we are able to move in and out of them based on the requirements and context of the situations in which we find ourselves.

The final task that Abercrombie discussed was how students would evaluate a written report from an experiment published in an authoritative and well-regarded scientific journal. The nature of bias has been studied in depth, and aesthetic, ethical, religious and political opinions can all affect our judgements. But the students were surprised to discover that, although they considered themselves to be 'scientists' with the ability to think logically and rationally, this was not the case with more subtle factors also affecting their assessments. Although they had all been taught the correct protocols and methodologies for experiments, such as standardising conditions and changing one factor at a time, students made varying assessments of the author's claims. For example, some students were affected by the status of the author, even though the report was vague and the experimental design inadequate. Many students were disturbed by the fact that their scientific judgement could be swayed so much by whether or not they trusted people in life. In everyday life, we are continually evaluating evidence, and we too may not be aware of making any judgements either.

In discussing the effectiveness of her course of free discussions compared to the more usual teaching methods by lecture, Abercrombie felt that the discussions had been of benefit in teaching students to understand the key differences between description and inference, something they had not been able to understand when comparing and describing the hand X-rays. Inferences, of course, are important, because it is inferences rather than descriptions that can lead to action – for example a doctor reaching a conclusion with a diagnosis based on what he observes in a patient. Abercrombie also saw a reduction in the number of false inferences in her students, due to the students being more critical of the evidence before them. But, as has already been noted, the process of change was not an easy one for many students who, despite their youth, remained inflexible, much like their older professors who could often appear to be wedded to their theories and hypotheses.

The greatest challenge that students faced was the changed view of the external world and their relationship to it. In particular, the course showed them just how limited the implicit assumptions of a nineteenth century world view were, as well as the assumption that a student was a passive receiver of information from the outside world through his or her senses. Some examples of the students' revelations were:

> It's as though my world has been cracked open.
>
> But you can't have all the world a jelly.
>
> I daren't walk downstairs in case the stairs are not there.[24]

Some became frightened at losing the comfort of a fixed and eternal world existing independently of the vagaries of human needs, and this could potentially be due to the fact that the students were now seeing changes in themselves:

> I can't trust myself now, let alone anyone else.[25]

When some students did change their opinions, they were sometimes jeered. This is an interesting emotional reaction, since science is supposed to be free of value judgements. How can scientific knowledge advance, when changes of opinion are not approved of? Other sources of hostility appeared to come from deep held schemata on one's own position in society, demonstrated in one student's views on classification, which led to a long discussion by the other students in his group, who attempted to correct what they saw as his confusions:

> Classification brings order into beautiful chaos, the state
> where actions and statements are not compared and
> unduly criticised. Classification is the major enemy of
> all individualistic tendencies but we, unfortunately, live

in a civilisation where individuals are sacrificed for the common good.[26]

In summary, the design of the course, with the teacher there to facilitate discussion rather than to impart knowledge, demonstrated to the students their own personal involvement with their perceptions of the external world. A significant outcome was that their beliefs in the stability and independence of the external world, and their confidence in their ability to secure reliable information about it, was shaken. Deep held beliefs in authority were also questioned. However, Abercrombie's task was to lead the students to relinquishing their security of thinking in well-defined channels, and to find recognition based on ambiguity, uncertainty and open choice.

Perhaps the greatest lesson we can take from this exploration of seeing, is that to see well is an act of humility. When we are stuck in ego, we never stop to contemplate and to ask ourselves if we really have seen and noticed all that there is to see in our field of vision. Our ego can act as blinkers on a horse. This is particularly true when we look at how we see other people. Have we really seen the people around us as they truly are? Can we really see who those people are who fully epitomise the essence of the purpose, mission and values of our organisation, whichever level they may be in the formal organisational hierarchy? Or does our fear of competition, insecurity and desire for personal achievement at the expense of others place a blindfold over our eyes? Finding this level of humility takes courage and strength, but when we are able to let go of our insecurities, as Abercrombie's students eventually were able to do, we find that we have fresh new holonomic eyes for absorbing, appreciating and comprehending at a deeper level, the totality of the vibrant, living and creative organisations and ecosystems of which we are a part.

4. Goethe's Way of Seeing

Goethe's Greatest Achievement

Until now we have been examining the disciplines of phenomenology and science, and looking to see if we can discover aspects of both that can help those of us in business to develop our ways of thinking. In doing so, we have begun to consider more deeply concepts in systems such as the whole and the parts, and also the manner in which our conceptual way of thinking is an intimate part of how we see. One way in which can begin to make this new method of thinking more comprehensible and concrete for us is to study the scientific works of Johann Wolfgang von Goethe (1749–1832).

Many people know Goethe only through his literature and poetry, with his lifelong work *Faust* considered to be one of the greatest contributions to modern European literature. Goethe, though, was far more than a poet and a writer, and when you study his life you are left with a sense of wonder and bewilderment at his genius, especially when his scientific body of work opens up to you. His work, covering plants, animal morphology, colour, clouds, weather and geology, has on the whole been ignored in the scientific arena, because many scientists, both during his lifetime and up to the present day, have considered his science to be unworthy of the name, being the work of a romantic dilettante, unable to understand mathematics. Nothing could be further from the truth, and it is important not only to study the results of Goethe's work, such as that on morphology, of which Goethe is the founding father, but also to understand the nature of his way of thinking, knowing and penetrating into the phenomena of organic life.

Goethe was born in Germany in 1749. As a student, between 1765 and 1768, he studied law at Leipzig, but this bored him and while there he also enrolled in science courses which covered anatomy, electricity and magnetism. Goethe took a keen interest in medicine, as well as studying philosophy, but (in his own words) the works of Gottfried Leibniz and Christian Wolff 'simply refused to become clear to me'.[1] His studies were curtailed in 1768 due to illness, but through the visits of his physician he developed an interest in alchemy and the writings of Paracelsus.[2] In 1774 he wrote *The Sorrows of Young Werther*, the novel which led to his worldwide fame, and which also led him to being invited into the court of the eighteen year old Duke Karl August in Weimar, which became his permanent place of residence until his death in 1832.

Goethe was closely associated with the Romantic Movement, predominantly due to his close relationship with the poet, playwright and philosopher Friedrich Schiller, who, along with many other great proponents of the Romantic Movement, was based in Jena, just a few miles away from Goethe in Weimar. While Goethe and the Romantic movement both saw limitations in the science of their time, the abstract idealism of the natural philosophy developed by Georg Hegel was almost diametrically opposed to the deeply empirical nature of Goethe's scientific methods, which were entirely based on systematic observations, as we will see.

Goethe was a man deeply grounded in reality, living a life completely in the everyday world, in which he was an excellent administrator of the Duchy of Saxe-Weimar, in charge of the forestry, mines and market gardens, and actively involved with the affairs of the tiny state. Goethe emphasised in his writings the importance he attached to having such a physical and practical life, and so his great works should not be seen as those of a whimsical poet, but rather as a great and active doer, for whom the description 'prolific' appears to be woefully inadequate.

Goethe would rarely write or articulate his methods, having 'no organ for philosophy' as he put it.[3] His own methods were described back to him by his friend Friedrich Schelling, who saw that what he himself was doing in thought, Goethe was doing in practice. However, some researchers have developed methodologies directly from and inspired by Goethe, and these cover areas as diverse as biology, genetics, landscape, spirituality and business strategy (such as the work of Otto Scharmer).

If we study Goethe, we too can begin to enter into his way of seeing, which is designed to move us away from our everyday mode of seeing, which is so theory-driven. It could be said that Goethe's genius lay in his perceptive abilities and his powers of observation. Goethe felt that his own genius in perception did not come from abilities he was born with, but through long and systematic observation of the subjects in which he was interested, particularly plants. This makes Goethe worth studying, because while many of us will only be able to listen to the music of the great composers such as Bach, Beethoven and Mozart, with Goethe it is as if we can step into his shoes, really seeing the vibrant livingness and complexity that he saw in nature.

Before we look at some of Goethe's different scientific studies, it is worth contemplating what his greatest achievement was, in order to place his studies in a wider context.[4] Prior to Goethe, it was thought that it was not possible to understand life, as in living organisms. We sometimes think of the mechanistic world view as being dominant in science during Goethe's era, viewing the universe as a massive clockwork machine, a world view inspired by a naive understanding of Newtonian classical physics. While there were philosophers such as Baron d'Holbach (1723–1789) who, in works such as *The System of Nature* did conceive of nature as pure mechanism, it could be argued that the more prevalent view, epitomised by Immanuel Kant (1724–1804), was that there was a fundamental difference between inorganic and organic life, but that the secrets of organic life would never be accessible to the human mind.

When thinking about a simple inorganic mechanistic system,

we can explain the movement of bodies that use mass, direction and velocity, and so long as we know the starting conditions, we can predict the outcome. This is well known, and Newton's mechanics (only slightly modified) were good enough to get us to the Moon. The key point here is that these factors, including heat and weight and time, are all available to our senses. We do not have to go beyond our senses to access them; we can perceive them directly. We can explain the workings of a machine if we understand the interactions of each of its parts. The unifying principle of the machine lies outside the parts, that is, it lies in the plan in the head of the builder.

A plant is not like a machine. The relationships of the parts do not appear to follow one from another, but appear to be guided by an inner principle which is not perceptible to the senses. Kant wanted to say that it was this inner guiding principle which was not accessible to human logic. The human capacity for knowledge was believed to end at the level of organic nature.

Another way to understand organic life is to say that one part of a plant, for example, does not determine another part. In a plant, it is the whole which determines the parts, but this whole is not a super-part, it is not a top down hierarchy, it is not the controller. Goethe used the term 'entelechy' to refer to the way in which a plant has the ability to make itself out of itself, something a machine cannot do. But note that we are not talking here about one physical plant reproducing itself into a new plant, for these are just two physical manifestations of the inner guiding principle.

'The plant', therefore, as Goethe understood it, was more than the physical plants that we can see. Goethe was able to comprehend the guiding principles which led to life creating itself out of itself, but this comprehension was not through the logical mind, but through intuition. Living organisms, therefore, can only be comprehended through an 'intuitive concept', and unlike machines, they need something more than just our sense perceptions to comprehend them. In this view of nature, we become less focused on each individual instance of a plant, and instead know the plant as an entity that is never stationary, never at rest; it is constantly reshaping itself, transforming, and therefore 'it can only be truly comprehended in its becoming, in its development'.[5]

Rudolf Steiner described Goethe as 'the Copernicus and Kepler of the organic world'.[6] Although the nature of organic life was known long before Goethe, it was Goethe who discovered its lawfulness. In Goethe's time, the overriding paradigm in understanding plant and animal morphology was classification, where efforts were directed in searching for all the differences between species. For Goethe this could never succeed, and he felt that he was able to perceive the same underlying lawful principles across animals and across plants.

If we look at Charles Darwin (1809–1882), we see that his theoretical foundations are often presented as outer influences working mechanically on organisms. Goethe understood organisms as having an ability to take on many forms, which were contingent on outer conditions, that is, the environment. Hence, as Steiner puts it, 'external conditions are the outer inducement for the inner forces to manifest in a particular way'.[7] What does Steiner mean by this? We find the answer in Goethe's discovery of the intermaxillary bone, a little bone found between the lower and upper jaws of animals, and a bone which, prior to Goethe's discovery, was not thought to be present in humans. Hence, in the mindset that is always looking for differences, this was seen as a central trait distinguishing humans from animals.

Goethe though, was able to conceive of the existence of the bone in humans, because whereas others sought difference, he was able to see unifying principles which were present in all organisms, but which manifested concretely in different species. Hence, when Goethe undertook many observational studies of skulls, his way of looking enabled him to perceive the bone in humans, but only in extremely young babies, since the bone 'disappears' as the child grows. This bone is not easy to see, because seeing it depends on the quality and condition of the skulls being examined; but there is something in the way of looking which enables the bone to be seen, whereas previously it was missed.

Let us now fast forward to that branch of complexity theory which views organisations as well as organisms as living systems. W. Edwards Deming, the great management theorist, suggested that 97% of what management does cannot be measured.[8] This strongly echoes Henri, who points us to the intrinsic dimension of organic life which can only be perceived in the intuitive mind, and which also cannot be measured or described using Cartesian or Euclidean logic. The deep study of Goethe's way of seeing is directly relevant to business. We see this in the way in which Toyota have for many years invited executives from all their major competitors to tours of their production lines. Toyota's system has been much studied but almost never replicated. Just as the majority of scientists have failed to comprehend Goethe's dynamic way of seeing and understanding plants, business executives with their mechanistic mindsets cannot see or understand Toyota's living production systems.[9]

Toyota do not need expensive external management information systems to run their plants, something that Thomas Johnson calls 'the information factory'. This is because the information necessary for running Toyota's production plant is intrinsic to the actual production line itself, due to the way in which the plant is organised. Toyota also have a profound management philosophy, and this is implicit to such an extent that Mike Rother, who has studied and written extensively about Toyota, says that even people from Toyota cannot articulate it, just as we cannot articulate the lawful dynamic principles of the One plant.[10] The only way to reach an understanding of Toyota's production plant is via Goethe's way of seeing an organism, and that is via one's intuition.

While a few scientists who were contemporaries of Goethe did understand his great achievement exactly, the vast majority did not, and perhaps this is still true today, a situation exacerbated by the fact that Goethe's 'delicate empiricism', as he called it, is either not considered to be science, or not considered at all. But now, with the growing interest in chaos and complexity theory, the time is now ripe for a reappraisal of Goethe and recognition of just how fundamentally important his main insight and contribution to science was.

The Act of Distinction

Having examined the act of 'seeing', we now need to consider the act of 'distinction'. This is critical in order to understand how thinking phenomenologically allows us to overcome seemingly paradoxical concepts. Just as we did with the act of seeing, we also have to direct our attention upstream into the act of distinction, and not get distracted by the outcome, the objects which have been distinguished. Our common way of thinking about distinction is that it is a way in which we are able to perceive separate objects. In this way, everything about the way we think directs us downstream. It takes effort for us to direct our attention upstream into the act of distinction, but we can use certain illustrations to help us.

Figure 4.1.

The ambiguous drawing in Figure 4.1 can be seen either as a duck or a rabbit. The duck is looking to the left, and the rabbit is looking to the right. Just as we saw with the Necker Cube (Figure 3.1), we can switch between seeing the two different meanings. However, if we think about the figure itself, it is not duck and rabbit – it is duck/rabbit. The reason we can say this is that the duck is the rabbit and the rabbit is the duck. It is not partly duck and partly rabbit. The key here is that the figure is simultaneously both duck and rabbit.

How does this relate to the act of distinction? We must

not confuse the act of distinction with separation. If we go upstream into the act of distinction, we discover that there are two simultaneous movements. On the one hand, when we distinguish between two entities 'a' and 'b', we *difference* them ('difference' here being used as a verb). And, simultaneously, we also *relate* them. So, just as the figure above is duck/rabbit, we have to understand the act of distinction as differencing/relating.

Another key insight of phenomenology is that 'lived experience' is intrinsically holistic. How can this be? Well, we have to stay focused on the act of distinguishing, and not on the objects that have been distinguished. Within the act of distinction, although there are two movements of thinking – differencing and relating – it is one single act of distinction, and therefore we can say that the act of distinction is a single whole, which although containing two movements of thinking, are related intrinsically, thus preserving the wholeness.

If this point is understood, then it can be seen that the act of distinction is intrinsically holistic, a statement which at first sight seems to be entirely paradoxical, since the way we normally think about distinction is that it is fundamentally reductionist. It is only paradoxical if we lose sight of the act of distinguishing. Therefore, we could also say that lived experience is intrinsically holistic too, since being upstream, it deals with the 'coming-into-being' of objects, and not the objects after they have been distinguished, where the only aspect that can be perceived is the separation. While this may still seem abstract, some concrete and real examples will help to explain why it is important to understand this concept. The examples that Henri uses come from the history of science,[11] and we will follow these with our more mundane example, so as to show how common this facet of seeing really is.

If we go back to the picture of the giraffe (see p.59), it could be said that in order to see the giraffe, not only do we have to already have a concept or a mental model of a giraffe, but we have to be able to see 'giraffe-ly'. This word is directing us to think about the act of seeing dynamically. As we have said before, seeing involves something that is non-sensory, – the organising idea. This may sound as if it is a thing, perhaps a static representation in the brain, but it is not. It should be thought of as a processing or organising within the act of seeing.

This should become much clearer when we consider our first example, one of the greatest triumphs in science, the distinguishing of clouds. If we look at the sky nowadays, we can see a number of types of cloud, and it may be the case that we wonder what the great accomplishment was, simply putting labels on the clouds. But before 1803, when Luke Howard published his seminal paper *On the Modification of Clouds,* many of the world's greatest thinkers had already tried to classify the clouds to no avail. It was as if they were seeing what we first see in the picture of the giraffe – just a meaningless jumble of shapes. Many scientists felt that it was simply not possible to classify clouds into different types. Once we go back upstream, before the clouds were first distinguished, we can better appreciate just what an achievement it was.

Howard was not just giving labels to different objects. He spent many years observing clouds, and not only was he able to distinguish the three main types – cirrus, stratus, and cumulus – he was also able to distinguish, and thus describe, their inner order and dynamics, which led to their modification of one type into another, based on changing atmospheric conditions. Howard did not classify clouds based on secondary characteristics; his discovery was a unitary act of differencing/relating, in which the different cloud types are at the same time both different from each other and dynamically related to one another.

The next example comes from psychiatrist Oliver Sacks. In his book *The Man who Mistook his Wife for a Hat,* Sacks discusses the work of neurologist Guillaume-Benjamin Duchenne (1806–1875), who, in the 1850s, was the first person to describe the disease muscular dystrophy. By 1860, after Duchenne's original description, many hundreds of cases had been recognised and described, so much so that his student Jean-Martin Charcot said, 'How come that a disease so common, so widespread, and so recognisable at a glance – a disease which has doubtless always existed – how come that it is only recognised now? Why did we need M. Duchenne to open our eyes?'[12]

We can think of 'describing' as the act of distinction. However, there is more to this phenomenon than simply people suddenly noticing something that had not previously come to their attention. Did Duchenne discover muscular dystrophy? Or can we say that in some way he created it? Or was the act of distinguishing/relating in some mixture of both of these things? This is an important question, as we can now begin to appreciate the concept of 'being' in phenomenology.

Iain McGilchrist has an interesting way of describing the mixture of objectivity and subjectivity by saying:

> We neither discover an objective reality nor invent a
> subjective reality, but that there is a process of responsive
> evocation, the world 'calling forth' something in me that
> in turn 'calls forth' something in the world.[13]

When something appears, we normally think of the object as existing fully before anyone describes it. Heidegger talked about things being freed in order to be, and Henri describes the act of distinguishing as 'releasing things into being'. The reason Sacks used the example of muscular dystrophy was that he found the example very similar to his experiences with Tourette syndrome. He had never seen a patient with Tourette's before, but in 1971 Sacks was featured in a newspaper article in *The Washington Post* about cases of his patients with 'tics'. Following publication of this article, he saw a patient called Ray:

> The day after I saw Ray, it seemed to me that I noticed
> three Touretters in the street in downtown New York. I
> was confounded, for Tourette's syndrome was said to be
> excessively rare. It had an incidence, I had read, of one in
> a million, yet I had apparently seen three examples in an
> hour. I was thrown into a turmoil of bewilderment and
> wonder: was it possible that I had been overlooking this

all the time, either not seeing such patients or vaguely dismissing them as 'nervous', 'cracked', 'twitchy'?

Was it possible that everyone had been overlooking them? Was it possible that Tourette's was not a rarity, but rather common – a thousand times more common, say, than previously supposed? The next day, without specially looking, I saw another two in the street. At this point I conceived a whimsical fantasy or private joke: suppose (I said to myself) that Tourette's is very common but fails to be recognised but once recognised is easily and constantly seen.[14]

Our own example of this is much more mundane. In 2009, Simon purchased a new car (second hand, but new to him). He came across a car he had never seen before at the Vauxhall dealers, nondescript but highly practical, and perfect for his needs in terms of space for his mountain bike. It was a Vauxhall Meriva, which was in the category of Mini People Carriers (MPV). No sooner had he finished the test drive and left the dealership to think about the purchase than he began to see Merivas everywhere on the roads. He could not believe how popular it was, a car that he had never known about before. As Henri puts it, the act of distinction 'theres it', and once Simon had distinguished Merivas, there they all were for him to see.

Goethe's Theory of Colours

It is not really possible to study Goethe's *Theory of Colours*[15] without having access to a small glass prism. Prisms can be purchased cheaply from many shops on-line. Although expensive prisms for scientific use are available, for these experiments the types of prisms that are used for teaching children about colour are more than adequate. A Google search using the term 'optical glass prism' should help you to find a few places to purchase them. The ones that we use are 5 cm long, each side being 2.5 cm.[16]

Although Goethe was studying the psychological and physiological aspects of colour perception, his experiments were created in such a way that anyone can do them with the minimal of equipment (unlike Newton's theory of light, which required a room to be set up in a very specific manner). The phenomena being discussed can be perceived rapidly and in a way in which a group can almost immediately come to complete agreement.

The first exercise we would suggest you do is to go to the internet

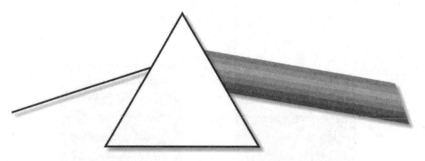

Figure 4.2. Schematic of light through a prism.

and find a number of different examples of artistic impressions and illustrations of light passing through a prism and forming a spectrum of light. We emphasise 'artistic impressions' and not actual photographs, since it is possible to find many different interpretations of how light passes through a prism. One famous drawing is on the front cover of Pink Floyd's album *The Dark Side of the Moon*. In this representation, a ray of light on the left can be seen in the form of 'grey' light passing through the prism (and then gradually fading), and the spectrum of seven colours begins to form immediately on the opposite edge of the spectrum to which the light entered. Other artistic impressions may well have no visible light inside the prism (e.g. Figure 4.2), while others may have all the colours being represented inside.

With Goethe's experiments, we begin by looking through the prism at a picture which simply consists of black and white. In order to see this, it may take you some time to locate the border between dark and light. One side of the prism has to be flat on top, so that it is pointing downwards. It will be in the exact opposite orientation to the prism shown in Figure 4.2. You may need to hold the picture higher up than the prism to locate the border. Using pieces of black and white card rather than the illustrations in this book may help as well.

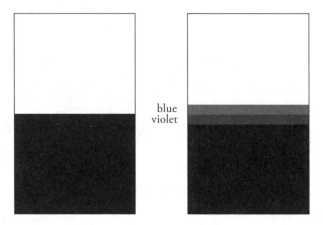

Figure 4.3 & Figure 4.4.

For the first experiment, we will look at a picture (Figure 4.3), which consists of white above and black below. Although we can also consider these to be 'dark' and 'light', this terminology can be a little confusing, so for now we will stick with 'black' and 'white'. What is seen when you look through the prism is extremely interesting. At the boundary of the black and white, two bands, violet and blue, can be seen (Figure 4.4). This becomes even more interesting when you look through the prism again, but this time with black on top and white below (Figure 4.5). You should now be able to see two very different bands of colour, red and yellow (Figure 4.6).

It is important that you really do carry out these exercises yourself, as an additional question needs to be asked, which is where exactly are the bands of colour? Do they cross the boundary, or do they lie on top of either the black card or the white card? Does the location change for the two different orientations of the black and white cards?

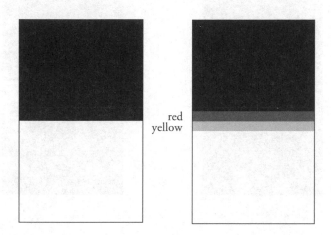

red
yellow

Figure 4.5 & Figure 4.6.

We can now ask ourselves a simple but potentially deceptive question: 'Where is the colour?' This question is asked with that specific wording in order to help you to think about your prior conceptions about light and colour, since most of us grew up being taught that white light consists of coloured light, and that the prism separates the colours. Is that really the case? In conducting these two experiments, it is important to point out that, in Goethe's way of science, we aim to stay with the phenomena as long as possible; at this point it is important not to begin to develop theories about how and why the phenomena arise, even though the shock of encountering these phenomena seemingly goes against all that we thought we knew about light.

So far we have only seen four colours. In order to see more colours, we have to create a slit. When you look at a white slit on a black background (Figure 4.7), we see five colours, with green in the middle (Figure 4.8). If you have purchased a prism to try out these experiments, it is also worth using squares of black and white card; you can then play with the size of the strip, in order to observe how this changes the phenomena you see. When the strip becomes a little wider, you do not still see the five colours described, but perhaps only four or three.

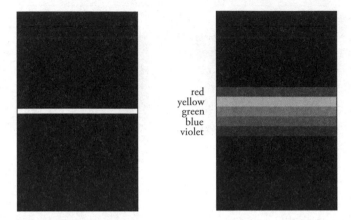

Figure 4.7 & Figure 4.8

In the contrary position of a black slit on a white background (Figure 4.9) we see an entirely new colour, ruby-magenta, which does not occur in Newton's seven-colour spectrum (Figure 4.10). Note also the inversion of blue and violet, and red and yellow. Once you have completed these experiments, if you have not already done so, look around your room through the prism. You will see all the colours that you saw previously, but it will now make sense, as these colours are only seen at the boundaries of black and white, or dark and light, such as a chair leg or window bar.

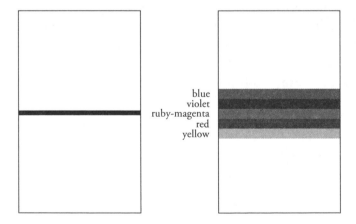

Figure 4.9 & Figure 4.10.

We can now begin to appreciate the differences between Goethe's theory of colours and that of Newton. For Goethe, colour arose at the boundary of what he termed 'dark' and 'light', and therefore the phenomena of colour were seen as arising from a dynamic relationship between opposites. Goethe conceived of the first two phenomena (Figures 4.4 and 4.6), where just two colours each were seen at a boundary, as 'primary phenomena', whereas for Newton, the whole spectrum (Figure 4.2) was a primary phenomenon.

In order to understand Goethe's motivation and reasoning, it is first worth reviewing Newton's theory of colour and light. Although Galileo had conceived of light as something mechanical, it was Newton who first sought to provide experimental proof of this theory. He first presented his experiments in 1671, in a letter to the Royal Society of London. At this time, his proof was not universally accepted, and many distinguished scientists, among them Robert Hooke, whose own theory of light was the most widely accepted, criticised Newton for not providing complete and adequate proof of his premises. Here, the criticism suggests that it was Newton's theorising about the phenomena before carrying out the experiments which drove the design of the experiments. However, by the time Newton published *Optiks* thirty-three years later, when he was President of the Royal Society and the most highly regarded scientist in Europe, no one was in a position to take him on and argue against him, Hooke having died in 1703.[17]

At school, we are taught that there are seven spectral colours, each with their own frequency and wavelength (see Table 1).

violet	668-789 THz	380-450 nm
blue	631-668 THz	450-475 nm
cyan	606-630 THz	476-495 nm
green	526-606 THz	495-570 nm
yellow	508-526 THz	570-590 nm
orange	484-508 THz	590-620 nm
red	400-484 THz	620-750 nm

Table 1. The seven colours of the spectrum.

Both Goethe's experiments and other phenomena (such as that of coloured shadows, where we do not see a shadow in the colour of the light causing it, but its complementary or opposite colour) show us that there is no simple relationship between perceived colour and its wavelength. In the 1950s, photographer Edwin Land carried out some landmark experiments with coloured shadows and photography. Contrary to the still widely accepted trichromatic theory, with the three pigments in eye seen as responding to the peak absorption of the wavelengths at 419, 531 and 558 nm, he concluded that 'the natural image depends on the random interplay of short and longer wavelengths over the total visual field'.[18] Interestingly, Land was greatly criticised for not being a professional psychologist and having no real understanding of that academic discipline, but what we see in Land is a professional who was steeped in the phenomena without being misled by preconceived theory. This allowed him to first notice this phenomenon in some photographs that he had been processing, and which therefore aroused his curiosity.

Goethe, likewise, had been curious about colour, having undertaken a tour of Italy in the years 1786 to 1788, when he had met many different artists, all of whom could verbally account for their skills apart from that of colour. Goethe then wondered if it would be possible to develop a theory of colour, and borrowed some optical equipment from his friend Hofrat Büttner of Jena in order to replicate Newton's experiments. Although he had set up a room as a camera obscura, as required by Newton's methodology, due to much pressure from his friend, he was forced to return the equipment; but before doing so, he looked through the prism out of curiosity. In Goethe's words:

> I remembered well that everything appeared many-
> coloured, but in what manner was no longer present to
> my mind. At that very moment I was in a room that had
> been painted completely white; I expected, mindful of the
> Newtonian theory as I placed the prism before my eyes, to

see the light that comes from there to my eye split up into
so many coloured lights.

How astonished I was, then, when the white wall,
observed through the prism, remained white just as before;
that only there, where darkness adjoined on it, did a more
or less determinate colour appear; finally, that the window
bars appeared in the liveliest colours of all, whereas no
trace of colouring was to be seen in the light grey sky
outside. It did not take much deliberation for me to
recognise that a boundary is necessary to produce colours,
and I immediately said to myself, as if by instinct, that the
Newtonian teaching is false.[19]

Goethe was well versed in Newton's theory of light, but when
he published his *Theory of Colours (Zur Farbenlehre),* some of his
forceful arguments against Newton were factually incorrect. This
aspect of his theory appears to have led many critics to reject his
entire theory. But so long as we are aware of these limitations, we
can look more deeply into what Goethe was doing, and what he
was trying to achieve. Goethe was attempting to account for the
qualities of colour in his phenomenological experiments. He was
staying within his own experience without theorising, unlike the
scientific dogma of his time, which followed Galileo's division of
the world into primary and secondary qualities.

It was with Galileo that natural philosophy, as science was then
called, started to distrust the physical senses, trusting only that
which could be quantified, such as distance, time and mass. This
is expressed in the following way by Lord Kelvin (1824–1907):

In physical science the first essential step in the direction
of learning any subject is to find principles of numerical
reckoning and practicable methods for measuring some
quality connected with it. I often say that when you can
measure what you are speaking about, and express it in
numbers, you know something about it; but when you
cannot measure it, when you cannot express it in numbers,

your knowledge is of a meagre and unsatisfactory kind;
it may be the beginning of knowledge, but you have
scarcely in your thoughts advanced to the state of Science,
whatever the matter may be.[20]

Goethe's 'experiments', or exercises, in *The Theory of Colours* stay within the phenomena as much as possible. To appreciate them we have to make changes to the way in which we differentiate between an experiment and a theory. Goethe's exercises can be seen as a single 'experiment', which consists of perceiving the phenomena in as many different ways as possible. His emphasis is on the seeing of the phenomena, whereas for Newton the role of the experimenter is one of an independent observer viewing an external phenomenon, a colour spectrum projected on to a wall.

Newton was well aware of the phenomena seen when looking through a prism, and many critics of Goethe felt that the phenomena could be understood in terms of light rays. But what is a light ray? It is a line of infinitely small width. It is not a three-dimensional beam, but a mathematical construction used to describe quite accurately the diffraction of light. This can lead to confusion, because Newton did not consider psychological or physiological explanations in his experiments with light, whereas Goethe's theory was focused more on the psychological and physiological, although that would be to miss his deeper insights into the notion of colour arising from the relationship between physical light and 'dark' and 'light'.

Goethe did not use mathematics in his methodology. Instead, his progression of exercises was designed to help his readers to build up a clear understanding of the phenomena as a whole. In order to have this deep perception, Goethe first carried out physical experiments, to gain as exact a description of the phenomena as possible, and then these same experiments were played through in his mind, both backwards and forwards. This activity helped to develop, in his words, a new 'organ of perception', where perception and intuition became more objective, with the phenomena now dwelling deep inside the scientist. This activity also draws our attention to the fact that there is theorising in all seeing, as we have discussed previously.

The philosopher David Hume (1711–1776) denied that human consciousness could perceive necessary connections between phenomena, stating that 'the human mind never perceives any real connections among distinct existences'.[21] This stance comes from an extreme identification with the analytical mode of consciousness, and his impact on our subsequent science and philosophy has been enormous. His view is in direct contrast to that of Goethe, who ultimately was searching for the 'hidden lawfulness' in nature. In the science of colour, from a Newtonian perspective, there are no relationships between colours. This is a science which focuses on quantity. But in Goethe's approach to colour, we are able to experience the colours as belonging together, a qualitative dimension of the phenomena.

Goethe's complementary way of science is, therefore, showing us how objective truth (in the form of necessary connections) can be revealed by our subjective senses. The hidden laws are not revealed in our visual perceptions (our sensory impressions), but they are in our faculties of intuition.[22] Goethe was not attempting to provide an alternative mechanical explanation of light, but rather to allow nature to reveal the wholeness of the phenomena to the scientist by experiencing that wholeness in a holistic mode of consciousness.

We can see these principles or archetypal phenomena when contemplating the blue of a cloudless sky, and the reds and oranges of the setting sun. As the sun sets, light passes through a greater proportion of the atmosphere, and thus, in Goethe's way of seeing, the atmosphere acts as a darkening agent or medium. In this way, the warm colours appear – reds, oranges and yellows. However, when we look upwards at a blue sky, we are not seeing light (from the sun), but in fact we are seeing darkness passing through an atmosphere filled with light. For Goethe, darkness is just as dynamic or active as light, equal and opposite, and so it brings forth the cool colours.

Goethe does not lead us into a reduced conception of light

as either waves or particles, but rather as a way to understanding how light in relationship gives rise to colours. It is useful to pause and really try to comprehend the magnitude of what Goethe achieved, since his methodology has much that is common to mathematics, where theorems are developed from axiomatic first principles. Goethe stays dwelling in the phenomena, which he then works hard to reproduce as precisely as possible within his imagination. This then allows him to see within his intuition, at a very deep level, a hidden principle of nature.

Perhaps we can also see this same process at play within Newton's active intuition, when he first developed his concept of gravity. This did not develop logically, as dictated by the inductive methodology outlined by Francis Bacon. Newton saw an apple fall from the tree, and within his intuition he was somehow able to see that this was the same falling or action between the Moon and the Earth. We can also see this in Galileo's fascination with the slow swinging motion of the altar lamp hung from a high ceiling in the cathedral of Pisa. As the arc increased, the lamp would speed up, and as the arc decreased, so would the speed.

Galileo was able to see more and more deeply into this phenomenon, and only after this initial period of dwelling in the phenomenon did his experiments begin. Therefore, we can think of scientific discovery as a form of object recognition, and if we do so, this leads us to the realisation that we can train ourselves in this intuitive way of thinking, and open up our own organs of perception, allowing us to develop new insights in our own spheres of work and life.

The Metamorphosis of Plants

The Oxford English Dictionary first defines 'dynamic' as: '1, energetic, active, potent'. If we look at the other dictionary definitions of the word, we find: '2, Physics *a,* concerning motive force (opp. Static). *b,* concerning force in actual operation'. If we then consider this definition, we find one meaning relating to 'the branch of mechanics concerned with the motion of bodies under the action of forces', and a second meaning, which is more interesting in that it relates to ethics as well as physics: 'the motive forces, physical or moral, affecting behaviour and change in any sphere'. So here in the dictionary definition of dynamics we find both physical and non-physical aspects.

Gregory Bateson has said that the major problems in the world are the result of the difference between how nature works and how people think.[23] Our concept of the word 'dynamic' is based on our mental models of physics, or forces acting on bodies, and this is a very mechanical conceptualisation of reality. This mechanistic way of thinking, though, is entirely inadequate for us when entering into an exploration of the organic world and the phenomenological world in which we experience ourselves.

In our analysis of colour, we introduced the concept of dynamics when discussing the dynamical relationship between 'dark' and 'light'. Here though we experienced phenomena without resorting to abstract concepts of what light actually is as a physical entity. Nothing in effect moves when we consider the dynamics of dark and light; rather, it is an intuition of a deep organisational principle within nature. For this reason, we emphasise again the importance of carrying out Goethe's experiments yourself with a prism, so that you can really experience the phenomena that we are describing.

In working with Goethe's theory of colours, we begin to get a new feeling for the word 'dynamic', which for many people signifies a process in time. In reversing dark with light, we begin to get a sense of an inorganic phenomenon relating to dynamic relationships out of time. This work on colour is incredibly powerful in its ability to inspire in us a profound questioning of the scientific paradigm that places so much emphasis on primary qualities and quantifiable measurement. The experiments help to illuminate the insights from those philosophers who draw our attention to the loss of meaning and loss of lived experience, for which science either fails to take into account, or which it dismisses as subjective, therefore telling us nothing about reality.

In Goethe's experiments, we are able to develop a collective consensus on what are qualitative phenomena, something that should make us much more conscientious about how we conduct our own studies in our corporate, business or organisational lives.

Only now, two centuries after Goethe developed his way of seeing, are we able to appreciate his insights. Goethe said that 'the history of science is science itself'.[24] In studying the history of science, we cannot separate the science from the social order in which the science was carried out. It is rare for new scientific insights and discoveries to be readily absorbed and integrated at the point of discovery. Often, our mental models and constructs of reality still bind us to the prior order of thinking, and Goethe, too, struggled to find the language to describe his own novel insights into plant growth and metamorphosis. We can see this struggle in the third paragraph of *The Metamorphosis of Plants* where he writes:

> We will familiarise ourselves with the laws of
> metamorphosis by which nature produces one part
> through another, creating a great variety of forms through
> the modification of a single organ.[25]

In the first part of this sentence, Goethe misleads us into thinking that one adult plant organ (for example, a leaf) can actually change into another (for example, a sepal). Many students of Goethe have made this mistake, and they therefore miss the deep insights of this dynamical way of seeing. In the second part of the sentence, Goethe does manage to express his theory, whereby the great many forms of plant organ arise through the modification of a single organ.

This single organ is not a fully formed adult organ, which can be touched, studied and described. This mysterious single organ can only be grasped in the intuition of the scientist. Does this mean it does not actually exist? No – far from it. Goethe is pursuing one of the highest forms of science, where his faculty of perception is so great that it will allow him to develop theories of plant growth that only in the last decade or so modern science has been able to verify as correct.[26] This is a prodigious achievement, and it is another example of objective laws being able to be perceived correctly in the intuition of the scientist.

In this section we will focus on Henri's teachings of Goethe, and we will also examine Goethe from a philosophical point of view, in order to delve into certain aspects of his way of thinking and seeing. Goethe saw phenomena dynamically, being able to perceive dynamical processes that reveal deep principles of organic life, which only in the last thirty years or so we have begun to be able to model, with modern computing and the mathematics of complexity theory. The value in studying Goethe is to be able, over time, to develop this same organ of perception that enables us to be far more dynamic in both our thinking and intuition.

There are a number of reasons why Goethe's way of seeing is so difficult for us as westerners to grasp. Even some of the most well-regarded authors on Goethe, past and present, have failed to truly grasp his dynamical way of seeing. The very dynamics of seeing lead us away from it, to the end product of what is seen. There is something about how 'seeing' works that contributes to us not noticing it in our normal lives, and not being taught how to see in this manner, so that by the time we are adults and arrive at university, we are not even aware that another way of seeing exists. Henri puts it this way: 'The dynamics of thinking promotes its own eclipse'.[27]

Goethe directs us into the sensory experience and away from the verbal, logical, conceptual and abstract mind. In our lives, we start off as children sensing the living qualities of a leaf; but as adults, when we are out in nature, if we are not mentally present we tend only to see the leaf as an abstract *category*. The verbal intellectual mind is an excellent tool for dealing with the logic of dead solids, but when we move into an analysis of dynamic organisms, our minds encounter paradoxes, which they are unable to resolve within their own way of thinking.

Goethe awakens us to a more holistic and dynamical way of seeing, which transforms the way in which we come to know living organisms. In following Goethe's methodology, we plunge right into the sensory way of knowing, and from there we relive the experience of what we have observed in our imagination. When we recreate phenomena in our minds, it is important not to embellish the phenomena with elements that we ourselves have created. There is, therefore, a dynamic process of paying close attention to phenomena, imagining the phenomena, and then going back to check how closely our imagination fits in with what we have observed. Simply doing this with a branch can be quite an eye-opener, since it can reveal to us just how little we are able to observe in the first instance.

One of the best summaries of what Goethe can teach us comes from Goethean scientist Craig Holdrege, who says that we need to 'learn how to think like a plant lives'.[28] Goethe's thinking became the same as the movement of the growth of the plant, writing that 'if we want to behold nature in a living way, we must follow her example and make ourselves as mobile and flexible as nature herself'.[29] Goethe was able to perceive the deeper dynamics of the plant in its growth. One way to express this is that he was able to perceive *movement* in a single plant. A good starting point for understanding this is to look at a water lily (Figure 4.11).

In the water lily, there are petals, and then rings of stamens standing up. But you will notice, if you look closely, that what look like stamens seem to be an intermediate organ of part-petals and part-stamens. The overall effect is to see a movement of a single organ, gradually turning from petals into stamens. This effect is what Goethe refers to in *The Metamorphosis of Plants*:

> Anyone who has paid even a little attention to plant
> growth will readily see that certain external parts of the
> plant undergo frequent change and take on the shape of
> the adjacent parts – sometimes fully, sometimes more, and
> sometimes less.[30]

Another example of this comes from the wild and cultivated rose, in relation to where the petals are and where the stamens are.

Figure 4.11. Water Lily.

In some flowers, you will notice that where you were expecting petals, you see stamens. What we get from this example is a sense of an underlying formative principle, which relates to an internal relationship between two different types of external organ. It is this relationship that we need to perceive in our intuition, and not the separate parts of the plant in isolation.

We should not think of this movement as one external organ transforming or metamorphosing into another organ. The leaf does not transform into the sepal. What is happening is that there appears to be one single form, which can dynamically have a number of different external forms. Thinking about the story of Proteus, the Greek god who could take on many forms, animals in particular, will help us with this point. When we think of one of these forms – for example, a pig or a serpent – we do not think of it as being the true Proteus. It is more a case of there being one Proteus, who manifests in many different forms.[31] In plants, we can see this if we look at the very earliest, embryonic stage of a plant's life, that of the meristem. We can almost see in photographs from electron microscopes the coming-into-being of the different organs out of this one form, with the sepals, stamens and leaves all having a striking similarity in their appearance.

It is not just the organs that we can think of as being derivative from one form. We can think of there also being just one plant, which comes to presence in the many physical ways, depending on the location and environment in which the plant grows. Goethe was struck by this during his tour of Italy. His observations did not lead him to seeing many different varieties of one type of plant, but the *same* plant being itself, differently.[32]

We are now back to thinking about the relationship between 'the One' and the many. The concept of the hologram is useful in helping us to overcome our Cartesian minds. As explained previously, when holograms were first created, they were constructed using holographic plates. These plates, unlike modern holograms, had a very interesting property. Imagine seeing a picture of a flower in the hologram when it is illuminated with light. If you were then to break the plate in two, what you would see in one of the halves is not half a flower, but the whole flower.

In normal thinking, if we have a whole and split it into parts, we no longer have a whole; we have two parts, which are separate and no longer whole. This would happen if you had a photograph and tore it in half, as we have seen previously in Chapter 2. With a hologram, however, we can say that it can come to presence in two separate parts, while still retaining its wholeness. Therefore, something can be both whole – a unity, or 'One' – and, at the same time, many. So, when Goethe talks about the one organ of the plant, or the one plant, we have to think that what he is talking about is something that we can neither perceive with our senses, nor describe in language or symbols by abstracting what is common from the many parts. There is some kind of dynamical and holographic process that results in the final forms of the physical plants and their organs, and it is this dynamical process which Goethe is perceiving in his intuitive mind. An example of this comes from John Seymour, in his book *The Countryside Explained*:

The potato is not grown commercially from seed, but from sets, which are just potatoes, and so all the potatoes of one variety in the world are *one plant*. They are one individual which has just been divided and divided. When you produce a new variety you have to first of all fertilise the plant with the pollen of another one. But when you have got your new variety, after that the breeder arranges for the new variety to be multiplied by setting the actual potatoes from it. And if it proves a popular variety the original half dozen or so potatoes on the first ever plant of that variety may turn – by division and subdivision – into billions and billions of potatoes, all parts of that same plant. It would be interesting to know how many billions that first King Edward potato had turned into.[33]

Having thought about these different examples, we can now return to Henri's notion of 'differencing/relating'. In order to understand this, we cannot simply think about separate flowers in a static manner in their maturity. A key difference between a hologram and a plant is that the One plant has the ability to create new forms of itself. So we can say that the plant 'self-differences/self-relates'. Note that this is not written as self-differences and self-relates, as that would imply two separate movements.

Goethe's dynamical way of thinking contrasts dramatically with what was called 'archetypal anatomy' in the nineteenth century, championed by Richard Owen (1804–1892). In this instance, the approach was to attempt to find everything that plants had in common. If we take an adult plant as our starting point, we can see how Goethe, in his movement of thinking, goes back upstream towards the coming-into-being of the plant, and this is where he finds the unity in the one organ which self-differences. In stripping out all the differences, the movement of archetypal anatomy goes in the opposite direction from Goethe, further downstream, where nature consists of dead categories, and the dynamical living aspect of nature is entirely lost.

How else can we attempt to grasp this concept of the One

plant organ? We can go back again and contemplate the image of duck/rabbit (Figure 4.1). To reiterate the point, what you are seeing is not duck and rabbit; you are seeing duck/rabbit. Within this picture, there is an 'intensive' distinction. The same is true for the single plant organ before it has come into being in the form of any number of adult organs. It is a single organ which has an intensive dimension, and what we discover here is the extraordinary idea of 'self-difference' instead of 'self-sameness'. This is the idea that something can become *different from itself* while remaining itself, and not becoming *something else*; otherwise, there would be no self-difference. It is within these words and ideas that we begin to discover the dynamics of nature, which are so vastly different from, or perhaps alien to, our mechanical conceptions of reality. As Henri puts it, 'there is *other* without there being *several*'.[34]

Our thinking about organic life and the complexities of dynamical processes is completely transformed by this way of thinking. When we think of the One plant manifesting in different physical forms in different environments, we can no longer think of just the environment as causing these changes to take place. There is also some aspect inside the plant that is able to actively respond to the external circumstances; the plant is not passive in its response. The plant has its own contribution to make in the process of its coming-into-being, which is more like a conversation.

Holdrege has described this well, and he warns against us thinking that these different forms are somehow already contained within the seed of the plant. We have to think in terms of dynamic and emergent processes:

> Imagine that you are holding a groundsel seed in your
> hands before planting it. Depending on how, when, and
> where you plant the seed, a limitless variety of forms
> can arise. All these potential forms are not, of course,
> stored in the seed. The concrete forms are emergent
> characteristics that arise out of a germinal state and

develop in the interplay between the plant's plasticity and the environmental conditions. In particular surroundings the potential of the plant is evoked, but what appears is only one manifestation of the myriad ways in which this plant could develop.[35]

In this passage, Holdrege is saying that there are two potential traps that we can fall into. The first is when we think mechanically, perceiving the plant as if it were a physical object, simply being determined by external causes. This is 'finished product' thinking, or as Henri puts it 'like trying to get to the milk by way of the cheese'.[36] The other trap is when we make a switch to organic thinking, where we imagine the various forms that are already in the plant, waiting to come out when the circumstances are right. Getting into this way of seeing the coming-into-being of the plant is not easy, as Holdrege further explains:

> The plasticity connected with the seed is, however, limited. The characteristic features of a variety (or, more generally, of any given species) are recognisable despite different conditions. There is something similar linking every generation. What is this something? It is a limited plastic tendency. This sounds abstract. It is, in fact, very difficult to find adequate words for what, in this case, stands before the mind's eye. It cannot be drawn and it cannot be adequately represented in any scheme or model.[37]

We always need to keep in mind the differences between plants and machines. The difference is summed up excellently by Ronald Brady, who described plants as having the 'potency to be otherwise'. Machines lack this potency:

> The forms of life are not 'finished work' but always forms *becoming*, and their 'potency to be otherwise' is an immediate aspect of their internal constitution – i.e. of their representative function – and not something to be

added to them. Their 'potency' is 'self-derived,' in that it is inherent in their identity with the whole. The *becoming* that belongs to this constitution is not a process that finishes when it reaches a certain goal but a condition of existence – a necessity to change in order to remain the same.[38]

Henri's work was based on leading us to a point whereby we can come to realise, through our own experience, the limitations in our thinking that have come from both Plato and Aristotle, or as Henri suggested, a misunderstanding of these philosophers. In his classes at Schumacher College, Henri told us that it took him many years of philosophical work before everything became clear to him. He also told us of his own struggles with his ego as he battled to move into this new way of seeing, even though he felt that he had had some staggering insights in those instances when he had made that shift.

During these classes with Henri, our friend Rebeh asked him about the role that feelings and thoughts played in this concept of science, and Henri's reply was fascinating. In terms of your thoughts and feelings, you have to just leave them where they are. Rebeh then asked him about how you should *look* when making observations. Were we meant to begin this work with an open and focused appreciation and attention? For Henri, this work, or mode of science, is not a neutral experience:

Feelings and appreciation develop, and I find that what happens to me is I get an expansion of the heart. Sometimes I experience it as if it is written into the heart. But that comes later. It can happen spontaneously. Your feelings are not just being subjective; it is feeling, not emotion. This is a key thing. Feeling becomes an actual organ of perception itself. This is beyond exact sensorial perception. Feeling itself becomes an organ of perception and that is what it should be. When it is emotion it is not. When we are emotional our feelings are screwed. We do not actually have perceptive feeling when

we are emotional, but that is the time we think we really
are. When it calms down, there is perception through
feeling and it is very fundamental. This is when we pick
up the more subtle things that are there. This is when the
feeling of acknowledgement comes. Acknowledgement is a
feeling that grows, and you should leave it at that, and you
should not then say 'I acknowledge it' as that is not there
in the feeling, as you have put a separation there.[39]

This also relates to another point that Henri has made about our
rational and logical minds, which when working in a Cartesian
manner can only relate to solid objects. A phenomenological
approach can help us to become more attuned to what is alive
and what is living. For Henri, with his radically different way of
seeing, one that is upstream and which focuses on the coming-
into-being of things, modern science as we know it has no access
to the livingness of organic life. Modern science is only a science
of dead objects:

The big thing about the sensory world is that this is
where the livingness is, and you become more
attuned with what is alive and what is living. The
verbal intellectual mind cannot reach this. The verbal
intellectual mind brings us into contact with what is dead
in things; but we often think it is the most wonderful
thing of all. You come to this understanding of this
dynamic movement in life. The verbal intellectual mind
is perfect for dealing with the logic of solids and finished
objects.[40]

This insight has huge implications, allowing us to begin to
understand just why humanity is so destructive towards nature.
Trapped in our logical and rational minds, all that we are able
to perceive is our separateness from nature, a disconnection
which arises from our being lost in our abstract and conceptual
way of thinking; we have long since discarded any reverence for

our sensory experiences through which we experience an intense connection to nature, not just in our thoughts, but in our hearts too. It is not enough just to study complexity and complex systems using only one part of our minds, through logic and abstraction. A deeper way of knowing is required, allowing us to break free from the traps of our perceptions. 'Re-cognition' is a term coined by Emma Kidd, a phenomenologist and practitioner of Goethean science, who is helping people to reconnect back to the natural world. She introduces this new term in the following way:

> We are so caught up with what we 'know' that we forget to be amazed by the mystery, and all that we as of yet do not 'know'. In my dissertation I explore a holistic, phenomenological way of seeing through the work of Goethe, which challenges this separated knowledge; inspiring and reinvigorating a sense of wonder with the world, and re-connection to nature. I feel that the re-cognition of the world which is achieved through this holistic way of seeing is fundamental for any attempt at 'Sustainability' and that only through inspiring wonder and deep connection with life, will we collectively imbue our actions on the Earth with the respect and reverence needed for us to survive. In re-cognising the wholeness of nature, we are re-cognising the nature of wholeness and what it truly means to be whole, and part of a whole, on this earth.[41]

This concept and process of 're-cognition' is extremely powerful, but it can only be fully appreciated once it has been experienced. At Schumacher College, Goethe's work really comes alive for students when studying the dynamic nature of plants in the beautiful gardens of Dartington Hall where the college is based.[42] Few of us have the opportunity to dedicate such a large amount of time to this way of studying. In the final section of this chapter we will describe an exercise which we run with business executives over the course of hour or so, which gives the participants an opportunity to experience holonomic thinking for the first time.

Working Blindfold

We first introduced this exercise into a dialogue group that Maria runs in São Paulo, involving business leaders and executives responsible for business strategy in their organisations, which range across transport, banking, construction, education, manufacturing and public services (government). On this occasion, the group was meeting to discuss sustainability in relationship to strategy, and we had designed an exercise to help everyone explore sustainability, not through their thinking minds, but via the sense of touch, feeling and intuition.

Everyone was given a blindfold, and then a piece of clay, which they could shape and mould in any way they wished, so as to create a piece of art which expressed their connection to nature. In the background, an audio track of birdsong and flowing water was played, which both maintained their meditative states and engendered a sense of being immersed in nature. It really was quite remarkable to see not only what was created in clay, but also the insights that everyone shared during the discussion of this exercise.[43]

One participant, Henrique, created a sphere in which he placed one of his fingers. He spoke with his finger still inside it. At first he started to think about how man was destroying the environment, but then, as his finger played and went inside the clay, it made him realise that nature also protects humanity. He realised that, although we do interfere with nature, if we do so in equilibrium, the environment will protect us. Patrícia, another participant, made a similar abstract shape which was wrapped around her hand. This had the same message: if we take care of nature, nature will take care of us.

Mônica made some recycling pots, and began by telling us how her team at work engaged in many sustainable activities, such as recycling and reducing energy consumption. Mônica told us how, when her new babysitter arrived and asked what her recycling programme was, she realised that although she was sustainable at work, she was not applying this thinking at home. Carla told the group that the sounds of the river and birds had taken her back to her childhood, and so she had made a tree, a river, sun and grass, reminding her of playful days. Nicolas, who worked for a car manufacturer, created a car and also depicted sand. He was very proud of what his company was achieving in terms of making their products recyclable, and that he too liked to be out in nature to relax.

Figures of men, women and children were created by a number of participants. Pedro told us that in fact he had not thought about sustainability until he had children, when his outlook changed, and so he created models of a father and child next to a tree. Jayme had wanted to create a man with a much larger head than body, so as to show how much our thoughts have the desire to control nature. In his figure, one arm did indeed partly break, as if to show this damage within the model itself. Roberto created a man in a meditative lotus position, to show how happiness comes from within, and not from external objects.

Finally, Alice created a mother and child in an embrace, which for her best represented our mutual relationship with nature, each embracing and protecting the other at the same time. Alice also said that at her company, two cleaners were also instructors in the company recycling scheme. It was fantastic to see an organisation realising that each and every member could contribute creatively to a programme, and that ideas did not always depend on those at the very top of the hierarchy.

This particular meeting had been structured around the themes of sustainability and the dynamic way of seeing. We saw how everyone had been entering into all four ways of knowing – thinking, sensing, feeling and intuition – which triggered these wonderful insights of our relationship with nature, insights which could not always be fully articulated in language. In opening people up to an exploration through feeling and intuition, the rest of the day's dialogue and discussion on strategy, as it relates to sustainability, was more profound and wide-ranging, generating ideas of real practical value.

PART II

The Dynamics of Nature: From Biology to Business

5. Living Systems

Seeing the Organisation Whole

The mantra of business today is: 'If it can't be measured, it can't be managed'. The problem that we are facing is not the decision to measure or not to measure, since measurement is a fundamental aspect of business management. We have to rethink our understanding of what measurement is, and how it relates to our conception of systems as authentic wholes. We need to allow the way in which we measure systems to point us towards a deeper understanding of the meaning of systems. This dilemma is particularly true in relation to the measurement of sustainability metrics. For example, how do we measure human values such as love, peace, righteousness and truth?

We have an obsession in business with quantification, and our spreadsheets flatter us with our ability to make minor changes to some assumptions, and thus to be able to predict in minute detail what the impact of these changes will be. A business spreadsheet may be *complicated,* but it is almost never *complex.* Every cell in the spreadsheet has a well defined mathematical relationship with all other cells. An expert in accountancy may draw up the various formulas, such as the system used for depreciation, and while these may certainly be complicated, we know that the same change to a single cell in the spreadsheet will always result in the same change to the calculation. The business world is linear, and in terms of the spreadsheets worked on for business case proposals, projected revenue and profits always increase, even ten years into the future.

What exactly is the key underlying assumption that has driven this obsession with spreadsheets? One possible argument is that business today, especially in western economies, is driven by management by objectives, also known as 'management by results'. Business activities are based on this system, whereby the business sets quantifiable targets, which are then managed via centralised control. In this world view or way of thinking, limitless growth in production is possible, and continual growth in consumption and production are both necessary and desirable goals.

Our present culture in society makes it almost suicidal for politicians to discuss anything other than growth; indeed, the British Prime Minister, David Cameron, stated at the start of 2012, in the context of a worsening economic crisis in Europe, that growth was his number one priority:

> Let me start with growth. This was rightly the focus of today's meeting. It has to be our number one priority, not just today, but every time we meet. My message to other leaders was clear: we've got to be bold and decisive. EU action should match the ambition that we are showing back at home. So it's a step forward, I believe, that we've agreed today to accelerate the legislation that will do the most to generate growth, to consider a clear plan at our March summit to cut red tape, to remove barriers to trade in services right across the EU and to make it easier to do business online – the so-called digital single market – across a market with half a billion customers.[1]

While our politicians can only talk about growth, it is interesting to consider the statistics provided by Arie de Geus, who tells us that 'the average life expectancy of a multinational corporation – Fortune 500 or its equivalent – is between forty and fifty years. A full one-third of the companies listed in the 1970 Fortune 500 had vanished by 1983'.[2] Another more recent study of European and Japanese companies, cited by de Geus, has shown that the average life expectancy of all the firms investigated was just twelve and a half years.[3]

De Geus spent his entire managerial career at the Royal Dutch Shell group of companies, working there for twenty years before coming across these statistics. He has said that it took him another decade for the actual implications of the studies to sink in. Although there is no consensus in terms of what exactly is the cause of such high mortality, de Geus sees the problem in terms of both the prevailing *thinking* and *language* of economics, a way of thinking which is unable to perceive organisations as living systems.

This idea – perceiving the organisation as a living system – has also been taken up by Thomas Johnson and Anders Bröms, who take the view that 'management by results' can have unfortunate consequences, which are counterintuitive and not easily recognised. This is because short-term goals are affected by long-term forces, which create a positive feedback loop. The serious side effects from short-term interventions such as lay-offs, cost-cutting on training, maintenance and customer service, for example, all affect the fundamental health of the system as a whole. These also lead to demoralisation of the workforce, customers and investors.[4]

In addition to this feedback loop, an increasing trend since the 1970s has been the belief that successful managers can make decisions without being familiar with the company's products, technologies or customers. The trend has been to recruit top managers who have been taught on MBA programmes that place a primary value on generic financial reporting, and far too little emphasis on understanding the very DNA of the company itself. In his seminal studies of the history of accounting, Thomas Johnson showed how this practice of using information from financial accounting procedures to run a business only dated back as far as the early 1950s, after which it took off rapidly, spreading globally.[5]

We will revisit 'management by results' in the context of the case study on Toyota (see Chapter 7). For now, it is important to look at the world view, or mode of thinking, which lies behind modern business practice. Not surprisingly, we find that this way of thinking is mechanistic in the extreme; it is exactly the same philosophy of scientific management as that of Frederick Taylor, dating back to 1911.

Scientists have struggled intensely over many centuries to adapt not only to new facts, but also to entirely new world views – world views so radical that they have shaken the scientists' very concept of reality. This revolution in thinking has not yet permeated business to any significant degree. It is not access to factual information that prevents management from implementing new ideas. Over the last few decades, management has seen many different fads come and go, achieving greater or lesser success – for example outsourcing, centralising, decentralising, downsizing, globalising and many more. These ideas all fit into the overall manner of thinking which encompasses management by results in the desire for limitless growth.

Johnson and Bröms have provided us with an archetypal case study which encapsulates the nature of seeing described in Part One of this book, demonstrating the need for new mental models, inspired by living systems, which we will explore in this second part. The case study comes from the period shortly after World War II, when automobile manufacturers were struggling to produce a variety of cars at a low cost. Johnson and Bröms report a meeting in 1982 between Eiji Toyoda, head of Toyota Motor Corporation, and Philip Caldwell, head of Ford Motor Company. At this meeting, Toyoda is reported to have said: 'There is no secret to how we learned to do what we do. We learned it at the Rouge'.[6]

The Rouge River Plant was built by Ford during World War I, and became a world success story, producing fifteen million Model T cars by 1927. This plant was visited by executives from all the major car manufacturers, including General Motors, Chrysler and Toyota. What becomes clear in this case study is that there was something radically different about what the executives from Toyota *saw* in their visits compared to what their western counterparts were able to see. The difference in their thinking, which was reflected in their seeing, allowed them to develop a unique production system, which operated at a much lower cost while achieving higher quality, less waste and with far more stable earnings compared to their competitors.

Toyota appear to have solved a great paradox of quality, variation and cost, in a manner that even those who have studied their operations extensively have been unable to understand or explain, let alone copy. The ability to solve paradoxes in business is the same ability to resolve paradoxes encountered in nature and science; and part of the solution lies in the ability to perceive the *intrinsic* dimensions of a system, which cannot be accessed through quantitative methods or mechanistic thinking. Mechanistic thinking is not enough, and it is for this reason that this book has been designed to help take the reader through this movement of thinking, to a point where the reader begins to understand systems as an organic and dynamic whole. Toyota's executives were able to *see the company whole.*

If we return to Goethe, we find in him someone who was not opposed to mathematics; rather, he saw in nature phenomena which were not susceptible to scientific measurement:

> The mathematicians did not find out the metamorphosis
> of plants. I have achieved this discovery without the aid
> of mathematics, and the mathematicians were forced to
> put up with it. To understand the phenomena of colour,
> nothing is required but unbiased observation and a sound
> head; but these are scarcer than folks imagine.[7]

So far, we have discussed Goethe's way of seeing in terms of colour and plants. We can also examine how Goethe's way of seeing can be applied to the study of animals, following the work of Wolfgang Schad, most notably *Man and Mammals* (1971). The way in which we categorise mammals today originates from hierarchical taxonomies, based on the work of Carl Linnaeus (1707–1778). Members of each category, such as jaguars, tigers and cats, share key structural features and other characteristics. Darwin's *The Origin of Species* (1859) gained a new significance with the concept of a single ancestor back in time. This was fine so far as it went, but there still remained the problem of how to explain mammals with very similar characteristics, but which were only very distantly related, perhaps separated by oceans and continents. The traditional explanation was that these mammals evolved under similar external environmental conditions.

That is fine, but is there another way of viewing this same situation? There is – by rethinking what an organism is. It can be seen not just as the product of external conditions, but also as a result of their *intrinsic* organising principles, which then interact dynamically with external conditions. This was the approach which Schad developed.[8]

Schad helps us to understand animals in terms of a threefold distinction. If we think of the *quality* of the life of a harvest mouse, it lives nervously, continually at risk of being eaten by a predator. We can perceive its primary orientation in its nervous and sensory systems, with the head and anterior as the major centre for these organic systems.

A bison, on the other hand, can be thought of as quite the opposite of the harvest mouse, with the bison's focus on its digestive system, as it seemingly goes consciously inwards as it grazes leisurely. The primary orientation of the bison is, therefore, focused on its limbs and digestion, which are primarily towards its posterior. These two mammals can be seen to have opposite forms (accented anterior or posterior) in reciprocal relationships with the functions (metabolic and limb).

When it comes to the leopard, a carnivore, its predominant systems are metabolic (circulatory and respiratory). At one moment the leopard is intensely alert and hunting prey, muscles tensed and ready to spring; at another moment, having gorged on its prey, it is lazily sprawled out in a tree, its awareness now going inwards to its digestion.

Schad used his threefold system to classify mammals, and in doing so he provided a convincing argument for having discovered a formative principle, which is why the same motif can be found across diverse mammals whose relationships are not immediately apparent in the earlier form of classification. This principle only becomes intelligible when the relationships among phenomena are understood in their wholeness. This perception of 'wholeness' comes from both scientific and artistic consciousness. When perceiving phenomena, the underlying organising principles appear in the imagination, in the authentic '*belonging* together'.

When we try to abstract common principles, we are taking a system apart, looking at parts which are already separate, and trying to put them together. This 'belonging *together*' is counterfeit if we only look at external relationships, which we ourselves have synthetically created, such as the taxonomy of Linnaeus. It is only once we have experienced in our intuition an authentic whole that we come to meet that whole, in a way in which it comes to presence in the parts. Note that, in this sense – in relation to the example of Schad and mammals – 'whole' here refers to a dynamic process, which results in the wholeness of the animal.

Order and Chaos

In thinking about chaos and complexity, it is important to understand the concept of 'order' and the relationship between order and 'chaos'. We have to be aware that the new sciences of complexity and chaos can, and do, use these terms in a way that is somewhat different from their commonsense definitions in everyday life. What we will find is that chaos is not necessarily the opposite of order. A system at one level can be chaotic, but at the same time can display a behaviour which shows a surprising and unexpected level of order. While this may seem counterintuitive, we will discuss various systems in nature – chemical, biological and social – to help the reader to understand these points further.

Most people have heard of the 'butterfly effect'. This is probably the best known metaphor to come out of chaos theory. It suggests that the flapping of the wings of a butterfly in Rio can result in a hurricane the other side of the world, in (say) Singapore. The butterfly effect is an interesting example of chaos and complexity to start with, since it enables us to introduce some of the key concepts of this discipline.

In the early 1960s, Edward Lorenz was attempting to develop a series of mathematical equations to model weather systems.[9] He was focusing on how the weather changes due to convection currents. He used just three time-varying quantities: the convective flow, the horizontal temperature distribution and the vertical temperature distribution.[10]

The behaviour of this system is 'fully determined'. Nothing is random. We can explore the behaviour of the system further by plotting out the x, y and z variables on three axes. When we do, we notice the distinctive shape that the plot takes (Figure 5.1).

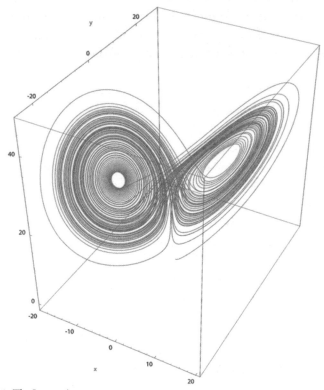

Figure 5.1. The Lorenz Attractor.

The system traces out a path which can be seen to revolve around two fixed points, although the path traced never actually crosses itself. In visualising the equations in this manner, we can begin to appreciate some qualitative aspect of the system as a whole, in that although it is a chaotic system, there are two points to which the system seems to be attracted. These points are called 'attractors', and in this instance, the attractors are called 'strange'. At some point, the system will flip unexpectedly from one semi-fixed state to an entirely different one – hence the term 'strange attractor'. This can be contrasted with a 'simple attractor', which could be the final resting place of a swinging pendulum.

Lorenz described his system as being one of sensitive dependence on initial conditions, but he also coined his term 'the butterfly effect' to describe these types of system more poetically. In contemplating these types of system, with such sensitivities, we can think about the notion of order, and of our very human, scientific and political desires to impose order on nature, on societies and on business, from the outside. As managers, we still treat the living systems in which we work as mechanical, deterministic, and ones that can be adequately modelled using spreadsheets. We are inclined to perceive some form of order in our worlds, where often there is none, or none as we currently imagine order to be.

The word 'order' is one that our politicians seem to love. Shortly after the attacks on the World Trade Centre in 2001, the then British Prime Minister, Tony Blair, spoke at the Labour Party conference, and for him the attacks were a great opportunity:

> This is a moment to seize. The Kaleidoscope has been shaken. The pieces are in flux. Soon they will settle again. Before they do, let us re-order this world around us.[11]

Blair's thinking comprehends 'order' as a concept which can be imposed externally upon a system, enabling an outside agency to control that system. US politician Zbigniew Brzezinski famously used the metaphor of chess in *The Grand Chessboard: American*

Primacy and Its Geostrategic Imperatives, suggesting a level of control and understanding of the rules of the game that could be bordering on the delusional and megalomanic. In this world view, countries, economies, armies, and even multinational corporations are just seen as pawns which can be sacrificed and fought over in order to win the great game of geopolitics.

The order in nature that we will be discussing is not an order that is imposed externally, but an intrinsic aspect of the system, which manifests in the relationship between the parts of the system. In Part One, we looked at a conceptualisation of the whole, whereby neither the whole dominated the parts, nor did the parts have primacy over the whole. Many systems also demonstrate other surprising behaviours, surprising to the extent that scientists are not in agreement as to the meaning of these behaviours.

One of the most influential thinkers in this area was Ilya Prigogine, the 1977 Nobel laureate in chemistry who, along with his colleagues, developed a distinct and still controversial concept of chaos.[12] For Prigogine, there are two forms of chaos, one being passive, and the other active. A passive form of chaos can exist when a system is in equilibrium or maximum entropy, so that no organisation exists. Active chaos occurs in systems which are in states that are far-from-equilibrium. When a system is in this state, the system does not break down, as may be expected, but new systems or new levels of order emerge. This form of chaos is 'active, hot and energetic'.[13]

The view of reality proposed by Prigogine is radical, and, as we have seen with quantum physics and Einstein's theory of relativity, it challenges our fundamental assumptions about the building blocks of life. In particular, Prigogine challenged long-held scientific assumptions about time, the notion of reversibility and causation. Prigogine argued that, for many centuries, there was a conviction that the world was simple, and that the fundamental laws of physics were time-reversible. Because Newton's laws of motion did not have a single arrow of time built in, they could work backwards as well as forwards. Prigogine did not see the laws of nature as time-reversible. For Prigogine, Newton's illusion of the irreversibility of time is not an illusion at all; in fact, it plays a key role in the process of 'self-organisation':

> The artificial may be deterministic and reversible. The natural contains essential elements of randomness and irreversibility. This leads to a new view of matter in which matter is no longer the passive substance described in the mechanistic world view but is associated with spontaneous activity.[14]

If we are to understand organisations as living systems, it is important to understand Prigogine's view of systems. To do so, we have to return to our journey through the history of science, and look at the great shift in conceptual thinking with the introduction of the first non-classical science, that of thermodynamics. Newton's laws were really the laws of trajectories, and these laws displayed lawfulness, determinism and reversibility. These mathematical laws were structured in such a way as to suggest that, if all the velocities in a system were somehow reversed, the system would go backwards in time, that is, the system would retrace its steps. Although in our everyday world we never experience any system going backwards – examples being a dropped piece of toast rising from the floor, the pieces of a smashed cup mending themselves, flowers going back into their bulbs, people growing young – these events in classical physics were treated as just as probable as any others.

This changed in the nineteenth century with the introduction of thermodynamics, the first science of complexity, introducing new processes which were dependent on the direction of time. Prior to this new thinking, irreversible chemical and physical processes were viewed as 'nuisances, as disturbances, as subjects not worthy of study'.[15] But these systems are dynamic, in that the systems are not studied in isolation, but in relationship to their surroundings, where energy, heat and chemicals are transferred between the system and their surrounding context. It is these open systems which Prigogine studied, naming them 'dissipative structures', because the dissipative processes play an active role in determining the system's formation, structure and behaviour.

Thermodynamics is the science of the correlation of variation in the properties of pressure, volume, chemical composition and temperature. The introduction of thermodynamics came in 1811, with the mathematical description of the propagation of heat in solids by Baron Jean-Joseph Fourier (1768–1830), who proposed that heat flow is proportional to the gradient of the temperature. In this formulation, a solid, liquid or gas is a macroscopic system, which consists of an inconceivably large number of molecules, and yet its behaviour is described by a single law. When applied to an isolated body, the effect of heat propagation results in the distribution of temperature until homogeneity is reached.[16]

The overriding image of the clock in the mechanical cosmos of classical physics was replaced by the conception in the industrial age of the cosmos as a reservoir of energy which would eventually run down, fully exhausted. This conceptualisation really came about in the formulation by Lord Kelvin in 1852 of the second law of thermodynamics, and with the introduction of the concept of 'entropy' in 1865 by Rudolf Clausius (1822–1888). This is worth examining, since this law is much cited, but often misunderstood when being applied as a metaphor outside of science.

'Entropy' is a useful term to understand, and it has been applied to a wide variety of systems, including information systems. In chemical terms, it enables us to distinguish between physiochemical transformations where either energy is exchanged in a 'useful manner' or energy is irreversibly wasted. Irreversible processes can be the result of heat loss and friction, for example, and in these instances, entropy is said to increase. Since energy cannot be created, only transferred, the production of entropy is an expression of the occurrence of irreversible changes inside a system. In an isolated system where there are no exchanges with its environment, the entropy flow is, by definition, zero.[17]

Another significant conceptual change in physics was introduced by Ludwig Boltzmann (1844–1906), who sought to use the theory of probability when describing thermodynamic systems. This was a break from the past, where everything was determined in terms of initial states and the laws of motion. Boltzmann's 'order principles', though, could not be applied to open systems, be they biological cells or cities. (An open system is one which continually interacts with its environment, the interaction consisting of a flow of energy, material or information). These systems were not only open, but also existed because they were open. If they were cut off from their environment, they would lose their sources of sustenance and die. Living systems appeared to go against the second law of thermodynamics, in that they evolved to ever greater levels of order and to levels of ever increasing complexity. It was in these types of system that Prigogine developed his descriptions of dissipative structures.

One of Prigogine and colleague Isabelle Stengers' favourite examples of a dissipative structure was the phenomenon known as the 'Bénard instability'. This effect is created in thin layers of liquid compared to the proportion of surface. It is a dissipative system, because heat is applied below and heat is allowed to escape from the upper heat-conducting layer. When this system is first set up, the flow of heat is continuous, travelling by conduction, and it can be said to be in near-equilibrium. As the heating continues, the difference between the hot layer and the cooling layer above takes the system into a state which is far-from-equilibrium, and it becomes increasingly turbulent. If you were to look at the system in this state, it could be described as 'near chaotic', or reaching a state of 'near disorder'.

What happens next is the really interesting part. The behaviour changes entirely, and the point at which this happens is known as a 'bifurcation point'. This will be fully defined later, but for now it can be thought of as a change of state of the system. In this instance, large-scale convection currents emerge, resulting in a lattice of hexagonal cells appearing on the upper surface. Here, we have a system where order appears out of chaos. Another interesting observation is that, as the heat is increased, the rate of loss of heat also increases. The system experiences increasing entropy production, but demonstrates increasing order:

The convection motion produced actually consists of the complex spatial organisation of the system. Millions of molecules move coherently, forming hexagonal convection cells of a characteristic size.[18]

A second example of a dissipative system, which can help us to understand chaos, complexity and order in chemistry, is the 'Belousov-Zhabotinsky reaction', also referred to as the 'BZ reaction'. This is a form of rare chemical reaction, discovered by the Russian chemist Boris P. Belousov in 1951. Although he attempted to publish a paper on the reaction, it was rejected for being unscientific, on the premise that chemical reactions *cannot* oscillate, because that would violate the second law of thermodynamics. This affected Belousov so much that he decided to leave science, and he would not live to see his work belatedly recognised after his death in 1970. His work was continued by A.M. Zhabotinsky, under the direction of biochemistry professor Simon Schnoll.[19] In 1959, Zhabotinsky modified the reactions slightly to make them more visually striking, with bright and easily seen bands of colour (Figure 5.2).

Figure 5.2. The Belousov-Zhabotinsky reaction.

The reactions can only be fully appreciated when seen, and there is a high quality video on Youtube, entitled *Belousov Zhabotinsky reaction 8 x normal speed,* which allows you to see the progression over time. What exactly is the series of reactions which leads to this stunning visual appearance? The full sequence consists of a number of separate reactions, resulting in a complex array of interactions between organic and inorganic compounds. Within this system there is also a complex interaction between autocatalytic positive feedback and time-delayed negative feedback.[20]

We do not need to have any knowledge of chemistry to appreciate the qualities of these types of system. As Prigogine and Stengers tell us, 'such a degree of order stemming from the activity of billions of molecules seems incredible'.[21] Our previous mental models of chemical systems may well have consisted of an image of billions of tiny particles, all colliding randomly in time and space in a chaotic manner, and in this scenario there would be no possible mechanism for self-organisation to emerge. For order to emerge, there would have to be some form of communication. For a form of communication to take place, the system has to act as a whole. When we study the behaviours of these systems as a whole, we realise that the same models can be applied not only in biological systems, but also in social systems. We begin to perceive similarities in the behaviour of systems which have extremely different physical constituents.

Although the BZ reaction in total is immensely complex, it has been studied a great deal, and it can be understood conceptually in the following simplified equations:

(1) $A \Rightarrow B$
(2) $A + B \Rightarrow 2B$
(3) $B + C \Rightarrow 2C$
(4) $C \Rightarrow D$

The reaction starts with the compound A and some C. An autocatalytic reaction takes place, resulting in the generation of compound B. This can be seen in (2), where the presence of B leads to the creation of more B. Then a second autocatalytic process (3) takes over, reducing the amount of B and increasing the amount of C. The system will then oscillate between these two reactions until the supply of A is used up, or until the waste product D clogs up the system.[22]

Once the study of the BZ reaction began to spread through the scientific community, biologists also became interested, as they could see the same patterns which emerged from chemical systems in totally different systems – living systems. This is fascinating, because in chemical oscillations although the molecules are simple, the reactions are complex. In biological examples, the reaction sequence can often be much more simple, but the actual compounds involved – such as acids and proteins – can be highly complex and specific. One of the best examples of a living system that exhibits this behaviour is slime mould, the Acrasiales amoebas (*Dictyostelium discoideum*).

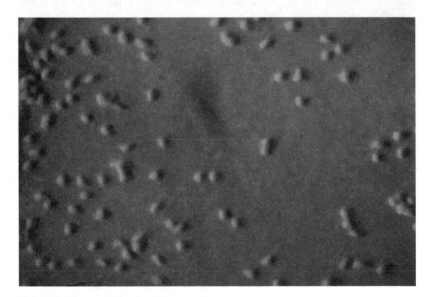

Figure 5.3. Slime mould as free living amoebae.

Slime mould is a fascinating organism to study, because it has two distinctive phases in its lifecycle. When food is plentiful, in the form of bacteria, this species exists as free-living and independent amoeba (Figure 5.3). However, as soon as food becomes scarce, something quite extraordinary happens; the previously independent amoeba begin to act as a coherent whole. After an eight-hour interphase process, some of the amoeba start to aggregate around cells, which act as centres, sending out chemical signals consisting of cAMP (cyclic adenosine monophosphate), a molecule which is involved in the regulation of energy in all cells (see Figure 5.4). There are two forms of action. In the first instance, cells which receive the signal then repeat the signal by sending it out to other cells. In the second instance, cells receiving the signal move towards the origin of the signal.[23] This behaviour is shown in the beautiful black and white films of biology professor emeritus John Bonner, who has studied slime mould for almost forty years.[24]

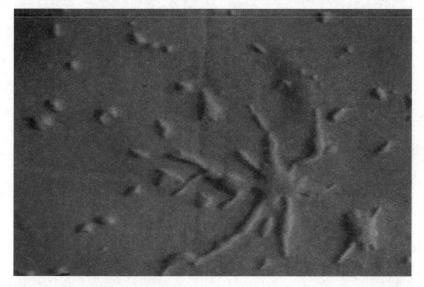

Figure 5.4. Slime mould aggregating.

Around each centre, several thousand cells will amalgamate and start to form a new, multicellular organism. Previously identical cells will begin to differentiate into different cell types, forming a fruiting body (Figure 5.5). This new organism consists of a base, a stalk which rises up from the base, and a fruiting body made up of a ball of live spores, which will be able to survive the absence of food and water. Therefore, not only do the cells differentiate, but those making up the stalk will eventually die, sacrificing themselves for the greater good of the whole.

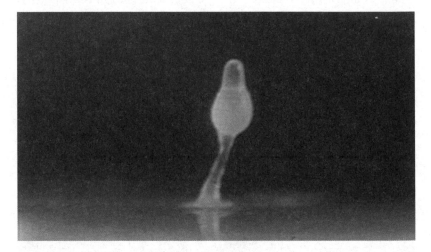

Figure 5.5. Slime mould fruiting body.

To understand this behaviour, we can use the same simplified equations that we used to understand the BZ Reaction. In the case of slime mould, it is cAMP which acts as a catalyst, stimulating its own production. However, if all cells started to send out cAMP as a signal, the entire area would be awash with the chemical, and this would serve no purpose. An enzyme, phosphodiesterase, is secreted by the amoeba and destroys the cAMP, resulting in there being a direction of signal, which controls their movement. The signalling works in such a way that it cannot travel backwards, and so a form of order arises spatially.[25]

Both the BZ reaction and the behaviour of slime mould can be referred to as 'self-organisation'. This is where a system has the capacity to generate patterns spontaneously, without any specific instructions telling it to do so.[25] There is no plan or blueprint which exists prior to the system acting as it does. The patterns are the result of the dynamic relationships which exist between the parts. As we have seen in two very different physical systems, it is not the nature of the molecules involved which determines this behaviour, but their dynamical properties in relationship.

Bifurcation

The word 'bifurcation' is occasionally found in business literature. It has a number of definitions, and the simplest way to think about it is as a fork in a road. The road splits in two; hence there is a bifurcation point at the junction. However, bifurcation plays an important role in complexity and chaos theory, and so it is worth examining mathematical models closely to understand the path from an initially stable system into a complex, then chaotic one.

We can use the population growth equation developed in 1845 by Pierre-François Verhulst (1804–1849), which describes the way in which a population develops in a closed area.[27] This equation uses the concept of mathematical normalisation in order to be able to compare different sized populations. A population of this type can be said to vary between 0 and 1, that is, the maximum size of a population is 1. The equation is:

$$x_n + 1 = rx_n(1 - x_n)$$

In this equation, r is a fixed constant representing the birth rate, and x is the size of the population. The value of x at time n feeds back into itself, resulting in a new value of x at time $n+1$. For values of r between 1 and 3 the system settles down to a fixed value. For values of r between 3 and approximately 3.4494, the system oscillates between two values, and for values of r which are just a small percentage more, the system oscillates between four fixed values. This equation can be plotted as shown in Figure 5.6. Note that the x axis does not show time; it shows increasing values of the constant *r*. The *y* axis demonstrates the value of *x* to which *x* settles down after a number of iterations of the equation.

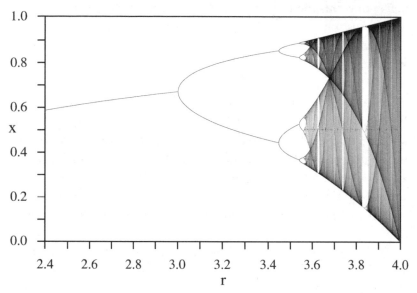

Figure 5.6. Bifurcation diagram.

With values of *r* higher than 3.56, the system becomes chaotic, with *r* not settling down to any fixed pattern at all. However, within all of this chaos there are interesting vertical bands of white, the first one appearing where *r* is approximately 3.7, and a much wider one around *r* = 3.8. These are windows, where the system exhibits stable behaviour. These periods of stability and predictability amid such chaotic behaviour are known as 'intermittency'.

Prigogine and Stengers studied bifurcations in chemical processes, leading them to call for science to recognise that we are entering a new era, one which seeks to understand the relation between 'being' and 'becoming', and the relationship between 'permanence' and 'change'.[28] To understand Prigogine and Stengers' explanation of bifurcation, we begin by examining a simple chemical reaction, one that is at equilibrium or near-equilibrium (Figure 5.7). The *x* axis in this instance shows a parameter λ, which represents the concentration of a substance. X represents the action of chemical X. As the value of λ increases, the system reaches a bifurcation point at which two possible stable solutions emerge. According to Prigogine and Stengers, the macroscopic equations cannot predict the path that the system will take.[29] Unlike our previous examples, *randomness* now enters the picture.

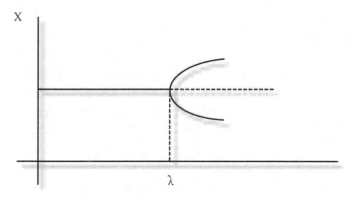

Figure 5.7. Symmetrical bifurcation diagram.

Not only does randomness play an unexpected part, but so does the history of the chemical process, in that the path taken by the system can depend on the history of the concentration of X. This too is totally unexpected. Interestingly, Prigogine and Stengers note that only recently has it been discovered that when a system is in a far-from-equilibrium state, external fields, such as the gravitational field, can be 'perceived' by the system, and this will impact on the behaviour of that system. This amazing sensitivity of a system could potentially play a role in the way in which complex dynamic systems adapt to their environments.[30]

At the level of cells in biology, systems begin in a state of homogeneity, with all cells being of the same form. During the development of an organism, these cells begin to differentiate, in terms of their spatial location and physical form. Prigogine and Stengers suggested that bifurcations in the form that he has studied play a vital role in the way in which life appears to be able to spontaneously self-organise. For much of the time, organisms develop in a deterministic manner, but at crucial moments, bifurcations with random elements also play an important role, and these are the moments when our deterministic explanations break down. In this way, the order which we perceive in living systems emerges from chaos. 'Today we believe that the epoch of certainties and absolute oppositions is over.'[31]

Evolution

Henri Bortoft, with his background in the history of science, made some interesting observations to us about Darwin. According to Henri, interest in Darwin only began in the 1950s. As he wryly put it:

> Darwinism was invented in 1959. It was the centenary
> year of Darwin, and some decided to put Darwin on the
> map. Darwin more or less petered out after the early 1900s
> to the end of the 1920s. When I was at school in the
> 1950s you could do biology without mentioning Darwin
> or Evolution.[32]

So far we have concentrated on attempting to point out how mechanistic thinking in science can limit the mode of thinking and knowing in all other fields of human endeavour, a limitation rooted in our ways of seeing. But when we study Darwin, we also see how science itself is limited by the prevalent social and political orders of its time, in that Darwin was heavily influenced by the concepts of market capitalism of Victorian England, based primarily on Adam Smith's economic theories, which saw people competing ruthlessly for scarce goods.

In Darwin's early work it is possible to see distinct similarities with Goethe's work on plants, which is not surprising as Darwin was greatly influenced by Goethe. It was through his work on barnacles that Darwin discovered that variation was everywhere, ubiquitous. Previously, he had thought that variation was quite restricted. But after studying barnacles for eight years, he saw that they were continually changing in form, almost as if there were no species.[33] In this phase of his research, Darwin was entering into active seeing, and his achievement was to stay in the seeing without being influenced by the current scientific dogma of his times. As Henri put it:

> Before he did his work with barnacles, Darwin had believed that variation is the exception in nature, occurring only in times of crisis. His barnacle work changed that. Here he found that there are no unvarying forms, and that barnacle species are, as he put it, *'eminently* variable'. What made the work of classification so difficult was that 'Every part "of every species" was prone to change; the closer he looked, the more stability seemed an illusion'. Barnacles, he told Hooker, are infinitely variable; and in the context of his theory of what he called 'the transmutation of species', he went further to see variations as incipient species. There is a switch in gestalt here, like the reversing cube: in one perspective the phenomenon appears as the variations of a species, whereas in another perspective the very same phenomenon appears as the initial stages of new species. Goethe and Darwin both encountered the organism's 'potency to be otherwise' which is the self-differencing dynamic of life. But whereas Goethe saw this unceasing variation phenomenologically, so that he understood it as the expression of life itself, Darwin wanted to explain it (in this regard he thought more like a physicist). He eventually 'found' an explanation in the key to the success of Victorian capitalism: the division of labour.[34]

By the 1960s, Darwinism was becoming a prevalent force. Darwinism is not a mechanism as such. It is the belief that the internal changes in organisms are selected and come first, and not the environment. This is taken to be a constant. One person who saw things differently was the late Brian Goodwin, a friend and colleague of Henri.[35] While mainstream science is atomistic, Goodwin saw features of wholeness in the development of organisms. Graduating with a PhD in Biology, Goodwin then went to Cambridge to study mathematics, where he took a great interest in non-linear dynamical systems, in which features of wholeness are found. Goodwin was, therefore, one of the few biologists who had really mastered the new mathematics of complexity in a way which could not be matched by the majority of his peers.

Goodwin was most well-known for his work on morphology, the study of how organisms grow. At Edinburgh, he studied under C.H. Waddington, who, like Goodwin, believed that organisms should be studied as wholes. We have already considered Schad's work, inspired by Goethe, in this field; Goodwin, too, was a great proponent of this alternative perspective. Goodwin's main argument was that an understanding of genes was not enough to be able to explain the properties of organisms. You should not reduce an organism to the properties of genes alone; rather, organisms have to be understood as dynamical systems, with distinctive properties which characterise the living state.[36]

Just as the concept of survival of the fittest pervades business and economics, so does the metaphor, sometimes applied literally, of DNA. 'It's in our DNA' is frequently found in strap lines and advertisements, and the metaphor suggests that some quality, such as high quality, security, customer service, safety, etcetera, runs through every aspect of the company. Interestingly, the metaphor of Richard Dawkins' selfish genes would later be extended by him to the concept of the 'meme', an idea that can replicate using the same structure or mechanism as DNA itself. This terminology too was enthusiastically taken up by the business world.

Goodwin wished that people would come to understand not only the good parts and achievements of Darwin, but also the limitations of Darwin's theory. In Goodwin's view, a genetic program is restricted, in that it can only specify when and where in a developing embryo particular proteins and other molecules are produced. The molecular composition is not enough to be able to explain physical form. 'In order for evolution of complexity to occur DNA has to be within a cellular context; the whole system evolves as a reproducing unit.'[37]

Emergent Properties

Goodwin told a very interesting story about one of his lectures at Schumacher College, describing the process of ventricular fibrillation and sudden cardiac arrest. At the very time when he was describing the different stages of activity of a heart, from a healthy beat to the very regular periodic activity of a fibrillating heart, he became unwell. (A healthy heart has a regular average or mean heart rate, but chaotic variability between successive heart beats). Although some of the class thought that he might be acting to demonstrate his point, it soon became apparent that his condition was serious enough to require an ambulance to take him to the local hospital for emergency treatment. It was quite a synchronicity for Goodwin, this incident occurring during a class on cardiac dynamics.[38]

A heartbeat can be explained in a similar manner to the waves travelling in a BZ reaction or those which are formed by slime mould. Through electrical stimulation, waves travel through the muscular tissue, resulting in muscular contraction. This same muscle tissue requires a period of recovery, during which it no longer responds to any signalling. The heart then, is an example of an 'excitable medium' (a medium which goes into stable temporal and spatial dynamical states), and in terms of the health of the overall organism, too much order in the heart (by way of an inflexible regularity) can lead to fatal consequences, one example being sudden cardiac arrest.[39]

A normal healthy heart exhibits chaotic behaviour. This sounds like a paradox; but in fact, in a healthy heart the average time between heartbeats is constant. If you were to measure the actual gaps between heartbeats, you would discover a chaotic pattern. This average heartbeat can be thought of, therefore, as one type of strange attractor. The healthy heart maintains continuous sensitivity to unpredictable demands on it from the rest of the body by continuously changing, so that it never gets stuck into a pattern. The origin of the chaotic behaviour is not yet clear, but it does point to a dynamic and emergent property of the *whole* which affects the parts.

The study of social insects, such as ants and termites, presents us with many paradoxes. Ants and termites have tiny brains, and therefore at the individual level their behaviour can be seen as extremely disorganised, or chaotic; it cannot be described as in any way intelligent. But when they are studied collectively, as a whole, their behaviour is seen in a very different light, to the extent that we are still at a loss to be able to explain how their achievements came about.

One amazing example is the phenomenon of termite mounds. Termite mounds have all the qualities that we humans would want from a home: security, heating, air conditioning, self-contained nurseries, gardens, and sanitation systems. These mounds really have to be seen to be understood in all their glory, such as in the many television documentaries by David Attenborough, who takes us deep inside these structures.[40]

Australian termites are known as 'magnetic termites' due to their ability to build mounds which are wide, yet extremely thin. The mounds are oriented north-south, which allows the wide panel to catch the heat from the morning sun; but at midday, when the sun is high, the razor-like quality of the mounds minimises the amount of light falling on the structure. Termites normally retreat underground to avoid the heat; but, because of flooding in that region of the world, only this design of structure can prevent the termites from overheating in the day or freezing at night.

In Nigeria, termites are able to build structures which can reach 15 m (50 ft), the most complex and sophisticated of all termite mounds. To put this in perspective, if termites were the size of an average man, the structure would be a mile high. The basement of the mound reaches 1.8 m (6 ft) below the surface, and there are shafts which go much deeper to the water table, where worker ants bring up mud, building concentric veins, which hang from the ceilings of the cellar. As the mud cools, the evaporating water has the effect of drawing up cool air into tunnels above. On the outside of the mound there are pores which allow oxygen to enter and carbon dioxide to be expelled.

Termites build gardens, where they cultivate their own food in the form of a fungus, which can only exist at the very precise temperature found inside the mounds. Wood, which is hard to digest, is stored, and then eaten; the fungus, which is much more nutritious, is cultivated on their dung. Given that there will be somewhere in the region of 1.5 million insects living in the colony, all of which are generating heat, the termite mound is built to ensure that not only are the termites living at temperatures suitable for themselves, but this temperature never varies by more than two degrees around thirty-one degrees otherwise the fungus would perish.

The air conditioning solution of termite mounds is so successful that their design has been copied by architect Mick Pearce in the construction of the Eastgate Centre in Zimbabwe. This building uses 10% less energy than an equivalent one with conventional heating and air conditioning; the owners saved a further $3.5 million, because this traditional equipment did not have to be installed. Retailers in this shopping centre also pay 20% less rent than other tenants in the surrounding area.[41] Pearce describes his approach as follows:

> Architectural expression must construct a balance between
> the natural, social and economic environments in which
> a project is sited. My models are drawn from nature from
> copying natural processes, which I study through the new
> science of biomimicry.
>
> I have become increasingly interested in the
> development of a new relationship between the city
> and nature. This has a wide-ranging influence on my

architecture. The termitary, which I used to develop
the concept for Eastgate, has become the basis of my
conceptual method. Like a termitary, built structures for
humans must work as a complex, self-sustaining organism
in which each part supports the activities of the other.[42]

A number of studies of ant colonies have shown that ants, too,
can be considered to be an excitable medium. When just a small
number of ants are placed together, their behaviour is chaotic. But
as the number of ants is increased, a sudden transition to ordered
behaviour is observed. Individual ants have periods of rest, and
when they are together in a colony, their behaviour as a whole
was shown in one experiment to suddenly switch from chaotic
to rhythmic every twenty-five minutes.[43] The colony took a rest
twice every hour. The important observation here is that there
was nothing in an individual ant's behaviour that could lead to
the prediction of this ordered behaviour in the colony.

   This order at the level of the whole is a clear example of an
'emergent property' in an excitable medium, and it is the same
system as that observed in hearts, slime mould and the chemicals
of the BZ reaction. So it does not matter what the complex system
is made out of; what is important is the dynamical organisation
of the whole – in other words, the 'relational order' of the system.
To really understand a complex system, therefore, a study of just
the parts is not enough; you have to study the whole, and, in
doing so, to be prepared to discover surprises, due to the fact that
unexpected behaviour will emerge.

   Another question now arises. Is this behaviour truly unexpected?
A related issue is that of evolution, and, in particular, the
mechanisms and principles that enabled intelligent and sentient
life forms to emerge from the primordial soup on our planet,
billions of years ago. While Darwin's work *The Origin of Species*
has dominated thinking on evolution for more than 150 years,
new discoveries are now being made by the emerging science of
complexity, revealing ever greater swathes of 'spontaneous order'
in what were previously thought of as purely random systems.

This concept of spontaneous order is now a great challenge to those biologists who believe in natural selection as the sole source of order in biology. One of the greatest proponents in this area is Stuart Kauffman, who, for the last few decades, has been developing a theory of emergence. His work builds on the studies of dissipative structures by Prigogine and Stengers. Kauffman makes the important point that, if we are to understand complex systems such as cells, ecosystems and economic systems, we may at the same time be forced into giving up our dream to predict the details of such systems.

This is because, as we have seen in the previous mathematical examples, non-equilibrium systems can be thought of as computers carrying out algorithms, and in many cases we are able to discover and model these algorithms. There is, however, only one way in which to discover the behaviour of such an algorithm, and that is to watch the details unfold. As Kauffman puts it, these systems 'are their own shortest descriptions'.[44] We no longer have a model of a system; rather, the system is the model in its most compact form. The consequences of moving to this world view are, therefore, profound. We have to give up the pretence of being able to make long-term predictions.

Probably the most common or everyday scientific conception of evolution is that of Richard Dawkins, where life evolves as a result of cumulative selection. Although there may be huge differences between simple organisms millions of years ago and the complex organisms and organs of today, each successive change in the gradual evolutionary process is simple relative to its predecessor, having arisen by chance. This cumulative process is directed by non-random survival.[45] Life, though, did not evolve gradually; there were phases that saw the sudden spawning of many new life forms in a short space of time, one well known example being the 'Cambrian explosion'. Stephen Gould termed these periods 'punctuated equilibrium'.

The discovery of the helical structure of DNA in 1953 by James Watson and Francis Crick revolutionised molecular biology. This discovery led them to understand heredity as a result of the transmission of information contained in the genes of cells. The new metaphor was that of the computer and the computer program – the organism being the computer and the genome a program which encodes the organism's development and response to the environment – whereby all of the information required to create a new organism was contained purely within the DNA. It was this assumption which led to the creation of the genome project in the 1980s and 1990s which promised to reveal the greatest secrets of nature and life, but the results of which entirely failed to match its predictions.

The central prediction was that humans would turn out to have many more thousands of genomes than far simpler forms of life. This assumption was the result of a way of thinking which saw biological organisms as essentially the same as machines, whereby knowledge of the parts was enough to be able to understand the whole. Researchers have since discovered that single genes are rarely responsible for just one particular function in an organism. In fact, the action of a gene is a result of the actions not only of other genes as well; the overall *context* of the cellular environment also influences the actions and behaviours of the genes.[46]

The findings of the human genome project shocked many people. It had been expected that humans would have approximately 100,000 genes, since humans were generally regarded as the most complex of organisms.[47] The reality was that humans actually had around 30,000 genes, far fewer than predicted. To put this in perspective, caenorhabditis is a tiny worm, around 1 mm long. Its patterned body is comprised of exactly 969 cells, and it has a simple brain of approximately 302 cells. Caenorhabditis has a total of 18,000 genes. The eye of a fruit fly alone is considerably more complex than the entire caenorhabditis, but it has 5,000 fewer genes. This tells us that it is not the quantity of genes which determines the complexity of an organism, but how the genes are organised, that is, their relationships.

When thinking about randomness and probabilities in relation to the evolution of life on Earth, the numbers are far too big for most of us to be able to comfortably envisage. One way of viewing

Darwinian evolution is that the four billion years over which life has evolved is more than enough time for life to evolve through random mutations. But is it? An alternative argument, based on the probabilities of obtaining functioning enzymes, suggests not.[48] Kauffman compares the maximum number of attempts to create life which could conceivably have taken place – 2.5 x 10^{51} – with the probability of the actual number of trials required to obtain a functioning enzyme – 1 in $10^{40,000}$. Given that the total number of hydrogen atoms in the universe is approximately 10^{60}, in this conception, life could not have possibly occurred. But life did emerge and we humans exist today, so how can this huge discrepancy be explained?

Kauffman explains this mystery in terms of autocatalytic reactions in living systems. Living organisms can be seen as consisting of chemicals which have the capacity to catalyse their own reproduction. While the description of genes as the 'command and control centre' reduced living systems to being viewed in reductionist terms, autocatalytic sets exhibit the emergent properties of holism, whereby the whole exists by means of the parts, and the parts exist because of, and in order to sustain, the whole. Kauffman argues that the order which he studied arises spontaneously, a phenomenon he describes as 'order for free'. How can this possibly arise?

Kauffman created computer models of genes, whose activity and interaction were determined by simple rules. In this simulation, genes were ascribed a limited set of random logical functions, which reflected the gene's response to neighbouring genes. If you imagine that each gene can be in one of two states – off or on – and that there are 100 genes, then the total possible number of states in this system is 2^{100}. In reality, actual cells have thousands of genes, so the total number of available states is in the region of $2^{10,000}$, another inconceivably large number.

On running his simulation, Kauffman discovered that the system settled down into a cycle that lasted for an average of ten different states. In a much larger network, consisting of 100,000 genes which could pass through $2^{100,000}$ states, the system settled down into a regular cycle of just 317 states. Kauffman saw a pattern developing, whereby the number of cyclical states was the square root of the number of genes, that is, 10 is the square root of 100, and 317 is approximately the square root of 100,000. Putting this another way, although these systems could in theory explore an incredibly large number of states, in practice their dynamic behaviour was settling down into a greatly restricted total.

Kauffman reached the conclusion that much of the order that was seen in cells was not the result of Darwinian evolution, but resulted from the dynamic behaviour of the genomic network. This goes entirely against our intuitions as to what the requirements for order are. However, there is one requirement for cells to exhibit this type of behaviour: stability and flexibility. That is, the cells must not be too rigid in their behaviour, because otherwise, just as we saw in the example of the heart, the cells will not be able to cope with the complex environments in which they live.

Life, therefore, is the continual juggling between the demands of stability and flexibility. Living systems survive in the middle of these two extremes. The term 'on the edge of chaos' which is fundamental in complexity theory, was coined by Norman Packard in 1988 to reflect this aspect of complex systems.[49] Packard, along with Chris Langton, spent many years studying cellular automata in computer simulations.

Packard and Langton noticed that there was a region of transition between chaotic and ordered systems, where all parts were in dynamic communication with all the other parts. In this domain, the possibility for communication was at a maximum, the system neither collapsing in chaotic behaviour, nor becoming stuck in too rigid patterns. Langton and Packard suggested that this was of significance in evolutionary scenarios, since this transitionary state 'on the edge of chaos' was the optimum condition for maximum adaptability.[50]

Gaia

Having considered some of the smallest organisms, we can now examine the complexities of life at our level, in terms of people, animals, plants and the environment. It is tempting to simply envisage the environment as being a stable, or constant and neutral entity in the background, while individual organisms evolve slowly through gradual adaptations, which increase their chances of survival. Life, though, evolved as a tangled mesh of interactions, not only between organisms, but as a result of complex and dynamic feedback loops between both organic and inorganic life. Darwin was more than aware of these interactions when he observed:

> It is interesting to contemplate an entangled bank, clothed with many plants of many kinds, with birds singing on the bushes, with various insects flitting about, and with worms crawling through the damp earth, and to reflect that these elaborately constructed forms, so different from each other, and dependent on each other in so complex a manner, have all been produced by laws acting around us.[51]

Figure 5.8 shows a partial food web of the Northwest Atlantic.[52] Earth's food webs are so complex that we are still unable to determine at what level of simplicity the models break down in terms of descriptive value. Peter Meisenheimer provides us with an excellent summary of the impact on an environment when people fail to understand these great webs of relationships.[53] In the early 1990s, the Northwest Atlantic cod fishery collapsed, and many reasons for this were cited. The Canadian government believed that seals, a natural predator of cod, had to be culled in order to restore the overall stock. However, scientists from the Canadian Department of Fisheries concluded that, while there was no evidence of seals exerting any impact on the total mortality in cod, there was clear evidence of an impact from human activities.

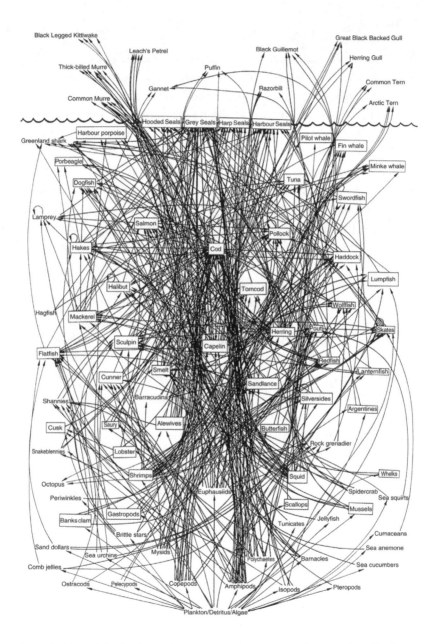

Figure 5.8. Partial food web showing some trophic interactions for part of the Northwest Atlantic.

The Canadian politicians were looking for a scapegoat to excuse their poor management, and so they blamed the seal population. But the reality was that as well as eating cod, seals also ate other animals, which were also predators of cod. It could well be that if seals were culled, then the cod would face even *more* predators from other predatory species. As Meisenheimer has pointed out, mythology for politicians can be more important than science, even scientific findings which come from their own biologists:

> Nothing much has changed since the cod disappeared.
> The political leadership still refuses to accept the analysis
> of their biologists. The prescription for a seal cull is now
> being presented as a 'common sense' solution that should
> be pursued regardless of the data. Common sense, of
> course, is a term used for mythology, bias, prejudice, and
> heart-felt belief when its proponents cannot justify their
> position with facts. Common sense, furthermore, is often
> very different from good sense.[54]

In this case study of North Atlantic cod, we see how, even with just a few competing or interacting species, the web of interactions can be unfathomably complex. But what about the complex web of interactions on a global scale? To understand this, and also to follow the change in thinking of the global scientific community, we have to go back to the 1970s and look at the great insight of an independent scientist, James Lovelock.

So far we have been looking at individual organisms as dynamic, self-regulating systems, which are capable of demonstrating a spontaneous level of order. But could this be true if we imagine the Earth to be, in effect, a self-regulating system? In 1972, when Lovelock first proposed this in the form of his Gaia hypothesis, he faced a widespread and hostile rejection. Lovelock then went on to develop the hypothesis with the help of both Lynn Margulis and an ingenious, yet simple, mathematic model, which he called 'Daisyworld'.[55]

Lovelock's primary insight, which departed strongly from the prevailing mainstream view, was not that non-biological processes were in control of the Earth, but that living systems were in fact tightly coupled with non-living systems. This means that the conditions for life on Earth are an emergent property of the entire set of processes, that is, the complex processes which occur between organisms, the atmosphere, rocks and water. Lovelock's theory suggests that the Earth is one single organism, of which we are parts. It is a truly dynamical, holistic and non-hierarchical view of the biosphere.

The idea first came to Lovelock in 1965, when he was working in the Jet Propulsion Laboratory at the California Institute for Technology. In the early 1960s, NASA was beginning to look at ways of detecting life on Mars, and their principal plan was to devise ways of sending probes to its surface, in order to be able to analyse the soil. Lovelock was not certain of the wisdom of this approach, and, when asked what he would do, he replied that he would look for 'entropy reduction in the atmosphere'.[56] Lovelock was saying that life was characterised (as we saw in the discussion of Prigogine's work) by dynamic and dissipative processes, which are able to counter the second law of thermodynamics and actively maintain conditions suitable for life.

Lovelock has described himself as having a 'flash of enlightenment' when thinking about the Earth's atmosphere, its composition, and of the composition of the air that we breathe. The chemical constituents of our atmosphere – methane, ammonia, sulphur gases, methyl chloride and methyl iodide – have a tendency to react with oxygen, and so they coexist in a far-from-equilibrium state. Because the air's atmosphere is so full of these unstable and almost combustible gases, something has to keep it in a state of equilibrium, the delicate conditions required to maintain life. Lovelock's first insight was that, in order for the atmosphere to remain constant, something must be regulating it, and that somehow life on the surface of the planet must be involved. As Lovelock noted, the science of the time was so reductionist and compartmentalised that very little thought had gone in to thinking about what exactly 'life' was.

The name for Lovelock's theory came to him one day when going for a walk near his home with the novelist William Golding, who suggested the name 'Gaia', after the ancient Greek mother goddess. The name 'Gaia Theory' evoked images of the world as animate, intelligent and alive, and it would come to capture the imagination of those people, the world over, who had an interest in both ecology and spirituality. For many, it evoked a sense of reverence for a planet which was alive and nurturing; to them the name embodied a new form of consciousness, where the planet became a 'being', which was to have a sacred relationship with them, rather than just a lifeless and soulless entity, which we could plunder and exploit without limit.[57]

In looking at the evolution of life on Earth, Lovelock proposed that life was a self-regulating emergent property of the biosphere, or Gaia, as a whole. It evolved as an entity, as did, for example, termite colonies. Unlike many non-scientists, who were inspired by the theory, from the majority of the scientific community came a violent backlash against the idea, since within it was the implicit notion of either 'teleology' or 'animism' – the notion that there was somehow a mysterious force consciously guiding evolution on Earth.[58] This was not what Lovelock was suggesting, but there still remained other rejections, based on scientific grounds rather than emotional misconceptions.

The criticisms which Lovelock did take seriously came from those who argued that planetary regulation, if it did exist, could not have come about through Darwinian mechanisms of natural selection. Evolutionary biologist W. Ford Doolittle argued that self-regulation had only come about through chance alone, and not through regulatory feedback mechanisms.[59] The way in which Lovelock would be able to counter the many and varied criticisms came to him in 1981, again due to another great intuitive insight gained from a surprising piece of luck.

Lovelock was reading some periodicals, and in one he happened to see some equations, which described the growth of the plantain, a wild English plant. Lovelock's intuition was to ask himself what a planet would be like with just two species of plant, both daisies, but one variety being light-coloured and the other being dark-coloured. These two types of daisy would have different albedos, meaning that they would reflect different amounts of sunlight, the light daisies reflecting far more light than the dark ones. Following this insight, Lovelock created a computer simulation based on this scenario, but there was also another critical assumption built in to the model.

Our sun today is approximately 25% brighter than it was 3,500 million years ago, and yet, across this immense time span, the temperature of the planet has never been too hot nor too cold for life.[60] In the lifetime of Earth, there certainly have been periods where it has been warmer than average, and there have been cool periods as well. But the average temperature has remained surprisingly stable, given the evolution of the sun in the same time period. As living systems, we humans are able to regulate our own body temperatures across an extremely wide range of temperatures. The concept is the same for the Earth, although many scientists have suggested that this is down to pure chance, an attitude which is hardly scientific to take.

Lovelock built in to his Daisyworld model an increasing luminosity of the sun. He populated his artificial world with white daisies, with an albedo of 0.75 (where the albedo can range between 0 and 1), and black daisies with an albedo of 0.25. He also assumed that there would be areas of the surface of the planet which would have no covering of daisies, and gave these an albedo value of 0.5. The results from the simulation startled him. At the beginning, the planet was covered with seeds from both black and white daisies. As the luminosity of the planet was initially low, the black daisies began to prosper, since they were better than the white daisies at absorbing heat from the sun, and were therefore more efficient at photosynthesis. However, there came a point when the planet was covered in so many black daisies that it began to warm up. Then, with a warmer planetary temperature, the white daisies began to have an advantage, since they were better able to cope as they reflected the heat.

White daisies began to spread across the planet, and at this point a reverse process kicked in. With so many white daisies reflecting heat, the overall temperature of the planet started to fall. When this happened, and the temperature dropped to a certain level, the black daisies once again would have a competitive advantage, and so an oscillation of the temperature started, around a point which could sustain life. This stable temperature was maintained against a background of a sun with an ever increasing luminosity. A point came when the luminosity of the sun was simply too great for the Earth's biota, and at this point life on Daisyworld collapsed and died.

The stable temperature could be described as an 'emergent property', due to the fact that there was simply nothing in the mathematics of Daisyworld which could possibly lead to the prediction of this as an outcome. Stephan Harding, a long time collaborator with Lovelock, has said that, even to this day, the equations still inspire Lovelock with a sense of wonder, due to their continuing mysterious behaviour.

Lovelock expanded Daisyworld to include even more varieties of daisy with different albedos. He also enriched the environment with rabbits, which ate daisies, and with foxes, which were predators of the rabbits. Our commonsense view of the world suggests that, with this added 'complexity' of far more species, Daisyworld ought to act in a far more 'chaotic' and unstable manner. Here we are using the words 'complex' and 'chaotic' in their everyday sense of the words, and not as defined by chaos and complexity science. Again, the outcome surprised Lovelock, because the introduction of more species led to an increasing stability in the overall temperature of the planet, even with occasional catastrophic events such as plagues or hits by meteors.

Daisyworld was important, since it became the basis for developing far more sophisticated models of Gaia, such as the long-term climate prediction models of the Hadley Centre in the UK. Harding has developed Daisyworld further in partnership with Lovelock, exploring the question whether or not complex ecosystems are better able to survive and recover from disturbances than less connected and more simple ones. This is now a vital debate, as huge global corporations move over to highly unnatural systems of monoculture, where crops are now seemingly less able to cope with insect outbreaks in tropical countries.

Harding has created a new version of Daisyworld, which has twenty-three species of daisy, with differing albedos, three herbivore species with more realistic behaviours, and more complex behaviours between the herbivores and the predator species. Another dimension was added, which meant that Harding could change the complexity of the food web, for example, by changing the number of varieties of daisies eaten by each herbivore. As before, increasing the complexity of interactions between all the species resulted in a stable global temperature. When Harding decreased the complexity of the food web, holding back the herbivores until only two dominant plant species had established themselves, the temperature began to oscillate wildly, in a manner quite unlike the more complex scenarios.[61]

The key finding here is that, in general, communities which are more complex are more stable. It is also noteworthy that this complex web of interactions includes both living organisms and their environment. In the case of Daisyworld, the environment is modelled in terms of ground, which is not covered in daisies. In reality, the Earth has many tightly coupled systems connecting organic and inorganic life, such as the long-term and short-term carbon cycles.

How does Henri's concept of '*belonging* together' relate to the manner in which Gaian scientists such as Harding build their systems models? Does Henri's criticism of General Systems Theory – that it can fall into a trap of modelling counterfeit wholes – also apply to the mathematical models of Gaia Theory? Or could, in fact, the opposite be true; that systems models could, indeed, somehow model the *belonging* together of parts?

These questions are of fundamental importance for anyone who is involved in developing systems models, and, indeed, any other forms of models. In 2009, during his Schumacher College lectures, Henri explored this question in detail with Stephan Harding, Philip Franses, and that year's Holistic Science students.[62] The concept of '*belonging* together' comes from

Heidegger[63], and for a long time Henri had felt that Systems Theory had missed this subtle concept:

> I used to have an obsession that there was something deeply wrong about systems theory. In a way, it coloured my whole attitude for quite a long time. For me it was quite easy to see that what people did in systems thinking was to tie things together, and that there may be ways in which things belong, which in systems theory are coloured over. I felt this very strongly in my personal life, and in human relations in organisations.

> I did feel that people who came in, with their diagrams, and their grids, and their management tools, and personality tools and so on were doing something that was very coarse, and there was something more subtle there. They were just obliterating this with their approach.

Philip helped to explain the difference between the subtle *'belonging* together' and the more coarse 'belonging *together'*:

> In a watch, the parts are brought together and that is how the watch works. In a plant, the stem, the leaf, and the flower, you can only imagine them; they don't have any existence except in their belonging as a plant, the whole plant.

So in a watch, parts belong *together,* but in a plant, the parts *belong* together. Stephan asked Henri about the relationship between his dynamical way of seeing and the systems models of Gaia that he had developed. The questions help us to understand the difference between what Henri refers to as 'dogmatic annunciation' and 'constructive conception':

> **Stephan:** Can you go from one to the other? Thinking of Gaia, it looks at the interrelationships between phosphorus, nitrogen and carbon; you make a model of

that, and you have got a systems model. In my experience, that model, if used in the right way, can bring you to the *belonging* together. You would not have got that type of belonging together if you didn't have the systems model to begin with. You couldn't have possibly seen it all. It happens at such a large scale, where some of these cycles are happening very slowly and invisibly. I think there is a way of bringing it together where you are conscious of what you are doing. You have created a system, but you are doing it to come to this more subtle form.

Henri: I can see that that could be the case. What you are doing, therefore, is that in your more systems approach, the belonging *together* is not dogmatic. It is a 'constructive conception'.

Stephan: You know what you are doing. You are aware of it.

Henri: This is the key thing.

Stephan: There is feedback between the two. They can inform each other. The better able I am to get into the *belonging* together, the better my systems model is going to be, the more correct it is going to be. And then that will inspire my belonging *together*. So you can do a kind of feedback. They help define each other. I think of this particularly in relation to Gaia.

Henri: What comes across is that it is not a 'dogmatic annunciation'. This is what you get in systems thinking – 'dogmatic annunciation'. What you are working with is what I would call a 'constructive conception'. The idea of a constructive conception is that it is *not* the truth. A dogmatic annunciation says it *is* the truth. A constructive conception has in it sufficient truth for it to be useful to take you on [forward]. What you said, that you need to be aware that you are doing it, needs to be underlined in red many times. It is the most important thing of all. You do things in full awareness of what you are doing. Our problem is that we don't. We do things without being aware of what we are doing. That's when things become dogmatic and we become trapped in them.

We can do all sorts of reductionist things, and they can be jolly useful. But you need to be aware when you are doing it that that is what you are doing.

It is important not to think in a dogmatic way when developing a model. The better you can see '*belonging* together', the better your model will be. There is, therefore, a feedback loop between the two aspects. You become more aware of your own thinking, and also aware of mental processes and experiences that would otherwise be hidden from you. Modelling should only really be done once you have this level of self-awareness – aware of what you are thinking and doing. When this happens, you are able to work more fully in a reductionist or mechanistic manner, but you do not become so entranced by your models that you confuse the models with the deeper truths of reality, the totality of which cannot be modelled explicitly.

Johan Rockström, director of the Stockholm Resilience Centre at Stockholm University, along with many of his colleagues, published a groundbreaking article, 'A Safe Operating Space for Humanity', in the scientific journal *Nature,* which gives us a much better picture, not just of the carbon cycles, but also of many other planetary systems, which act together as a whole to create what they term a 'safe operating space' for life on Earth.[64] The nine critical Earth system processes identified were:

- Climate change.
- Depletion of stratospheric ozone.
- Land use change.
- Freshwater use.
- Rate of biological diversity loss.
- Ocean acidification.
- Amounts of nitrogen and phosphorus inputs to the biosphere and oceans.
- Air pollution from aerosol loading and chemical pollution.

Rockström's work counters the previous belief that environmental change occurs in an incremental, linear and predictable fashion. His evidence indicates that this may be the exception, not the rule, and that long periods of gradual change may well, eventually, push us past thresholds that result in abrupt and potentially disastrous changes. In order to avoid such disastrous outcomes, radical action will be required, shifting our mindsets from consumption to that of 'active stewardship' of the world's ecosystems.[65]

It is interesting to compare the food webs in the North Atlantic, which we have discussed, with this new research on Gaia, which encompasses many different planetary systems. In the case of the North Atlantic, politicians ignored what their own scientists were telling them, perhaps for political reasons. In the case of the work of Rockström and his colleagues, we may not be able to take in the information because of the emotional magnitude of what our science is telling us. This is a new dimension of complexity science. It is one thing to be taught about these systems, how complexity works. But when discussing complexity, we have to think also about how much a person has been able to absorb emotionally, and whether they are still in a mechanical mindset even though they are using the models and concepts from complexity.

We can now revisit our discussion in Chapter 1 about mechanistic thinking, systems thinking and holonomic thinking (Figure 5.9). Systems thinking can be limited by an analytical mode of consciousness which is only able to comprehend belonging *together*. If we expand our mode of consciousness to a point whereby we begin to be able to see *belonging* together, the systems models that we develop will be enhanced. We should, though, avoid falling into the trap of assuming that the belonging together in a system is fixed. If we do this, then we run the risk that the systems which we develop will no longer be creative, and we stop anything new from emerging. When you develop a counterfeit system, you try to bring the parts together by connecting them together. But when you see that the whole 'comes-to-presence' within the parts, whereby each part is an expression of the whole, and that the whole can only be the whole because of the parts, and the parts can only be the parts because of the whole, then you can see the deeper kind of belonging together.

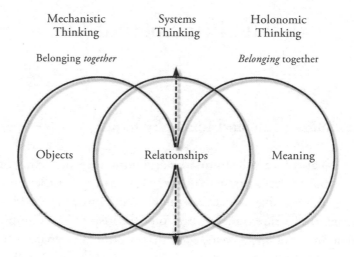

Figure 5.9. From mechanistic to holonomic thinking.

In thinking about complexity from a holonomic perspective, we come to realise that we can no longer separate ourselves from the environment. The environment and our ecosystems do not behave in a predictable and linear manner. This suggests that, in every way in which we act in our lives, we need to tread carefully and cautiously, because we are not able to predict the outcome of our actions. Businesses and investors, however, often rush into new markets, into new countries which have rich natural resources to exploit, with no thought about the wider implications.

6. The Principles of Life

Principles of Life and Living Systems

In this chapter we will summarise and bring together many of the points that we have discussed so far. The concept of the 'business ecosystem' is being used increasingly in the business world in an attempt to describe new business models, inspired by complexity science and ecology. *Investopedia,* in its online dictionary, offers a typical definition:

> The network of organisations – including suppliers, distributors, customers, competitors, government agencies and so on – involved in the delivery of a specific product or service through both competition and cooperation. The idea is that each business in the 'ecosystem' affects and is affected by the others, creating a constantly evolving relationship in which each business must be flexible and adaptable in order to survive, as in a biological ecosystem.

> The ecosystem model can also be applied to organisations such as hospitals and universities. This term is part of a recent trend toward using biological concepts to better understand ways to succeed in business. Advances in technology and increasing globalisation have changed ideas about the best ways to do business, and the idea of a business ecosystem is thought to help companies understand how to thrive in this rapidly changing environment.[1]

Although this seems to be offering a succinct summary of what we have been discussing, we will argue shortly that the concept of business ecosystems is potentially a counterfeit ecosystem. In their excellent book *Profit Beyond Measure*, Thomas Johnson and Anders Bröms summarise living systems as having three principal characteristics:

↓ Self-organisation
↓ Interdependence
↓ Diversity

To understand what a living system is, we need to ask the question: 'What is life?' Despite this question being posed by physicist Erwin Schrödinger in 1944, before the discovery of DNA, and before the discovery of the chemistry of metabolism by enzyme proteins, we still do not have a suitable or generally agreed upon definition. 'Life' is actually harder to pin down as a definition than this seemingly innocuous question may suggest.

In considering this question, we can draw on the work of the late Lynn Margulis, James Lovelock's colleague, who, with him, helped to turn his Gaia theory into the Gaia hypothesis. Margulis and Dorion Sagan begin their examination of the question of life by positing that the metaphor of life as a machine is not adequate to account for life, because machines do not have free will; they are unable to make their own choices, and, moreover, they are not able to create more of themselves from themselves. Margulis and Sagan also take the standpoint, like Goodwin, Kauffman and Lovelock, that Darwinian evolution is not sufficient by itself to generate evolutionary innovation.[2]

Two hundred years ago, thermodynamics was developed by scientists focusing on irreversible processes, which had been ignored as mere aberrations. Complexity science was developed by scientists and mathematicians also focusing on chaotic irregularities, which previously had been seen as nuisances. Likewise, Margulis, to her credit, focused on a peculiar aspect of human cells. Not all of the DNA in a human cell is contained within the nucleus. Some

DNA is contained within organelles, specifically mitochondria, which are parts of the cell outside the nucleus. Margulis' great achievement, which is now widely accepted in the scientific community, was to show how symbiogenesis (the origins of novel forms of life through symbiosis) was far more common than Darwinian evolutionists had ever conceived.

Life consists of five 'kingdoms': bacteria, protoctists, fungi, plants and animals. (Protoctists consist of a variety of microorganisms, such as algae, slime moulds, amoebas, etc.) There are two main types of living cell today – prokaryotes and eukaryotes. A prokaryote is a cell that has no nucleus, meaning that all bacterial cells are prokaryotes. Human cells, and those of animals, plants, fungi and protoctists, do have a nucleus and are therefore eukaryotes.

In the mid-1960s, Margulis argued that approximately 2,000 million years ago a new type of cell, the nucleated cell, came about; this was not by slow, gradual change of inherited characteristics, but by a merger between what were then free-living mitochondria and simple cells with no complex internal structures. This was considered a heresy at the time, despite the probability that Darwin himself would have been amenable to the idea, unlike his present-day disciples, the neo-Darwinists. In the 1970s, evidence supporting Margulis' view gradually accumulated, and in 1979 she won a Guggenheim fellowship. Two years later she published the book *Symbiosis in Cell Evolution,* leading her to be regarded as one of the most creative and respected researchers of her generation.[3]

We can no longer think of life on Earth as a hierarchy, with humans at the very top of the pyramid. We have to return to Koestler's concept of the 'holarchy', in which the constituents – holons – are both parts and wholes. A holarchy, as we have seen with Lovelock and Margulis' conceptualisation of Gaia, is different from a hierarchy, because there is no longer a sense of super-part, top-down control, or of one part controlling the other parts. Life on Earth is not a 'created hierarchy', but an 'emergent holarchy arisen from the self-induced synergy of combination, interfacing and re-combination'.[4]

Henri Bortoft continually urged us as students to contemplate that aspect of life which he described as the 'coming-into-being'. This notion can be extended to highlight our tendency to 'see' in terms of finished objects in relation to the concept of the word 'life'. Life is not a thing, and neither is life a property, restricted to those entities that we call organisms:

> Self-transforming, holarchic life 'breaks out' into new forms that incorporate formerly self-sufficient individuals as integral parts of greater identities. Life is distinguished not by its chemical constituents but by the behaviour of its chemicals ... The question 'What is life?' is thus a linguistic trap. To answer according to the rules of grammar, we must supply a noun, a thing. But life on Earth is more like a verb. It repairs, maintains, re-creates, and outdoes itself.[5]

A key characteristic of living systems is their ability to self-repair. The human body is quite amazing. We get a new stomach lining every five days, a new liver every two months, new skin every six weeks, and every year 98% of our bodies are replaced. These processes are the result of metabolism, a process which is fundamental to life. Humberto Maturana and Francisco Varela coined the term 'autopoiesis' to describe these metabolic processes. The term comes from two Greek words, 'auto' (meaning 'self'), and 'poiesis' (meaning 'making'):

> An autopoietic machine is a machine organised (defined as a unity) as a network of processes of production (transformation and destruction) of components that produces the components which: (i) through their interactions and transformations continuously regenerate and realise the network of processes (relations) that produced them; and (ii) constitute it (the machine) as a concrete unity in the space in which they (the components) exist by specifying the topological domain of its realisation as such a network.[6]

Autopoiesis, therefore, is the principle of living organisms being able to continually reproduce as a result of the internal organisation of the parts of those organisms. Autopoiesis is subtly different from self-organisation. We can think of a team being asked to 'self-organise'. A manager will provide the direction, the request to self-organise, and the team members – the individual parts – will then agree amongst themselves how best to organise their work. But once they start to work, their work unit changes. An autopoietic system, on the other hand, changes in order to remain the same.

Autopoiesis is not the same as replication. Viruses can be said not to be alive, since they lack sufficient genes and proteins to maintain themselves. DNA replicates itself, but it does so as a result of its relationships with many other parts of a cell. It does not replicate itself on its own. In this way, we can say that DNA is not alive, and so autopoiesis is a more fundamental characteristic of living systems than replication. The smallest cells that are known today, bacteria one ten-millionth of a metre in diameter, are the smallest known autopoietic units.

Our entire concept of the attributes of a 'gene' has recently gone through a radical re-appraisal, to the extent that biologists can no longer agree on what a gene is. According to Rick Young, a geneticist at the Whitehead Institute in Cambridge, Massachusetts, whereas a couple of decades ago it used to take him two hours to explain to his students what a gene is, now it takes an entire three months.[7] A key change is that, whereas previously RNA (ribonucleic acid, present in all living cells) was thought to be passive in the process of replicating information from DNA, it is now seen as far more active, and in fact may itself be able to pass on information, a role within the cell which was previously seen as exclusive to DNA.

Science philosophers Karola Stotz and Paul Griffiths carried out an experiment to measure the extent of working biologists' confusions and lack of agreement as to what genes are. In their study, geneticists had to evaluate fourteen different genetic arrangements, and to decide whether each one represented a gene, more than one gene, or none at all. Of the 500 biologists who answered, 60% were sure of one answer and 40% confident in another answer, with an insignificant proportion saying that they did not know, or had doubts.[8]

Living systems replicate, reproduce and evolve, but in order to do so, the living system has to be able to metabolise, a process in which the components of the system are continuously rearranged, destroyed, and rebuilt. In order to maintain their unity, living systems must create a local form of 'disorder', taking in energy, dissipating heat and noise, and being able to withstand a certain degree of uncertainty. The autopoietic view of life therefore differs from standard models of biology, where organisms exist against a static backdrop. The dynamic way of seeing life is to perceive organisms as interwoven into their environment in a holarchy, where the biosphere, as a whole, is able to maintain itself.

Our biosphere, and life on Earth, has evolved over the course of 4.6 billion years (4,600,000,000). As sentient beings, not only do we mistakenly place ourselves at the top of the hierarchy of the food chain, but, more often than not, we also fail to understand our place within the timescale of evolution. While there have been many attempts to help place the lifetime of human beings and our civilisation in context – for example, the final second of the final minute of the final hour in a period of 24 hours – the vast time spans of evolution were only brought home to us by going on one of Stephan Harding's 'deep time walks'.

Stephan invented the notion of a deep time walk in order to be able to teach Gaia theory to his students at Schumacher College. The idea is simple, but powerfully effective. On the deep time walk that we (the authors) went on, Stephan took us to a wonderful coastal path in Devon. The start of our walk was approximately 4.6 km from Dartmouth, our destination where our bus would be waiting for us. On this walk, each step that we took of one metre was the equivalent of one million years. The walk was done in a consciously meditative state, allowing us to really absorb the time spans, the eons and periods named by geologists, and thus to appreciate just how recent life, as we know it, sprang up in the context of the overall age of Earth.

At the start of the walk, not much happened in the first couple of kilometres. As Stephan described it:

> For the first 100 million years of the evocatively named Hadean Eon – the Earth was a broiling soup of molten rock, inhospitable to life as we can conceive of it. It is half a kilometre along our walk – or 500 million years before the Earth has definitely formed a solid crust and has acquired a thin covering of water.
>
> It takes about another 500 million years (taking us to three-and-a-half billion years ago) before we encounter the first incontrovertible signs of life: the prokaryotes or bacteria. A further kilometre (a billion years) takes us to two-and-a-half billion years ago and the formation of the first eukaryotic cells – the product of a wildly innovative co-operative bacterial breakthrough that eventually led to the appearance (around a billion-and-a-half years later) of the multicellular beings that populate our world – plants, animals fungi and protoctista: the algae, amoeba and such like. We also experience the first tentative wisps of free oxygen in the atmosphere and the appearance of large drifting continents poking above the seas.[9]

Figure 6.1 shows a simplified version of the 4.6 km deep time walk. The Cambrian explosion happens within the last half kilometre, or 500 metres. The format of the walk means that you can really feel the quality of evolution. In this final stage of the walk, events really begin to come at you every few metres or so. For example, the Cenozoic Eon (the 'Age of Mammals') begins a mere 65 metres from the end of the walk.

Millions of Years Ago	Event	Deep Time Walk
4,600	Archean Eon – Earth is formed	4.6 km
3,900	Life in the form of bacterial cells	3.9 km
3,500	Photosynthetic bacterial communities	3.5 km
3,300	Trace amounts of oxygen in atmosphere	3.3 km
3,000	Diversification of bacteria	3.0 km
2,500	Proterozoic Eon	2.5 km
2,200	Prokaryotic plankton in oceans	2.2 km
2,000	Mitochondria, ancestors to eukaryotes	2.0 km
1,700	Protoctists – second kingdom	1.7 km
600	Animals appear	600 m
541	Phanerozoic Eon – Appearance of fourth and fifth kingdoms: Plants and Fungi	541 m
541	Cambrian explosion – acceleration of evolution by an order of magnitude	541 m
245	Mesozoic Eon – 'Age of Reptiles'	245 m
65	Cenozoic Eon – 'Age of Mammals'	65 m
4	Appearance of human ancestors	4 m
1.65	Homo erectus and Homo neanderthalenis in Middle East, Africa and Europe	1.65 m
0.2	Homo sapiens	20 cm
0.01	Appearance of agricultural urban centres	1 cm
0.005	Appearance of cities	5 mm
0.002	Jesus	2 mm

Figure 6.1. The History of the Earth in relation to a Deep Time Walk.

Stephan really amazed us at the very end of the walk, when he demonstrated human civilisation in context. He produced a tape measure, but only the last few millimetres were required. Jesus was born two thousand years ago, which on the time walk is only two millimetres.

> The Holocene – the short geological blip since the end of the last ice age – starts at 1.3 cm (13,000 years) from the end of our walk. At 6 millimetres (or 6,000 years) from the end, recorded history begins in Mesopotamia and Egypt, and just one-fifth of a millimetre from the present day (200 years ago), the Industrial Revolution kicks in, triggering changes in the climate and biodiversity so profound that the era we are living through may well be dubbed by scientists as the 'Anthropocene'.[10]

The period from the Industrial Revolution until the present day was just the width of a fingernail compared to the distance that we had covered, and our own lifetimes far less than that. The deep time walk might sound like an extravagance when Stephan could have just gone through the dates traditionally in a classroom. But the time walk was deep because it was, perhaps, the closest that we could get to a Goethean way of experiencing evolution – in a sensory way, and in our intuition – which facts and figures cannot convey. The profound experiences of the deep time walk in which we participated are still with us today.

We are now ready to see if we can more fully answer the question 'What is life?' While there is still no definite answer, we have chosen to characterise living systems in a manner that combines the phenomenological way of seeing with the insights from complexity science. 'Life' is:

⭣ More a verb than a noun
⭣ Dynamic
⭣ Coming-into-being
⭣ Upstream
⭣ Creative
⭣ Ordered and chaotic
⭣ Simple and complex

- Co-operative and competitive
- Unpredictable
- Emergent
- Self-organising
- Autopoietic
- Dissipative
- Replicating and reproducing
- Evolving
- Diverse
- Holonomic

In setting out this list, we can begin to appreciate the many aspects of complexity science, biology, ecology and phenomenology which, if we study them in detail, lead us towards a greatly expanded world view. The list is designed to point us in a direction where we are no longer just seeing in a downstream manner, where we can only see finished objects; but, like the Necker Cube, we are able to switch our perspective and enter into a new way of seeing, via our intuition, that brings us into direct contact with the coming-into-being of living systems, the essence of 'livingness' itself.

Business Ecosystems and Living Organisations

Much criticism has been levelled at complexity science from within the business community, not only due to the fact that it is nascent science, albeit one that is becoming increasingly popular within a business context, but also because the way in which it can be applied in human systems is by no means clear. One criticism is that the laws which complexity science has supposedly discovered are still only computer models and not yet proven in the physical world. A second line of criticism is that social systems of which people are a part cannot possibly be compared to physical systems, because people are self-conscious and random, and since they have free will, the same laws cannot apply to them.

Michael C. Jackson has provided an interesting critique of complexity theory, seeing the value of complexity science in the metaphors that it brings to business thinking. His way of conceptualising systems thinking is through the lens of four different sociological paradigms. These paradigms are 'functionalist', 'interpretive', 'emancipatory' and 'postmodern'.

> Complexity theory, as applied to management in a variety
> of contexts, is very fashionable these days. Its advocates
> sometimes claim that it represents an advance on systems
> thinking. This is nonsense. With its emphasis on holism,
> emergence, interdependence and relationships, complexity
> theory is definitely a systems approach. Indeed, previous
> work in the systems field, on informal groups, group
> working, autonomous work groups, double-loop learning,
> organisations as information processing systems, open
> systems and 'turbulent field' environments, seems to cover
> much of the territory that complexity theory wants to
> claim as its own. Nevertheless, it has introduced a set of
> original concepts that help to enrich the functionalist form
> of systems thinking.[11]

We can contrast Jackson's approach to that of Henri, which comes not through 'lenses' of single 'paradigms', but from an expanded mode of consciousness, which approaches our being in the world via the four different ways of knowing (Figure 2.1). The limitation in Jackson's approach lies in his conceptualisation of holism. This is not the same way in which Henri conceives of the relationship between the whole and the parts. Remember that Henri coined the phrase 'counterfeit whole', in which the mistake of systems thinking was to see the whole as in some way superior to the parts. Following Henri's dynamic and holonomic way of thinking, we come to understand the whole more as an 'active absence', in which it cannot be directly understood; it can only be encountered in its active, yet absent, influence on the parts, where neither the parts nor the whole are primary.[12] For Jackson, though, coming from a systems thinking approach, the whole is primary, with the parts 'serving the purpose of the whole':

> Holism puts the study of wholes before that of the parts.
> It does not try to break down organisations into parts
> in order to understand them and intervene in them. It
> concentrates its attention instead at the organisational level
> and on ensuring that the parts are functioning and are
> related properly together so that they serve the purposes
> of the whole. Being holistic also means approaching
> problems ready to employ the systems language. For
> example, looking at organisations, their parts and their
> environments as systems, subsystems and supra-systems.
> All the systems approaches described in this book seek
> to make use of the philosophy of holism and the systems
> vocabulary associated with it.[13]

The value of complexity science goes far deeper than being merely a functionalist paradigm. While it is certainly true that it is a young science, the great discovery of phenomenology was more than one hundred years ago; and the schools of thought that we have been examining go back through Goethe to Plato, if we subscribe to the view that Plato has for the main part been misunderstood. This conceptualisation of the livingness of life, of the notion of the wholeness of experience, the dynamic coming-into-being of phenomena, of nature, is often lost in systems thinking.

In our characterisation of living systems, we have set aside two highly emotive and controversial aspects. These are 'consciousness' and 'purposefulness'. As Lovelock found to his cost, his proposal that the ability of Gaia to regulate its own climate came from an emergent dynamic interaction of its constituent parts, against great improbabilities, was interpreted by many scientists to be a statement that Gaia was a sentient being, consciously purposeful. Lovelock specifically said that this was not the case – hence his need to create the mathematical model of Daisyworld to demonstrate his point.

It is fair to suggest that the intelligence of nature has been greatly underestimated in science, and that many new experiments are continually surprising scientists with revelation after revelation. The examples which we highlight in this book suggest that, while of course no one is attributing the same quality of intelligence that humans have in other organisms, we may now need to think in terms of continuums, rather than consciousness and intelligence being exclusive to humans.

In 2000, a Japanese professor Toshiyuki Nakagaki and his colleagues demonstrated how slime mould had enough intelligence to be able to find its way out of a maze. The organism *Physarum polycephalum* has no brain, but it is still able to demonstrate complex information processing.[14] It has shown an ability to solve a problem by calculating the minimum-length solution between two points in a labyrinth. This sounds like a simple calculation for both humans and computers, but it is not.

In another experiment, Nakagaki placed food sources in various locations that were similar to railway and metro stations around Tokyo. As a result, the slime mould successfully formed the pattern of a railway system, remarkably similar to the complex and human-designed railroad networks of the Kanto region of Japan. This implied that slime mould could be used in the design of future networks. Atsushi Tero, from Kyushu University, southern Japan, who was also involved in this research, has observed that even with the computational power available to researchers today, the volume of calculations becomes too large for them. But slime moulds do not calculate all the possible options, and can gradually find the best routes.[15]

A second example which challenges our notions of 'intelligence' and 'consciousness' comes from the study of the human immune system. Here, the problem which our immune system must solve is how to distinguish *itself* from *other*. In the last two decades, neuroscientist Candace Pert and her colleagues have transformed our notions of health, mind and emotion by demonstrating that our brains, glands and immune systems, previously thought of as functionally separate, should in fact be seen as a fully interconnected single system, in which neuropeptides are the information carriers.[16] Previously information transmission had been conceived of only as an electrical network, not also chemical, that was based on neuron-axon-dendrite-neurotransmitter connections.

More recent research by Irun Cohen and Graham Jones has examined the whole notion of health as a dynamic state, which develops according to context. They developed a group of 300 proteins, in which Cohen and Jones could relate their dynamic state to the wider context of the whole organism.[17] In this view, the human immune system is seen as being capable of dynamic cognition, in which these molecules act as biomarkers, substances which can relay important information about the state of the system. There is continual feedback and monitoring of the system as a whole by its parts. Jones suggests that this self-referencing system, this looking-at-itself-looking-at-the-system, is fractal and holographic.[18]

Instead of looking at the body as a static machine, there is now a new notion of the body responding to its context. Cohen and Jones are developing new medical texts in which, by examining these molecules, they can judge if the body is healthy, or in some way disturbed. The key point is that Cohen and Jones themselves have a dynamic world view, one which understands the parts of a system in dynamic relation to their context. While this may sound abstract, this world view enables scientists to approach the subject matter that they are studying in new ways, which can result in much deeper insights and solutions to the problems that they are attempting to solve.

While self-recognition is clearly advantageous in animals, not only in their immune systems but also in recognising predators, it is less recognised in plants. Recent work indicates that physically connected roots recognise 'self' and reduce competitive interactions. Richard Karban and Kaori Shiojiri believe that they have produced the first demonstration of self/non-self recognition involving plant communication and defence.[19] In their tests, sagebrush shrubs had their leaves 'clipped', as if they were being eaten by herbivore predators, such as grasshoppers.

Unlike other examples of plant recognition that required direct physiological connection, the sagebrush in Karban and Shiojiri's study responded differently to cues of 'self' and 'non-self' in the absence of physical contact. The research indicated that chemical messages exchanged between plants allowed them to send out alerts when pests attacked, and even to discuss the presence of pollinators such as bees.

Having examined living systems and ecosystems from various perspectives, we can now extend this to an analysis of business ecosystems. Marco Iansiti and Roy Levien, writing in the *Harvard Business Review,* examined Walmart and Microsoft's business models, and related them to biological ecosystems. In this framework 'keystone organisations' focus on their core competencies, while developing a network of suppliers, distributors, outsourcing firms, makers of related products or services and technology providers, etcetera.[20]

Iansiti and Levien diverge from the way in which we have been conceiving of wholeness. Unlike ecosystems which thrive on diversity, with no species achieving primacy, keystone organisations do so in this type of business ecosystem. And, unlike metabolising autopoietic systems, these keystone organisations provide fixed and rigid platforms, on which other organisations depend.[21]

What is missing in business and economic thinking is a critical insight. Biological ecosystems are not out there, in some other country or continent, waiting to be studied, so that new business models can be created in the business environment. The great shortcoming of economics has been to fail to place business and economic systems within the overall ecosystem of the biosphere. Just as Gaia consists of regulatory feedback mechanisms between living organisms and non-living inorganic material, so the business world is very much a holon within Gaia.

David Peat captures well the true insights for business from complexity science.[22] He summarises these in four key lessons, which relate to the ethics and culture of organisations:

1. Transparency and Openness
   Nature organises itself to avoid blocks of any kind. In human systems, therefore, information and meaning should flow through systems unhindered.

2. Respect for Competition
   Natural systems flourish because of their inherent diversity. When one species begins to dominate, the system as a whole flounders.

3. The Role of Redundancy
   Nature does not often act in a way that appears to be maximally efficient. However, when situations change, nature systems are able to make adaptions to survive. Likewise businesses should look to maintain some level of redundancy so as not to become over-rigid and unable to make adjustments.

4. Accepting uncertainty
   The implications of complexity science suggest that business managers should give up their illusions of control. We now live in an age of incomplete information, and this can be challenging to managers.

Satish Kumar, one of the world's best known environmental campaigners, points out in his unique and gentle way that the words 'economics' and 'ecology' have the same derivative meaning, and therefore, economists should naturally be taught about ecology – but they are not. His following comments come from a talk that he gave at the London School of Economics:

> The study of the 'environment' is not the same as the study of 'ecology'. The environment is what surrounds us humans. This implies that humans are at the centre and what is around us is our environment. So 'environment' is

an anthropocentric concept whereas the word 'ecology' is more inclusive. Ecology implies relationships between all species, humans and the natural world.

Ecology and economy are derived from three Greek words: *oikos, logos, nomos. Oikos* means home: a place of relationships between all forms of life, sharing and participating in the evolution of the Earth community. *Logos* means the knowledge of our planet home, and *nomos* means management of that home.

Now what is taught at the LSE is economy; management of the home, and not ecology, the knowledge of home. How can anyone manage something they know nothing of? If you don't know your living room, bedroom, dining room, kitchen or garden how are you going to manage them? If you don't really know your mother, father, husband, wife or children, how are you going to manage those relationships?

So ecology should come before economy; knowledge before management. But at the LSE, as well as at most other universities, the study of the economy dominates. These universities are sending thousands upon thousands of young people into the world equipped with management skills but without knowledge of what they are going to manage. These graduates are half-educated, which is worse than being uneducated.[23]

Economist Georges Bataille (1897–1962) argued that classical economics was mistaken. The general economy was not human, but solar. His idea came from the fact that, in being able to photosynthesise energy from the sun, bacteria, protoctists and plants are the world's true producers and savers. Herbivores and carnivores such as ourselves are consumers, in so far as we eat and then temporarily store this photosynthetic energy. Spending, therefore, is not just a human economic problem; it has been a long term problem for life itself.[24]

One way to characterise a culture is, therefore, to look to see how a particular society is determined less by its needs and more by its excesses. In this view of the world, humans do not own anything at all, since ownerships rests with the biosphere. Although the amount of sun reaching the biosphere is, in theory, unlimited, the amount of resources within the biosphere are limited; but it seems that humans have not yet realised the implications. No single species in the long history of Earth has ever threatened the overall continual existence of life as a whole. Humans are now at risk, though, of irreversibly altering the complex systems of the planet's physiology.

Ultimately, the exploration of nature by using our faculties of thinking, feeling, sensing and intuition brings us fully into experiencing the dynamics of holonomic thinking. Satish Kumar and Philip Franses describe this as 'process and pilgrimage', bringing together the spiritual with the scientific.[25] For Kumar, the spiritual word 'pilgrimage' fully complements the more scientific word 'process', since a pilgrimage, too, is a journey, both literally and metaphorically (spiritual). In pilgrimage, nothing is fixed, rigid or static for the pilgrim; everything is always moving, changing and evolving. So this is the challenge. How do we remain fluid, flexible and not rigid? Life itself is a pilgrimage, if we do not get too fixed in one opinion, or one idea, and see how truth – like life – is always evolving.

'Deep Ecology' is the name given to a movement set up by a number of ecologists, including Kumar, Harding and their late friend, Arnae Ness. These ecologists are trying to solve the ecological problems that we face from a very deep level. They have a profound connection to nature and the natural world. In order to better explain what we mean by a 'deep connection', it is useful to read an account by Aldo Leopold, another of the founders of this movement.

In his book *A Sand County Almanac*, Leopold recalls a time when he was still young, and used to go shooting wolves. In one incident he was able to look into the eyes of a dying wolf, and what he saw shocked him into a new way of thinking, not just about wolves, but also about nature and his place within the natural world:

> We were eating lunch on a high rimrock, at the foot of which a turbulent river elbowed its way. We saw what we thought was a doe fording the torrent, her breast awash in white water. When she climbed the bank toward us and shook out her tail, we realised our error: it was a wolf. A half-dozen others, evidently grown pups, sprang from the willows and all joined in a welcoming mêlée of wagging tails and playful maulings. What was literally a pile of wolves writhed and tumbled in the centre of an open flat at the foot of our rimrock.
>
> In those days we had never heard of passing up a chance to kill a wolf. In a second we were pumping lead into the pack, but with more excitement than accuracy; how to aim a steep downhill shot is always confusing. When our rifles were empty, the old wolf was down, and a pup was dragging a leg into impassable side-rocks.
>
> We reached the old wolf in time to watch a fierce green fire dying in her eyes. I realised then, and have known ever since, that there was something new to me in those eyes – something known only to her and to the mountain. I was young then, and full of trigger-itch; I thought that because fewer wolves meant more deer, that no wolves would mean hunters' paradise. But after seeing the green fire die, I sensed that neither the wolf nor the mountain agreed with such a view.[26]

Kumar says that what we should strive for is a new trinity, a 'soil, soul, society' philosophy – soil for the environment, soul for the spiritual dimension, and society for the social justice that is essential.[27] He defines 'deep ecology' beautifully:

Giving nature a rightful place, and recognising nature's intrinsic value is the main idea of deep ecology. So there is a tree there. The tree is good in itself; the tree is not good because it is useful to humans. The tree is not good because it gives us a kind of oxygen, or firewood, or wood for the house, or flowers or fruit. A tree has intrinsic value. A river has a right to flow unpolluted, uncontaminated, undammed.

When we take something from nature for our survival, that is fine. That we should take with gratitude, not as a right, that it is our right to use nature. But we say it is a gift from nature, and we receive it with gratitude, and we reciprocate it, by looking after it, by composting it, by not polluting it, and by giving respect to it.[28]

Those in the deep ecology movement do not merely understand the science of ecology, the implications of climate change and our human impact on the world as an academic exercise, nor as series of statistics. In them we see people who have already made the great shift into a dynamical way of seeing, and this is manifest in their way of being. They are able to live their lives fully immersed in nature, without arrogance or ego, in harmonious relationships with all of nature. Nature is not dead to them, but alive in all its glory. Nature speaks in a thousand voices, and deep ecologists have started to listen. In the next chapter we will look at a number of businesses and organisations which have also started to listen.

Part III

The Dynamics of Business: From Economics to Holonomics

7. Applied Holonomics – From Biology to Business

Counterfeit Business Models

In this chapter we will be examining a number of businesses and organisations which we consider to be examples of holonomic thinking in practice. While sustainability is now becoming more firmly established in business and economic thinking, very few business leaders appear to have been able to make the leap over the point of liminality to true holonomic thinking, where systems are fully understood as authentic wholes.

The philosopher Martin Heidegger thought that a true understanding of the world did not amount to knowing facts about it, but knowing how to live in it.[1] What our case studies have in common is the deep connection not just to our ecological systems, but also to human systems – business, social, political, and educational systems. These can be thought of as 'worlds', which, when comprehended as a whole, lead to the development of authentic wholes. But before we examine these case studies, it is first worth examining counterfeit thinking so as to understand how an inability to see and think in authentic wholes can lead to misdirected thinking and evaluations of an organisation.

One example of this is Amazon. The book *Business Model Generation,* which is described by the authors, Alexander Osterwalder and Yves Pigneur, as 'a handbook for visionaries, game changers and challengers striving to defy outmoded business models and design tomorrow's enterprises', features Amazon heavily with two case studies, the first being their web services, and the second taking a more strategic look at how and why Amazon needed to diversify.[2] In contrast to Osterwalder and Pigneur's overview of Amazon's business models, a report on Amazon by the *Financial Times* focused on the human aspects of the business, stating that some workers walked between seven and fifteen miles every day at their new warehouse in Rugeley, Staffordshire. One manager said 'You're sort of like a robot, but in human form. It's human automation, if you like', and another reported that 'the feedback we're getting is it's like being in a slave camp'.[3]

Amazon have also launched another service called 'Mechanical Turk'. This allows anyone with a computer and internet access to carry out crowd-sourced jobs (which are described as 'HITs' – Human Intelligence Tasks). This sounds like a great new business model, but often the jobs are poorly paid, with workers signing an agreement which means that they are not covered by minimum-wage requirements. If employers reject work on any grounds, those doing the work have few options to complain and claim compensation for pay lost when they are not working.

So Amazon's business model, which on the surface seems to be cutting edge and next generation, in fact harks back to the beginning of the twentieth century and old fashioned Taylorism. This is not a paradigm shift from the industrial revolution; it is the industrial revolution, but with computer chips, security tags, and time and motion studies. If we consider the principles of scientific management proposed and developed by Frederick Taylor in the early twentieth century, we still see many organisations operating with the same philosophy, logic, hierarchy and power.[4] Why have these aspects of organisational life not changed, when we are aware that the world has changed and that we are now living in a very different reality from the one existing at the beginning of the last century?

This school of scientific management has greatly contributed to the construction of our mental models of production organisations today. Its philosophy was responsible for defining fundamental questions relating to production, such as productivity, efficiency, labour, and hierarchies based on knowledge and power. This form of production, born within the walls of the auto industry, the flagship of modern capitalism, ended up infecting all other industries, and even our model of functioning in other spheres of life. Its logic, grounded in scientific rationalism, where the whole was seen only as consisting of fragmented parts, increasingly forced us to turn away from seeing organisations as organic wholes.

For a long period, this way of seeing the organisation, seeking to optimise resources in the name of operational efficiency of each part, was able to respond to market demands and production. As the landscapes and ecosystems in which organisations were embedded began to change, this logic could no longer respond to, and meet the needs of, ever new management tools. The case studies which now follow show some organisations that are at the cutting-edge of innovation, sustainability, organisational change, education and production, and which are embracing a new organic logic, grounded in dynamic, non-linear holonomic thinking.

PUMA's Environmental Profit and Loss Accounts and the Balanced Scorecard

An article in *Nature,* written by thirteen economists and ecologists, reported on their project valuing the Earth's ecosystems in economic monetary terms.[5] Sixteen eco-services, including gas regulation, water regulation, water supply, soil formation, nutrient cycling and waste treatment, were modelled and valued at approximately $33 trillion per year. This figure compares with a global gross national product of approximately $18 trillion per year (although both figures are dwarfed by the derivatives market). The purpose of this study was to make the value of these services to humans more visible, with the aim of having them factored into policy decisions.

From a holonomic perspective, although these services are modelled in a systemic way, with the economists and ecologists noting how these functions and services are interdependent, they are still writing from a mechanistic perspective, which also includes the mindset of the industrial age, whereby humanity is at the top of a pyramid, the ecosystem of which is in service to people. In terms of the Jungian mandala, this type of analysis is driven purely from the thinking part of our minds, where there is no *feeling* in any way of being a holon within the ecosystem.

Although the ecosystems report was written with good intentions, the danger is that, as soon as a part of the biosphere is given an economic value, it becomes just another abstract economic entity on a spreadsheet; there is no intuitive feeling for the authentic wholeness, nor the complexity, of the living biosphere. The Earth's systems are not linear, and our impact on the biosphere means that systems can rapidly collapse into chaotic states. In that case, how do you place an economic value on the last 1,000 square miles of rainforest, for example?

PUMA SE is one of the world's leading sport lifestyle companies, which designs and develops footwear, clothing and accessories. Consolidated sales for the financial year 2012 were €3,270 million. PUMA became the first company to account for its use of natural resources by introducing new accounting procedures which enable it to place a value on the eco-services that it uses to produce its sports shoes and clothes. Jochen Zeitz, former chairman and CEO of PUMA, believes that this work is vital in shaping the future strategy of the company.[6] An Environmental Profit and Loss Account helps to identify negative environmental impacts, allowing a business to adapt rapidly and enabling it to align operations throughout the supply chain, working with people and nature, and not against them.

We certainly agree that PUMA should be applauded for their pioneering work. It is always interesting to examine what people understand by the word 'sustainability' and the related phrase 'sustainable development'. Is it only about maintaining current levels of consumption, or do we really need to look at whether or not the planet can actually withstand these current levels? These are difficult questions to ask of our business leaders, and we need to phrase them in a manner that is not aggressive, not confrontational, but in a way in which we can arrive at a joint understanding of just how much we need to transform, before we as human beings can say we are living on this planet in a truly sustainable manner.

It is interesting to compare the Environmental Profit and Loss Account with Robert Kaplan and David Norton's Balanced Scorecard methodology.[7] According to Bain & Company, the Balanced Scorecard methodology is the fifth most used management tool by business executives in the world.[8] It is not just a tool to increase stakeholder value in a business; its uses are far wider than that. The Balanced Scorecard links financial measures to operational measures, and translates organisational strategy into four classical perspectives: the financial perspective, the customer perspective, the internal perspective and the learning and growth perspective. As Robert Kaplan said, the Balanced Scorecard has shifted the focus of businesses from concentrating purely on shareholder value to understanding the need to include the community as well.[9]

David Norton has explained how there has been a shift in our economic models whereby 'the foundation of the world is now in intangible assets'.[10] The task that we face is to measure intangible assets; therefore, if we shift into a holonomic way of seeing, which is a higher level cognitive function than merely physical sensation (seeing physical objects), then we can start to make progress from mistakenly modelling counterfeit systems to being able to truly comprehend authentic systems. For David Norton, 'description is the ground level of the discipline'[11] and this very much echoes Henri Bortoft's exemplary work on the act of distinction and understanding the difference between *belonging* together and belonging *together* from a systems thinking perspective.

The Balanced Scorecard methodology links intangible assets, such as people's knowledge and competencies, to tangible results, that is, financial performance. There is often a pressure on managers and leaders to focus solely on results, but this can lead to a blind spot, that of time. In our Western paradigm a focus on the speed of growth has led us to lose sight of the time that nature requires to respond, transform, and grow. It is one of the great aspects of Balanced Scorecard that it refocuses our thinking back on time, showing that we need time to develop capacity, competencies and to improve processes, before we can improve the results. For example, the way in which Balanced Scorecard considers time in management systems – long, medium and short term – creates a fundamental link between operations and strategy. The short term is no longer seen as separate from the long term, but now acts in service to the long term.

The description of an organisation's strategy is contained within a model termed the 'strategic map', and as such it represents one of the most important ways in which an organisation develops shared vision and understanding across its divisions and departments.[12] Balanced Scorecard is not only used by businesses, but also by governments, as in Brazil, and many federal government departments and municipalities, such as the city of Porto Alegre, which is working with the methodology in their preparation for the World Cup in 2014. Another example is the city of Barcelona, which, following the Olympic Games in 1992, used the methodology to address many different strategic issues facing the population. This project became a huge success, helped by a visionary leadership. In a manner which echoes the philosophy of Kumar and Franses on process and pilgrimage, Kaplan observed that 'the very act of translating the strategy into a strategic map transforms people'.[13] People become more committed to the strategy and are better able to develop consensus, two key pillars of Balanced Scorecard. As our world becomes ever more networked, companies and organisations are co-creating their strategies with stakeholders, and this is now happening in many countries around the world such as South Korea, Singapore and Chile.

Balanced Scorecard can be seen as an entire management philosophy, but for those who do not have holonomic vision, many aspects can be easily missed when implementing it. While many businesses and organisations still aim just to maximise the performance of separate parts, such as teams, divisions, and profit centres, Balanced Scorecard allows a more nuanced relationship between the parts and the whole. The 'whole' in this context is articulated in the strategic map, representing the vision and the purpose of the organisation. Members of the organisation are encouraged not just to maximise their best locally, but to do what is best for the overall strategy, for now they can see the whole.

With this more systemic vision of the whole organisation, resources can be reallocated to any problematic aspect of the organisation which requires the most effort and attention. One of the key activities is the communication of the strategy to all members of the organisation, which can also include wider stakeholders. By bringing people into the process, you are creating meaning for them, and allowing them to understand the relationship between the parts and the whole. The whole is not imposed on them as a 'super-part' (counterfeit wholeness); activities enable people to better understand their own contributions. Engagement with people is not just through rational thinking, but through feeling, linking them emotionally with the strategy, thereby motivating them and helping them to develop their own performance.

Performance of the organisation is further enhanced by the strategic map, in that it encourages focus, allowing people to better understand what they can and cannot do. The values of the organisation become aligned with the way of doing things, the culture, such as the way of treating customers and suppliers. Balanced Scorecard is an open system, in that it encompasses all the issues facing an organisation, such as sustainability and community relationships. Every major issue which has an impact on the overall performance can be given the same level of importance as financial matters. For all of these reasons, Balanced Scorecard can contribute to fostering a collective sense of authentic wholeness in an organisation, when implemented by a conscious leadership from a wider holonomic perspective, with a strong sense of values and purpose.

Visa Inc.'s Chaordic Organisation

Visa Inc. is a fascinating organisation, and it is often cited as one of the archetypal case studies of a business model which has been explicitly designed from biological systems thinking. Their model provides much food for thought in terms of the success that can be achieved with this new way of thinking, but it also shows just how difficult it can be to implement a vision in its entirety.

The founder and first CEO of the Visa organisation was Dee Hock. In the 1960s, Hock was a vice president of a Seattle bank. In the mid-1960s, Bank of America had launched the first credit card, the BankAmericard, and soon faced competition from MasterCharge, formed from a partnership of five other American banks. But Bank of America's system quickly ran out of control, with even children, pets and convicted felons being issued with cards. Bank of America called a meeting with its licensee banks, of which Hock's bank was one, to look for solutions. When Hock suggested that they should look for a systematic solution, he was placed in charge.[14]

Hock's key insight was that the command-and-control organisational structures were no longer suitable to solve problems at the level of complexity that Bank of America was now facing. Just as scientists, notably Einstein, had been able to rethink fundamental concepts such as mass and energy, Hock stripped away all previous assumptions and began to redefine banks, money and credit cards. The design of Visa was based upon a single question: 'If there were no constraints whatever, if anything imaginable was possible, what would be the nature (not the structure) of an ideal organisation to create the world's premier device for the exchange of value?' After six months of discussions, Hock's team had arrived at the following principles for the future organisation:

- It must be equitably owned by all participants.
- Power and function must be distributive to the maximum degree.

⬇ Governance must be distributive.

⬇ It must be infinitely malleable yet extremely durable.

⬇ It must embrace diversity and change.[15]

When Visa was created in 1970, it was a non-stock and not-for-profit mutual corporation, owned by its 23,000 member organisations. These organisations were all owners, members, customers, both subjects and superiors of the Visa organisation. Although they competed with each other in the open marketplace, for Visa to work they all had to co-operate at a certain level as well, accepting cards from other members. However, within that framework, each member had the maximum amount of flexibility to decide how to implement its own Visa products, and this decentralisation was one of Visa's great strengths. In this way, the entire Visa system was able to evolve and self-organise.

In the early 1990s, Hock met Joel Getzendanner from the Santa Fe Institute, home to some of the world's most influential scientists working in the field of complexity and chaos theory. Hock had been studying the dynamic tension of far-from-equilibrium systems, which existed in their 'edge-of-chaos' states. He saw that this provided a strong metaphor for the Visa organisation, which itself created a dynamic tension between competition and co-operation among its members, resulting in the maximum amount of creativity and conditions for survival. Hock coined the word 'chaord' to describe this in-between phase, where order met chaos. He defined 'chaord' as:

1. Any self-organising, self-governing, adaptive, non-linear, complex organism, organisation, community or system, whether physical, biological, or social, the behaviour of which harmoniously combines characteristics of both chaos and order. 2. an entity whose behaviour exhibits observable patterns and probabilities not governed or explained by the rules that govern its constituent parts.[16]

Visa rapidly overtook MasterCard and became the world's leading credit card, which now serves approximately one-sixth of the world's population. In May 1985, Hock resigned from Visa, due to his belief that an organisation must not be driven by the ego of its leadership. 'Through the years, I have greatly feared and sought to keep at bay the four beasts that inevitably devour their keeper – Ego, Envy, Avarice, and Ambition.'[17] Hock kept a low profile after leaving Visa, but went on to promote the need to develop more chaordic organisations. This led him to champion the notion of chaordic leadership, a new type of leadership far removed from the top-down, controlling, authoritarian leadership still seen today, particularly in governments.

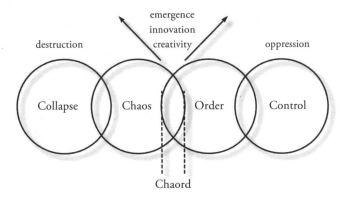

Figure 7.1. The chaord – the phase between chaos and order.

We can see the chaordic model in Figure 7.1. This image can serve as a mental model for managers who wish to nurture creativity and innovation in their organisations. In this model, some chaos is not seen as a bad thing, something to be managed out of existence. If this were to happen, the danger would be of the ordered organisation slipping into a controlling and authoritarian organisation, with no latitude for creative insights and new ideas to emerge freely. Likewise, with too much chaos, the organisation risks failure through collapse. Our businesses are not machines, they are living systems and therefore leaders have to continually search for a balance between pragmatism and perfection, a skill which requires flexibility, awareness, insight and discernment.

Kyocera's Amoeba Management System

Kyocera is a highly diverse global organisation, trading as a group of 229 companies, with around 71,600 employees, and generating an operating profit of $785 million from sales of $13,065 million (for the financial year ending March 2013).[18] The range of products that it manufactures includes ceramic components and products, semiconductor components, telecommunications, printing and imaging equipment, chemicals and optical equipment. It was founded in 1959 by Dr Kazuo Inamori, who, at the age of 27, established from the start a deep philosophical foundation for the company, the most essential part being articulated by the question: 'What is the right thing to do as a human being?' This stems from four basic principles: 'Don't be greedy', 'Do not cheat people', 'Do not lie' and 'Be honest'.[19]

Inamori developed Kyocera's 'Amoeba Management System' which was explicitly based on organisational principles found in cells, the building blocks of nature.[20] Amoebas are the profit centres, and these can expand, divide and disband as necessary. This creates a highly flexible structure, each cell being between three and one hundred members, who self-manage and self-coordinate their activities. Kyocera is dominated by a philosophical learning culture, where psychological rewards are emphasised above pure financial rewards. An important component of this learning can be seen in the daily routine of the amoeba teams, which have five daily operating procedures: Planning, Doing, Controlling, Acting and Checking.

It is not just a case, however, of subdividing a large organisation into small units. Creating amoebas depends on a deep understanding of the organisation as a whole, and for Inamori, there are three conditions which have to be met for an amoeba to form:

- ⇣ Amoebas must have clearly definable revenues and cost of sales in order that they can be fiscally self-supporting.
- ⇣ Amoebas must be self-contained business units.
- ⇣ Subdivision of the organisation must support the goals and objectives of the company as a whole.

Just like Visa, the management philosophy recognises that top-down management becomes inefficient in large organisations. Each team is responsible for creating their 'hourly efficiency reports'. While this may sound like a throwback to the days of Taylor's scientific management, they are not. These reports are created by each team, and through simple and transparent accounting procedures, they provide rapid feedback via morning meetings on how well each team is doing. This is what Kyocera calls 'Management by All', whereby all employees fully understand and fully participate in the business.

This is a holographic view of the employee; indeed, the corporate motto is holonomic: 'Respect the divine and love people'. It is extremely rare to find the word 'love' in any literature from such a large global corporation. Their motto is designed to inspire their vision: 'Preserve the spirit to work fairly and honourably, respect people, our work, our company and our global community'.

Gore Associates' Lattice Organisation and Genie Internet

W.L. Gore & Associates, Inc. is a privately-held company, founded in 1958. With annual revenues of $3.2 billion, Gore has 9,500 employees, called 'associates', located in thirty countries, with manufacturing facilities in the United States, Germany, United Kingdom, Japan and China. Although best known for their Gore-Tex® fabrics, Gore also operates in many other markets, including electronics, medical devices, and polymer processing.[21]

Gore is recognised globally as being one of the world's top organisations to work for. It believes that innovation is its core strength, and this is reflected in what it sees as its unique organisational structure. There are no job descriptions at Gore, no organisational charts, and no formal chains of command. Instead, Gore has what it terms a 'lattice organisation', based around a flat lattice network. In this structure, teams emerge naturally, based around perceived opportunities, and leaders also emerge naturally, based on their ability to attract followers, to get things done, and the reactions of their peers. 'We vote with our feet', says Rich Buckingham, a manufacturing leader in Gore's technical-fabrics group. 'If you call a meeting, and people show up, you're a leader.'[22]

This organisational structure means that those who work at Gore must demonstrate a high tolerance of ambiguity. In this structure, we can clearly see the principle of maximum creativity at the edge-of-chaos at work. Every individual is connected to everybody else, through direct communication. As a result, interpersonal communication is able to flow in all directions, not just up and down through a hierarchy. The network is kept as simple as possible, which inspires self-motivation as opposed to mandated performance targets, and it encourages spontaneous self-organisation.

Associates do not have bosses, but 'sponsors', who mentor them. Of course, not all associates wish to be leaders; some prefer to remain focused on their technical skills. Just as we saw with Kyocera, Gore also has a simple set of principles:

 ⬇ Try to be fair.
 ⬇ Use your freedom to grow.
 ⬇ Make your own commitments, and keep them.
 ⬇ Consult with other associates before any action that may hurt the reputation or financial stability of the company.[23]

The late founder, Bill Gore, believed that while people are motivated to join groups because they can accomplish more, the performance of a group peaks at around 150; and so, whenever a group reached between 150 and 200 people, he would break it up. He compared this maximum size to that of a tribe existing before the age of agriculture. In these tribes, everyone knew everyone else, but in larger groups the 'we' would become 'they', signalling the introduction of 'turf wars, the identification of enemies, and win-lose manoeuvres that eventually bring down even great companies'.[24]

Interestingly, this lattice structure does appear to be chaordic, in that there are some elements of hierarchical structures in place at Gore. This is due to the recognition by Gore that there are some limitations in this structure, and also difficulties, which he identified:

- ⇟ Stability and long-term constancy require a firm hand at the helm.
- ⇟ Decisions must be made. Complete consensus is never achieved.
- ⇟ There seems to be some upper limit for which the lattice is effective.
- ⇟ It's unrealistic for people to set their own salaries.[25]

While Gore's structure has evolved from the birth of the company, there is a danger in attempting to retro-fit or overlay new matrix organisational structures over the top of existing vertical structures. This type of strategy can often lead to increasing levels of complexity for employees, as decision-making, communications and accountability get mixed up and confused. One example of a successful response from a large and traditional blue-chip organisation comes from British Telecommunications, and the launch of Genie Internet, the world's first mobile internet portal in 1997.

Genie Internet, of which Simon was a co-founder, was created as a subsidiary of BT Cellnet (now O2), the mobile network division of BT. The original core team consisted of eight members from BT Cellnet, along with a small number of contractors who were responsible for the design and implementation of the platform, and the interconnection of the website with the cellular network. An early decision was made to install the Genie team in serviced offices in Richmond-upon-Thames, some distance from the head office in Slough, in order to allow the team to move rapidly without interference from existing business processes and corporate politics.

One decision which was not business-as-usual was to allow users from any UK network to subscribe to Genie, rather than making it exclusive to BT Cellnet customers. The agility that was afforded to the team allowed Genie to launch as a beta release (the first version of the service piloted with users but with bugs still requiring to be fixed) around two years before similar offerings from its competitors, leading to the development of an ecosystem consisting of a wide range of partnerships with content providers such as EMI, Virgin Records, Endemol, Channel 4 and MTV, systems providers such as Microsoft and UnwiredPlanet, and fixed internet service providers such as Freeserve.

BT Cellnet benefitted from offering services to customers on competing networks; a BT Cellnet Genie user on a monthly contract yielded 35% more ARPU (average revenue per user) than the average BT Cellnet base, with churn (the loss of customers to rival networks) on BT Cellnet overall reducing by 50%. So while existing businesses may not be able to move wholesale to the structures developed by Gore and Kyocera, it does make sense to contemplate new business models which involve elements of both competition and co-operation, as well as looking at which parts of the organisation can evolve to more agile and emergent structures which are better able to adapt to rapidly changing market conditions.

Toyota's Dynamic Way of Seeing

In Part One we outlined Toyota's production system, but now that we have covered complex systems in nature, we can examine their achievements in more detail. These are well worth studying, because Toyota has shown sales growth for forty years, while its US counterparts have stagnated; Toyota's profits exceed those of other car manufacturers; Toyota's recent market capitalisation exceeds those of Ford, General Motors and Chrysler combined, and Toyota is number one in global sales.[26]

According to Mike Rother, no other company in the world has managed to match Toyota in terms of its ability to systematically and effectively improve both on costs and quality.[27] The reason for this is that much of what Toyota does is invisible, in terms of management thinking and routines, with Toyota staff themselves often unable to explain or put into words exactly what it is that they do. This suggests that much of their thinking takes place not in the rational logical side of their thinking, but in a much deeper part of their intuitive minds.

It is not without reason that Mike Rother and John Shook named their book, which was the first to describe Toyota's mapping tools, *Learning to See* (1999).[28] However, despite the great success of this book, which enabled people to apply Toyota's methodologies, businesses still failed to fully replicate Toyota's success. It took Rother another ten years before he published his in-depth study, *Toyota Kata,* on Toyota's thinking, habits of behaviour and routines behind the methodologies – aspects that are very hard to see – explaining that it required many years of 'experiencing' in many settings and contexts, before he was fully able to make sense of it.

In order to understand Toyota's main insight, we have to go back to the 1920s, when they first visited Ford's production line, which had been developed to enable the mass production of a limited range of cars. Their business model was based on economies of scale. Any interruption to the production line to change over to producing different varieties of model would have introduced extra costs; so Ford achieved the economies of scale by limiting *variety*.

Toyota saw things differently. They wanted to introduce new methods, which would combine mass production with many varieties of models. This was seen in the west as a contradiction, which could not be resolved. Toyota understood that the fundamental secret to Ford's success was continuous flow, and because Toyota had limited resources, they would have to build their production lines in a single plant. Entering into a Goethean way of seeing allows us to understand that Toyota's way of production is much closer to an actual living system than those of Ford, General Motors and Chrysler. The latter were only thinking in terms of batched production, where a single model was manufactured as a part of a batch, after which the production line was switched over, ready to produce a new variety.

Toyota had a holonomic perspective, seeing the production plant whole, just as Goethe saw the whole, or archetypal plant in his intuition. Toyota understood continuous work flow in terms of every single part of the whole system, right down to the level of each work station. The whole was present in all of the parts. In this model, 'continuous work flow' meant that every step in the production process flowed at the same rate, including the rate at which finished units came off the production line.[29]

Toyota, therefore, did not focus on batches, but looked at every single aspect of every step in production to answer the question: 'How can we design each work step to progress the development of a single order?' After many decades, they began to perfect what is now known as the 'Toyota Production System'. Their system is one of maximum variety of models at minimum cost, because they only produce units which come from customer orders.

Like Kyocera's amoeba teams, Toyota nurture self-organising teams, who, more often than not, can solve any problems when they arise, thus avoiding disruptions to the 'pulse' of the operations, that is, the carefully timed pace of the production line. This seems to be very similar to the example of the human heart, whereby a small amount of chaos at one level results in a high degree of order at the higher level – the average heart rate.

Most traditional manufacturing processes require what Johnson and Bröms refer to as the 'information factory'. These are the systems, both physical and human, which are required for supervising, monitoring, controlling and reporting, and which result in expensive overheads. In contrast, Toyota have built a production system in which the information that directs operations is the work itself. The operations are not driven externally. This is how organic living systems operate. They do not have an overall command and control structure.

This is the most important lesson that Johnson and Bröms have taught us. To understand an authentic whole, and an authentic dynamic living system, we need more than just analytical thinking.

Every month, around fifty business executives from competitor car manufacturers visit Toyota's plants, free of charge, and no location is off-limits. Despite this unprecedented access, no other company has managed to imitate Toyota's system. The reason for this is that these visitors are stuck in their quantitative mindsets.

In business, the practice of management by results, using information from financial accounting systems to run a business, only really took off in the 1950s. This led to the situation in the 1970s whereby senior business executives were primarily from an accountancy background, believing that their MBA training in financial reporting was all that they would need to run a successful business. The trap, as Johnson sees it, is that management by results almost always has unfortunate and counterintuitive consequences, because it is neither systemic nor holonomic, and it is unable to recognise that it is the system itself which is the cause of these problems. By intervening to implement short term measures such as cost cutting, lowering prices and postponing investments in order to achieve financial results, the longer term systemic health of the system is weakened. This then results in even more drastic measures having to be implemented, which demoralise the workforce, customers and investors, and leads to even more instability.

The alternative to management by results is 'management by means', where the focus is on relationships. We noted in Chapter 4 W. Edwards Deming's observation that 97 per cent of the circumstances that affect a company's results are unmeasurable.[30] Managers today spend almost all of their time on that three per cent which can be measured. Toyota works in a qualitative way, focusing on relationships in their organisation at all levels, whereby each part reflects the whole in its entirety, with no part simply adding to the whole in a mere quantitative sense.[31] Toyota are able to intuitively comprehend the complex dynamic relationships where workers, machinery, parts and product all belong together harmoniously, and where, with a small amount of chaotic creativity, even the smallest teams are able to self-organise, and hence work in the most efficient and cost-productive manner, avoiding waste, just as nature does.

So, whereas the majority of businesses focus on short-term and bottom-line targets, seeing their organisations mechanistically, as a collection of parts, in which each part can be controlled and managed to achieve predictable outcomes, Toyota view 'results', as Thomas Johnson notes, as *'emerging* from a complex, non-linear process, in which people belong to, and patiently nurture, a web of relationships. Just as all of the components of natural living systems are interrelated, so it is in Toyota'.[32] The differences between mechanistic business thinking and holonomic business thinking can therefore be summarised as shown in Figure 7.2.[33]

Mechanistic Business Thinking	Holonomic Business Thinking
Low cost and variety cannot be achieved	Rich ends (variety) achieved via simple (low cost) means
Either/or thinking solved by problem solving	Problems dis-solve with changed thinking
Batched processes	Nature never produces the same model twice
Focus on quantitative results – Management by Results	Focus on quality of relationships – Management by Means
The organisation is a machine which can be optimised through the parts	The organisation is a network of relationships connecting people, customers, suppliers, the community and ecosystem
Focus is on the parts	Focus is on the whole, which comes to presence in the parts and is not a super-part (counterfeit whole)
Centralised top-down decision-making	Local decision-making
Profit is the goal of the organisation	Profit is a means, but not the purpose of the organisation

Figure 7.2. Differences between mechanistic business thinking and holonomic business thinking.

When we look at Toyota post the year 2000, we can see that for the first time in its history, they began to run into trouble. Between 2009 and 2012, Toyota had to recall approximately ten million faulty vehicles. In 2010, Toyota were fined $32.4 million by the US government for failing to swiftly recall millions of vehicles with faulty brakes and steering, and their profit for 2011 was half of that for 2010.[34] Johnson sees this as the result of their senior management team losing sight of the principles that first made Toyota great, and instead chasing profit targets. Instead of placing the root cause of the blame with Toyota, Johnson blames global financial institutions such as J.P. Morgan and Goldman Sachs, whose profits are not primarily made from helping businesses, but rather from their destructive trading activities, which they have learnt can be far more lucrative.[35]

In recent years, Toyota have had a cash balance of approximately $52 billion, which is seen by investment bankers as a great waste. Toyota have almost never sought loans for their business growth, a way of business that is anathema to the mental models of bankers, who cannot conceive of companies that never require loans or to issue stock. Toyota's mistake was to move from 'concrete' thinking (based in real-world, natural systems) to the 'virtual reality of financial abstractions, emulating almost every other big company in the last thirty years'.[36]

According to John Shook, a former Toyota engineer, Toyota had become 'addicted to chasing US profits'.[37] Shook also pointed out that there was a lot of 'non-Toyota thinking' when they opened their San Antonia US plant in November 2006, just before the global financial crisis hit. The biggest difference was that, whereas previously plants could manufacture many models, the San Antonia one was built to manufacture the Tundra, the largest pickup truck that Toyota had ever built. In 2009, in front of 400 Toyota executives, Toyota's honorary chairman, Shoichiro Toyoda, confronted the failures of the current management team. His grandson, Akio Toyoda, was appointed president in January that year, with the remit of refocusing Toyota on affordable quality, and returning Toyota to the fundamentals of its philosophy, which had served them so well for the first forty years of their life.

DPaschoal's Authentic Business Ecosystem

At the end of 2012, we (the authors) had the opportunity to record an exclusive interview with Luís Norberto Pascoal, President of DPaschoal, who shared with us his thoughts on his philosophy of business, long term sustainability and the social role of leaders. Group DPaschoal consists of six companies, the primary business focusing on automotive repair, with over 200 centres in Brazil. With a corporate motto 'We are not going to spend against the future', they have as their focus: innovation, sustainable financial performance and social responsibility. These stem from the group's philosophy which aims to benefit not only customers, but all stakeholders, especially the wider society. Luís Norberto's father, Donato Paschoal, founded DPaschoal in 1949. The group can trace their heritage back to one hundred years ago, when Luís Norberto's grandparents set up a grocery store, which also had a petrol station on the same land. Tragedy struck the family when they died, still in their forties, within the space of twenty days of each other. The food and stock in the supermarket deteriorated, and it seemed that all would be lost. Without new money, the petrol station could not be operated.

It was Luís Norberto's father, now an orphan at the age of twenty, who took responsibility for the family, the youngest being aged eleven. Old people from a retirement home helped him to restart the company, with one of them who knew him well giving him the necessary seed money. This experience had a great impact on him and his fiancée; they recognised the value that older people could provide for the young, with their experience and the freedom to do what they wanted. Luís Norberto summarised his father's philosophy as: 'You can't be sure of the future unless you seed good things for the future'.

It was as far back as the 1970s, when the term 'sustainability' was not widely used, that DPaschoal began to become aware of their wider social role. 'There is no need to be afraid of thinking about your own success, as long as you do not forget the future – the future of everyone – and not just your business.' In the 1970s and 1980s, Luís Norberto began to have conversations with many different experts about what 'sustainability' actually meant. He now sees evolution as a process where importance is placed on allowing different visions to appear and be heard, with the aim of developing proactive and not shocking ideas. For him, fanaticism of any kind, including the advocating of sustainability at any price, does not contribute to the achievement of plausible long-term solutions for business. 'Change can only come around if there is a common ground between those interested in sustainability and those in business. It cannot be one group against the other. Revolutionaries are needed to start a new wave, but they are not sustainable in the long-term.'

DPaschoal operate in a market which has a highly negative impact on the environment. Luís Norberto is very direct when he says that 'tyres and shock absorbers are bad for the planet when you produce, bad for the planet when you transport, bad for the planet when you use, and bad for the planet when you recycle. The whole chain is bad for the future. We work only with pollutants. It is necessary to reduce the impact on the environment.' Many years ago, he had to decide whether or not to carry on with the business. In the end, he decided that if he did not continue the company, someone else would fill the gap and sell tyres, so why should he not do the best possible? As a result, DPaschoal have the philosophy of selling the customer a new tyre only when one is really required, and not trying to sell new tyres when the old tyres have plenty of life left in them.

The first step towards having a sustainable business is to really understand what 'sustainability' means. For Luís Norberto, sustainability has four components:

⬦ Economic sustainability (profitable and able to invest in the long term).

↓ Industrial sustainability (being systemically sustainable in relation to your partners and industrial ecosystem).

↓ Marketing sustainability (avoiding greenwash marketing[38] and being sure about your promises and guarantees).

↓ Ecological sustainability (do not destroy the future to protect the present, and do not destroy the present to protect the future).

Luís Norberto explains his thinking as follows: 'I see this whole idea as a coin which always has two sides; protect the future by making good decisions in the present, but also protect the present, making decisions that will be very valuable in the future. Do what you can and should, but without destroying the future. Don't destroy the next generation in order to have what you want to have. This is the best definition of sustainable thinking in a business. Try to recuperate the future by using new technologies and innovation.'

Luís Norberto talked to us about his great dilemma in 2006, when, as previously mentioned, he asked himself whether he should stop working in his industry or continue with polluting naturally while doing the best that he could. How could he attempt to understand the challenges, rather than escaping from them? This is a dilemma now common among people who have an awareness of sustainability, while living in a consumerist society, which is continually inciting them not to be sustainable. It is not just a dilemma; it is also a challenge to promote a transition from a polluting reality to a healthier life.

Accordingly, Luís Norberto established the following philosophy in his business: 'Do not sell to your customer more than they need'. With this ethos, he established the practice of recommending the replacement of parts only when strictly necessary. 'With this principle, the loyalty of its customers and the revenue of the business increases, but in a sustainable way, minimising the impact on nature of the business.'

At that time, between 2005 and 2006, DPaschoal were reaching a peak in terms of financial results, but even so their leadership agreed to implement the radical new strategy. Initially the cost to the group was extremely high. Revenues fell dramatically, as customers were no longer sold new products, regardless of the condition and remaining lifetime of their existing parts, such as tyres, batteries, brakes and shock absorbers. There was also the impact on the manufacturers of these parts and vendors, who initially were angry, but now praise DPaschoal's initiative.[39] The vision was one of developing a relationship with the customer in the long term, and current sales are almost back to their 2006 high, with the group's turnover in 2012 approximately US $1 billion. DPaschoal are a remarkable example of a Brazilian business with both an awareness and a leadership which is focused on sustainability in the broadest and deepest sense. DPaschoal show that it is possible to generate impressive financial results, but not at any cost:

> It is important to remember that by being in the world, and acting in it, man is inevitably destroying, or at least modifying it. Farming is a great example. By devastating an area with large varieties of plant species, by planting a monoculture, people are changing and destroying nature and its diversity. If we think of a population of seven billion people currently living on our planet, the need for power takes this problem to its extreme. However, if we are conscious of this fact, we can act in such as way as to minimise the amount we do destroy, and, moreover, also act to recover what was destroyed via new technology, innovation and other principles, looking for solutions to ensure the sustenance of life in its fullness.

The entire chain of production, distribution and recovery of tyres is of a polluting and harming nature. 'If I change tyres 10,000 km before they are really worn, I'll be contributing to this increase and acceleration of pollution', says Luís Norberto. DPaschoal are developing new technology to lengthen the lifetime of tyres. The philosophy is emphasised in the training of their employees, who are made aware that this attitude will be better for all, and that it can therefore positively influence customers. The big question for Luís Norberto is how DPaschoal can be sustainable in every conceivable dimension, while working in an industry which is highly polluting and harmful to nature. The essence of DPaschoal is to answer this question with real actions. In order for their solutions to be put in place, the group began to invest in education many years ago. Education is seen as a major tool to promote the expansion of consciousness.

Education is perceived as relevant not only to the employees, but also to society as a whole – to children, customers, distributors, and the entire value chain of partners with whom DPaschoal interacts. According to a survey carried out by the group, in Brazil there are 500,000 mechanics. The fundamental question is who is training these professionals, each and every year, on new technologies, and bringing a greater awareness of how to make better and more sustainable ways of working? Every day, thousands of new cars with new technologies, parts and systems roll off production lines; so, who is training these mechanics to be prepared for this new technology? Luís Norberto's answer is that 'no one is teaching these people once they have left high school or technical school'.

After buying a car, usually the owner takes it back to the authorised dealers only during the period of the warranty. After this period, to avoid having to pay substantial sums to an authorised dealership, the owner goes to an independent mechanic, who the owner trusts. However, who is to say that this mechanic is being updated frequently about which oils are best, which parts require replacements, what repairs are required, etcetera? What is the extent of the mechanic's awareness of the best and most appropriate work to be done?

DPaschoal began three training programmes thirty years ago. One programme was *Training for Basic Mechanics,* mainly for women, in order to ensure their independence and to increase their security, especially when in unsafe situations (a factor of significant importance in Brazil). The more unaware you are of problems with your car, the greater the possibility of further damage and contribution to air pollution. Over 3,000 courses have been run since launch, although there is now more of a balance between men and women who attend.

The second education programme teaches large fleets how to train their employees and drivers to save tyres and fuel. 'In a two day programme in a big fleet you can save 20 per cent of the tyres. So, for a big fleet which buys 1,000 tyres a year, they can save 200 tyres. Only ten basic elements such as braking, pressure, alignment, etcetera, can result in a saving of 20 per cent in costs.'

The third programme deals with retreading truck tyres. 'If you use a truck tyre and you recycle, you have (say) one life, another 100,000 kilometres. But we do retreading very technologically, so the same carcass will be retreaded three times, so a carcass will give 300,000 kilometres. We can now retread truck and bus tyres which gives them three lives. The waste is very little.'

Twenty years ago, DPaschoal started to help public schools via a foundation. More recently, Luís Norberto has played a leading role in founding a number of important movements for the promotion of high quality public education, such as Faça Parte (which translates as 'Join', or 'Be a Part'), a volunteer programme for the promotion of education, and Todos Pela Educação ('Education For All'), in which Maria had the honour to participate as a partner consultant. In these movements, the main focus is to improve public education in elementary schools. The aim is to create more proactive citizens, who have the ability to influence the decision-making of government, supporting and working to promote the development of state policies with long term visions. Luís Norberto is, rightly, proud of the great achievements of these programmes:

> The overall goal was to change the way Brazil thought
> about education. Twenty years ago only 20 per cent
> of girls used to go to school in Brazil, mainly in poor
> areas. Now it is 90 per cent. Girls are now getting a

better education, and in some situations, better degrees than boys. We supported the decision by the Federal Government to have universal education for all in 1996. Now we have more girls in schools than boys. It is an amazing change for twenty years.

In 2011, DPaschoal followed up these educational programmes with another important example of concrete action, a programme called 'Maxxi Training', which aims to consolidate knowledge and enhance the training of entrepreneurs, managers, clerks, mechanics, automotive service repairmen, and others involved in their business ecosystem. DPaschoal began by establishing themselves as a 'distributor of knowledge', starting in Fortaleza, the capital of the state of Ceará in northeastern Brazil, with a 'Knowledge Fair' lasting four days. DPaschoal, as creator and director of the fair, provided local instructors, who were mostly engineers and supply companies, with around twenty to thirty classes taking place at the same time. The participants were students, mechanics and professionals in the region of Fortaleza, from twenty to sixty years old, and they were able to decide which topics interested them and on which courses to enrol. Luís Norberto told us about the start of the rollout of the programme, when it was so new that no one knew what it was about, nor what to expect:

> The first days would often begin with a suspicion that the great objective was in fact selling a product and service, but after the first lessons which demonstrated the ultimate purpose of education and dissemination of knowledge, a magical shift of perception occurred, a recognition of the satisfaction of getting something of value from knowing a little more. From that moment, everyone started to invite friends, relatives, colleagues, employees and other people, creating a virtuous trend and self-organised dissemination of knowledge and constant improvement. By the fourth day, the number of participants had increased fivefold. The initial goal of students for one year was to train 1,000

mechanics. The year ended with a total of 10,000 trained mechanics.

The programme is designed systemically. In addition to providing training, it facilitates and fosters important relationships and exchanges between professionals, so that everyone wins, especially customers and society. It develops in students an awareness that it is necessary to continue studying and learning, that is, it develops an awareness of the importance of education. If a badly trained mechanic installs a part incorrectly and damages that part, there are costs relating both to the need for a new part and also to any damage to the customer's vehicle.

> The whole programme is free to participants, the result of a partnership network between DPaschoal and key suppliers and agents in the value chain. After this program, companies said they reduced by 50 per cent the cost of repairs due to misuse of parts and equipment and they were also able to reduce the use of customer guarantees. This was simply due to greater awareness and knowledge!

You can only develop an awareness of sustainability if there is education. Only educated people can understand the importance of sustainability and will work with long-term vision. And only then will sustainability be a genuine part of the business, for example in the control of inventory, better use of materials and lower disposal of waste generation. One of the best ways to explain sustainability is by 'generating as little waste as possible'.

DPaschoal engage their 4,000 employees by making them all shareholders, thereby having an active interest in the business. Having a sustainable business and sustainable leadership means seeing all aspects of the organisation as an authentic whole: relationships with customers and suppliers, the treatment of raw materials, scrap materials and waste, consideration of the whole value chain and product lifecycle, and all aspects relating to employees and stakeholders.

DPaschoal are a private company, but they do have external investors. We asked if it would be possible for a publicly listed company to follow the same strategy, one which could initially result in lower annual revenue. Luís Norberto replied that there was always a strategy to grow the revenue: 'We are a selfish company and not altruistic. But we always think about the long-term.' It could be possible for public companies, he says:

> ... provided one has conscious leadership, human values
> and a clear vision of the need to generate results today
> for secure investments, but without killing the future.
> Leadership changes the world. They have the ability to
> inspire and influence others. No reality can be changed
> without a leader who has a clear vision of the future and
> the results which need to be achieved.

For this to happen across an organisation, Luís Norberto provides us with the recipe: the leader must first be convinced of the need for change, and where he or she wants to go.

> You need to communicate to others, explaining your
> vision, hearing suggestions, presenting, educating,
> constantly learning and reflecting on what works and what
> does not. Also, you need to have clear metrics to measure
> the progress of activities, as well as being able to promote
> the alignment of people, in the short and long term.
> There are CEOs, such as Paul Polman of Unilever, who
> do not have to be pushed by activists. He has the power
> of communication and vision. Leaders who have a clear
> vision of the future and who are good for the company,
> good for the planet and good for the shareholder, these are
> the ones who will be able to change the world.

For Luís Norberto, 'only conscious leaders will be able to promote this change'. One possible way to promote a change in attitudes and build a more equitable future is by recognising that everyone has the right to be respected, to have their opinions and freedom of expression. To lead is to enable the profound wisdom of each person to emerge from within themselves.

Why are we talking so much about education in a chapter on business? Because only a redesign of education can promote more aware citizens and highly qualified professionals, able to innovate and to find prosperous solutions for organisations, businesses and society. Today, we are in a complicated moment, resulting in a major crisis for all organisations, whether public or private. The educational framework which supports professionals does not currently favour sustainable thinking, long-term vision and the need for human values.

DPaschoal have a true ecosystem, where all of the parts *belong* together, helping to sustain each other. This can only be achieved with a common purpose and a sense of human values that comprehend the need for cooperation as well as competition. DPaschoal are not a rigid entity, but rather a living organisation, with porous boundaries, and sitting in true relationship with suppliers, customers, employees, the wider community and the planet. Their ecosystem is not counterfeit, because the vision and mission are not merely window dressing; these beliefs are sincerely held and reflected in every aspect of the organisation. 'Not selling' is not a paradoxical state; it is a long term strategy, which develops loyal customers and assures the long term resilience and survival of the group.

8. Mindfulness and Consciousness in Business

A Case Study in Leadership

Throughout this book we have emphasised the close relationship between the act of seeing and holonomic thinking. While it often seems to many that our understanding of the world is obvious, through philosophical or meditative contemplation we come to realise just how different our 'worlds' in which we experience life can be. Science aims to remove any trace of human subjectivity in the quest for objective truth, but most of us do not live our lives as scientists. It is through genuine dialogue and not through rigorous scientific experimentation that solutions to the complexities, challenges and creative quests can be found.

Otto Scharmer and Karin Kaufer define dialogue as 'a conversation where you see yourself through the eyes of another – and in the context of the whole'.[1] They have developed a four stage model which can be applied to many different personal, organisational, societal and economic processes:

1. Habitual awareness
2. Ego-system awareness
3. Stakeholder awareness
4. Eco-system awareness

Without an adequately developed level of mindful awareness and consciousness, genuine dialogue will never be able to be truly nurtured, since we are caught in the traps of our own egos:

> The blind spot in the twentieth-century toolkit of economics and management can be summarised in a single word: consciousness ... Today's real economy is a set of highly interdependent eco-systems, but the consciousness of the players within them is fragmented into a set of ego-systems. Instead of encompassing the whole, the awareness of the players in the larger system is bounded by its smaller subparts. The gap between eco-system reality and ego-system consciousness may well be the most important leadership challenge today – in business, in government and in civil society. [2]

In late 2012, we had the opportunity to meet Sergio Chaia, former president of Nextel Brazil, who has developed a leadership style in an intelligent and mindful way to manage both his organisation and people.[3] Nextel Brazil is an operating subsidiary of NII Holdings Inc., which provides mobile communications solutions to customers in Brazil, Mexico, Chile, Argentina and Peru. In 2012, Nextel Brazil ranked 162nd in the '500 Largest Companies in Latin America' list by *America Economia*. The company also ranked 157th among 'Latin America's 500 Largest Companies' and 21st among 'Latin America's Top 50 Technology Companies' by *Latin Business Chronicle*.[4]

Sergio has twice won the title of 'Executive of Value' in the category of telecommunications, a competition run by the newspaper *Valor Econômico*. He was also voted 'Executive of the Year' in South America by International Business Awards in 2010 and the title of 'CEO Parceiro do RH' ('the CEO who is the biggest champion of Human Resources') by *Você S/A* in 2011. During the five years when he served as president of Nextel Brazil, subscriber numbers multiplied fivefold, and turnover increased by the same proportion. In Sergio's words: 'When I put people into the equation, the results became even more substantial'.

One of the main factors highlighted by Sergio, and which led him to re-evaluate his life's project, was the discovery of Buddhism, and in particular the meditation on death (the imagining of what his burial would be like). Following this discovery, he decided to pursue a less lonely and more happy direction in life, one which would be able to combine impressive results with a style of leadership that could place more focus on the participation of others. In his words: 'A company which has genuine concern for people is a company which is able to build something different in the world'. When referring to 'people', Sergio means not only staff, but also the entire ecosystem – employees, customers, suppliers, the community, and society as a whole. Here, we are considering a vision of leadership which views its role in a radically different perspective from that purely of power and hierarchy:

> He who cuts the tree is man, the tree does not cut
> itself. Those who pollute rivers are businesses, rivers do
> not pollute themselves alone. Those who create toxic
> environments, ashes and uninhabitable regions are
> humans and organisations. It is crucial first to think about
> sustainability in your own internal environment in order
> to then think better about your relationship to the external
> environment. Creating sustainable human relations is
> what will generate a sustainable economy and a sustainable
> world. It is interesting to note here that biologists and
> environmentalists constantly reinforce our need to change
> the perspective with which we talk about sustainability.
> The right way is not 'save the world' and yes, including
> the human species. It is more that we need to think of
> our lives in a sustainable way, and this means our internal
> personal environment, our outer life, our relationships
> with those who are similar to us and all that surrounds us.

Thinking practically as a company, this attitude translates into a sustainable internal transformation, because, after all, 'it all starts from the inside out' and only then is passed on to customers, creating the foundation for the organisation's sustainability. This image of the leader as a role model leads us to a wonderful episode involving the great Indian master, Mahatma Gandhi.[5] A desperate mother took her diabetic son to Gandhi and asked him to recommend her son to stop consuming sugar and sweets. She was absolutely sure that her son would listen to the advice of Gandhi, a distinguished and respected personality throughout the country. With much care and attention, the great master heard the mother's request and, after a long silence, asked her to bring her son back to him three months later. With little understanding and clearly astonished and disappointed, the mother and son left the room.

Three months went by, and the mother then returned to Gandhi, very curious about what would happen. After some time in deep silence, Gandhi addressed her son softly, but firmly, saying, 'You have to stop eating sugar, as it is not good for your health'. Having said that, Gandhi returned to his silence. The mother, even more confused than the previous time, decided to ask why Gandhi had waited so long to say these simple words. Gandhi then replied, 'Because three months ago I also ate sugar!'

Sergio defines leadership as 'having the ability to shine with others, and with other people transforming results, themselves, yourself and the world'. This is a philosophy of leadership which Sergio says he is striving to achieve. In order to continue to learn, grow and transform, it is important to participate actively. Sergio says that, during each evolutionary stage of consciousness, it is necessary to make a decision: whether to get out of the game, or to continue playing. For Sergio, the better decision is always to keep playing; to keep on knowing himself, improving himself as a leader and making a difference in the world. We can choose to be either a commentator or a player. Sergio definitely does not want to be a commentator, staying out. Sergio observes that 'the corporate world is rotten, people are utilitarians, everyone is sad and this world is becoming more political. People hide behind companies, there is a fight of egos, everything is very poor and very negative'. Just being in the game offers the possibility of transforming and being transformed. As the Indian educator, Sathya Sai Baba, taught:

> Life is a challenge, meet it.
>
> Life is Love, share it.
>
> Life is a dream, realise it.
>
> Life is a game, play it![6]

For Sergio, the ideal organisation does not exist, because everything is being transformed, and everything is always evolving, whether genetically or energetically. Everything pulsates in every moment and turn; and, as everything is changing, so the ideal is also changing. There is, therefore, no watertight concept of 'ideal' which is achieved and comes to a conclusion. Since the ideal has a mutant characteristic, the ideal organisation must also have the feature of constant mutation. This ideal organisation, ever changing and evolving, will be in harmony if we are aware of its role in the world, expressed by its purpose. The clearer the purpose, the greater the assertiveness in decision making, which, when aligned, will always bring about the best results. Choices which are not in alignment with their purpose are expensive and hurt the organisation in every way. The financial results are seen as an expression, a consequence of those choices. The company which has a clear purpose is a company which has a soul, and is, therefore, conscious of itself, of others, and of its place in history.

Competition and Collaboration

Competition is part of the *modus operandi* of human beings. As we have discussed, if we look at nature, we see competition and collaboration happening all the time. In a holonomic view of any system, we understand that it is not one *or* the other, but one *and* another. Competition itself is not, therefore, something negative or destructive; rather, it is a form of development, which emerges naturally from the human desire to do better and to achieve more. We often have a mistaken view of competition, associating the word and its meaning with rivalry, the survival of one over the other. Indeed, a competitive process may result in the failure of one of the participants, but, when seen from the perspective of the system, it is part of the whole evolutionary process.

With honest frankness, Sergio recounts a time in his career when, on the eve of his anticipated promotion to president, the promotion was denied, due to his lack of ability to work in teams. This had been diagnosed using the 360° tool (that is, the practice of collating feedback from an employee's immediate circle) which demonstrated that his peers had not recommended his promotion due to an individualistic attitude in relation to his desire for personal achievement. After reflecting greatly on this episode, Sergio came to a very interesting conclusion: 'In a system where each party competes with one another, the end result is the individual victory of one party at the expense of the "loser", a clash which fails to maximise the potential of many individuals'. In order for the organisation as a whole to get the best out of everybody, a good leader does not promote or encourage competition between people, but, rather, encourages a virtuous process of competition for each to do their best. This point of view considers collaboration as a way to achieve your individual best.

This brings us to the definition of 'teacher' and 'disciple' in Indian culture. Those who are considered to be good teachers are those who can bring out the best in their disciples, and who are able, due to their extensive experience and levels of consciousness, to enable their pupils to achieve their true potential, allowing the next generation to overtake the former, in a constant process of evolution and improvement. Drawing a parallel with organisations, a good leader in a privileged position from the top has the opportunity to view the long term, and to look where the organisation should go, while also knowing the potential of his or her subordinates and enabling them to flourish and progress. It is important to emphasise the crucial difference between a dichotomous vision of *'or'* with a holonomic view of *'and'*. It is possible for all parts to grow and thrive, enhancing and promoting one another. 'The real leader is one who takes people where they could not go alone.' In other words, developing the potential of each one on behalf of the whole means giving people access to education, knowledge, challenges, a sense of achievement and of being a part of something significant.

In addition to being inspiring, the leader must be able to see how the organisation as a whole is progressing, instigating a process of crafting and refining individuals, so that the organisation can thrive. This does not mean that everything will always be wonderful and painless. It is important to note that this process brings losses, pain, challenges and risks, in the name of creating something better. In the course of this work, the leader constantly comes up against a big hurdle, which is the ego. This ego causes us to be stuck inside ourselves, unable to really see that which is all around us, denying us the ability to truly recognise other people.

After he had adopted the Buddhist philosophy of life, Sergio met a lama, who told him to be 'less intelligent and more wise'. He was referring to 'intelligence' as the ability to think fast, analyse, interpret charts, and to 'wisdom' as the awareness of knowing how to choose the best thoughts, so as to create better feelings and, consequently, better actions. Wisdom is seen as a way of being, and intelligence as a tool in service. Intelligence is in the mind that governs you, while wisdom is your consciousness, your 'higher self', which is able to know what is most appropriate for each moment, regardless of personal desires or feelings of limitation. Because wisdom does not have an ego (a strong sense of individuality and separation), it brings a greater freedom of choice and discernment.

According to the Indian programme 'Education in Human Values'created by educator Sathya Sai Baba, the great aim of education is the development of character. At the heart of the programme are five human values which are instilled in all students. These are love, peace, righteousness, truth and non-violence.[7] This approach to education enables and equips people not only to perform technical tasks, but also to develop wisdom and discernment, in order to give the individual the ability to make better choices in their path in life, from the point of view of everyone and not just themselves.

There is a beautiful story of an African educator, Victor Kanu, who created a school in Zambia which implemented this programme of education in human values. Kanu graduated from Oxford University, and then had a brilliant diplomatic career in the UK. However, a moment came in his life when he received an internal call from his heart to return to Africa and to work in education. Following this call, Kanu founded one of the most innovative schools in the world. The Sathya Sai School of Ndola, Zambia, provides students with a comprehensive education via an academic curriculum which has, at its core, the teaching of human values, as developed in India.

There are three explicit and inter-related aims which are spiritual and moral excellence, academic excellence and environmental excellence. The school provides young people with the skills necessary for a wide range of functions in any organisation, and it also promotes leadership for a better world, one in which humanity is more equitable and harmonious. The school was given the nickname 'Sathya Sai Miracle School' because it received young boys and girls who had been rejected from other schools due to their inappropriate behaviour and learning difficulties and transformed them into exceptional students who achieved an astonishing pass rate at the nationally held exams at grades 7, 9 and 12. The way in which the principles of human values are put into practice is, indeed, a miracle, because 'what seemed impossible became possible'. As well as achieving national recognition, it has also won awards internationally, receiving a Gold Star Award in Paris in 2005 in recognition of outstanding commitment to quality, excellence, customer satisfaction and innovation.[8]

In one of his speeches, Kanu drew attention to an important question, which is little reflected upon nowadays.[9] He asked whether the world today was more harmonious, peaceful, prosperous, safe, better to live in, and happier? The answer from the audience was, unfortunately, negative. Kanu also asked the audience what additional ingredient of education was required to guide the actions and decisions of students towards leading the world to a better level? In his opinion, what was missing from formal education was the pillar of human values.

An education devoid of values results in the loss of the ability to see connections and the dynamic relationship between the parts and the whole. Introducing human values such as love, peace, righteousness, truth and non-violence into education develops exactly what Sergio has stressed – not just intelligence, but also wisdom. The Indian programme was created with the explicit intention of producing future leaders who would receive an education infused with these values. We can refer to this as a form of 'holonomic education', one which prepares the individual not only for financial independence, which enables a dignified life, but also for a life of better choices, greater happiness and harmony. If we do not have this on a personal level, we will never have it at the social level – of households, organisations and society.

Sergio emphasises that 'there is no way for the world to be sustainable or for businesses to be sustainable if people are not sustainable, because everything is interdependent'. This is reflected in the beautiful American Indian saying: 'World peace resides in each individual'. Everything is interconnected, and awareness of this interdependence is critical in the business world. One example is Nextel Institute, which promotes education for young people living insecurely in dangerous regions, preparing them not just for work, but also for life. These young people will be the leaders, consumers and workers who, tomorrow, will be choosing the direction that organisations like Nextel itself will follow.

Sustainability is the understanding of action and reaction, the understanding that our existence on Earth is an ecosystem, which consists of feedback loops, both positive and negative. In thinking about the interconnectedness of life, we can again look to American Indians and their definition of sustainability, which is to 'take decisions now, thinking of the consequences for the seventh generation of the future'. Indigenous people come to decisions from a dialogue in which different members of the tribe sit in a circle. There is a difference between *consensus* and *acceptance,* which is fundamental, and they will only close a dialogue after they have reached a decision which covers the long term, and which has the understanding and acceptance of all. This form of decision making represents consciousness and discernment in practice, a detachment of their ideas towards collective wisdom and joint decision-making which is fully discussed and justified.

Our discussion with Sergio explored the relationship between giving and receiving. We are only capable of receiving to the extent that we can give. We are only able to receive satisfaction from the world to the extent that we can give satisfaction to the world. It is like a wave, which spreads and creates a positive motion of action and reaction. This is the essential basis for a sustainable business. So how should we deal with other organisations and people who have very different mental models and other styles of leadership and beliefs? Citing his son, who currently studies in a Waldorf school, Sergio says: 'The most beautiful pot is the one which has different flowers'. Sergio points out that it is essential to reflect on 'difference', a factor which can facilitate creativity and the environment to do things differently.

If we want a world where everyone thinks like us, then, once again, we are being driven by ego, by a desire for control and domination, which ignores interconnections. We can only cope with the complexity of today's world if we hear different voices and understand different perspectives. It is through active dialogue, without attachment to a desired outcome, that we can develop a more complete picture of what we are analysing. An awareness of the value of 'difference' can teach us much, because we do not have all the answers and, from a different perspective, it can enhance our vision and evaluation of the same issue. In a more complex world, where information is available to everyone all the time, asking the right questions is far more important than ascertaining the right answers. We have to look at the world through other lenses that are wider and larger than our individual perceptions.

Is Being Happy an Impossible Dream?

As well as researching and applying the best leadership practices, Sergio studies happiness and the scientific understanding of what it is to be happy. After many years, Sergio has concluded that there is no individual happiness without connections with others, and without those others also being happy. In this instance, 'others' refers to other people, other societies and nature. It is almost impossible to imagine being happy when enclosed in a cave, completely isolated from the world.

Buddhist economics, unlike neoclassical western economics, defines work as the result of three things: firstly, the means by which it is possible to obtain the resources needed to have a decent life; secondly, an opportunity to shape the ego and become a better human being when dealing with other people and with situations which are far beyond our normal comfort zone; and thirdly, an opportunity to put into practice distinctive and unique personal talents for the benefit of others. In Buddhist economics, work is a way to be happy. In the state of flow, when you are fully exercising your talents, any limitations or restrictions around you simply no longer exist. At that moment, everything becomes relative, and money becomes a means (in its original sense), not an end in itself.

One of the great insights from Einstein was that everything is relative. Sometimes, when we are not living our true path, there is a danger that we can get too caught up in our sensations and experiences, and we live in absolute terms. So, for example, we become influenced a great deal by marketing, by the media, believing that we do not earn enough, that we do not have the right clothes, or that we are not displaying the latest brands. But when we are experiencing flow, to say that everything becomes relative means that, if today we do not have enough money, we know that we can change our reality and in some way we will be able to earn more, if not tomorrow or next week, perhaps next month or next year. Opportunities open up to us as we become more open and less set in our ways and fixed in our thinking.

Discussing his relationship with money, and reflecting on the role of money in our lives, Sergio makes an interesting point. The key to having a healthy relationship with money lies in being able to distinguish between 'owning' and 'enjoyment'. Using money for enjoyment is good. When you use it for the acquisition of possessions, it is bad. Sergio says: 'Today, what I want is to have increasingly less and to enjoy more and more'. In an apparent contradiction, 'the more you have the less you enjoy' in respect of the things that you have, including your own money. For example, if you have ninety bags and one hundred shoes, surely you are not enjoying; you are possessing ninety bags and one hundred shoes, which could be being enjoyed by others. In terms of this sense of ownership, you develop a negative relationship with money, a relationship of slavery and not fluidity. The creature comes to dominate the creator, and not the reverse. Just as it is with intelligence, it is the mind that commands, and not consciousness and wisdom. Actually using those things which we own (as opposed to simply buying things for the sake of acquisition) can bring a great sense of flow, like the feeling of happiness when we use our talents for the benefit of another. This is related to how money is used and is not about having more, or less. To flow is to prosper. We can summarise this by saying that it is not what you have, but what matters is the relationship that you have with your possessions. It is not money which is the problem, but your attachment to it.

One way to give greater meaning to our actions in life is through meditation, of which Sergio is an active proponent. Meditation, regardless of its form, allows contact with your essence, a deeper connection with yourself and an expansion of your awareness of being in the world. Joseph Campbell, the great mythologist and author of *The Hero With a Thousand Faces,* has discussed how much of the time our meditations rarely manage to scale the heights of spirituality, but in fact often remain at a base level, for example focusing on worries relating to money. He demonstrates this with an example of a change in consciousness he experienced which was brought about by walking off the street in New York and into St Patrick's Cathedral, observing that:

Everything around me speaks of spiritual mysteries ...
My consciousness has been brought up onto another
level altogether, and I am on a different platform ...
Certain prayers or meditations are designed to hold your
consciousness on that level instead of letting it drop down
here all the way. And then what you can finally do is to
recognise that this is simply a lower level of that higher
consciousness. The mystery that is expressed there is
operating in the field of your money, for example. All
money is congealed energy. I think that that's the clue to
how to transform your consciousness.'[10]

A great bifurcation point in our global consciousness occurred in
1969, when man landed on the Moon, ushering in a new era in
the history of humanity. For the first time since human beings
began to stand upright and started our evolutionary journey, we
found ourselves in an entirely different environment from our
natural, earthly habitat. When standing on the Moon, humanity
saw with new eyes an alien land which had previously been
mysterious and distant. The American astronaut, Neil Armstrong,
commander of Apollo 11 and the first man on the Moon,
articulated the momentous occasion beautifully, saying that it
represented 'one small step for man, one giant leap for mankind'.
He was absolutely right. The view of Earth from the Moon
allowed humanity to have a new perspective on our planet,
heralding a major expansion of consciousness; the beginning of a
profound new journey, learning about ourselves, others and the
environment in which we live.

In an interview with journalist Bill Moyers, Joseph Campbell
pointed out that the photo of Earth, taken by the astronauts
from Apollo 17 (Figure 8.1) revealed to us an image which was
both surprising and disconcerting.[11] Humanity could observe
itself living on a finite planet with well-defined contours, a small
proportion of land in comparison to the full extent of water, and
a thin and fragile white layer between the black of infinite space
and the Earth's surface. It also brought home the reality that in

Figure 8.1. The Earth seen from Apollo 17. NASA image.

fact there are no physical or natural borders, and that it is cultural and man-made artefacts which separate nations.

From the perspective of a human being standing on the Earth, that which had previously been believed to have been infinite, was now seen from this external perspective from space as finite. According to Campbell, this moment marked the start of a new mythology and a new stage of consciousness for humanity; it brought the opportunity for more integration between people, as a result of the new awareness of our co-dependence, together with a greater care and connection with nature, resulting from our realisation of the fragility and finite resources. In this sense, it represented a unique moment, a sacred redemption made possible by advancing technology. This moment also opened up a new stage in research and studies on the sustainability of the planet and life of man on Earth. From then on, the image of the absence of boundaries would awaken the need for communication without borders, a dream which would become reality with the advent of the internet and the development of networks with a limitless capacity for communication.

These times of greater awareness about ourselves and of the

world around us bring up another challenge, and an old question, which haunts humanity: whether the pursuit of happiness is the purpose of life? This question has been extensively examined in Bhutan, a small Buddhist kingdom located in the Himalayas, between China in the north and west, and India on the east and south. In 1970, Jigme Singye Wangchuck, the King of Bhutan, decided to implement an extremely innovative policy for their government. Understanding that the goal of his reign was to ensure the happiness of his people, he gathered a group of experts from different areas to develop an indicator of happiness. This indicator would measure the degree of happiness of the population, and thus highlight more precisely which actions and attitudes should be developed to ensure happiness. After many conversations, surveys, analyses and reflections, the group developed an indicator which is now also being developed in other countries. This indicator is based on the principle that the concept of prosperity goes far beyond economic growth, an idea which is little understood.

Indicators of happiness are designed go beyond gross domestic product (GDP), which is considered by many to be the central measure of the economic health of a country. Concentrating on economic output leads us to lose sight of other factors which play a central role in the happiness of a nation. Because the goal is to measure development, prosperity and economic growth, indicators of happiness also measure the level of living standards, education, psychological well-being, health, use of time, cultural diversity and resilience, good governance, community vitality, and ecological diversity and resilience.[12] These nine aspects are the basis for the well-being and happiness of people, and should therefore be measured and be closely observed. These are the foundations which are the basis for our lives being worthy and dignified, with healthier and more prosperous relationships.

Prosperity is exactly what every organisation seeks: to be sustainable, long-lived, and solid. Interestingly, the word 'prosperity' comes from the Latin word *prosperitas,* meaning the condition of someone enjoying 'good fortune', thus happy, wealthy and flourishing. In such a concept of prosperity which includes physical, mental, financial, environmental and social aspects of life, 'growth' has a different meaning; it should not be designated as the number one priority, because the other attributes are just as important. From the perspective of prosperity, we see organisations in another light. Healthy relationships are recognised as extremely important and a goal to be achieved, and progress can only be recognised if prosperity is guaranteed. With holonomic eyes, the lenses through which we evaluate success consider the system as a whole, without overlooking the constituent parts. In a thriving organisation, values are the fundamental foundation of relationships, with economic and financial results being a natural result and neither the primary focus, nor the only factor to be pursued.

What we wish to emphasise here is the fundamental question of 'meaning'. We move in the world and we become enchanted with our reality only if we find a meaning in everything we do. This enables us to progress and create. When we shift into a holonomic mode of consciousness, we are able to move upstream and experience the coming-into-being of life. In this mode of consciousness, a higher level of consciousness than mechanistic consciousness, meaning *is* being.[13] As Joseph Campbell has written in *The Power of Myth*:

> People say that what we're all seeking is a meaning for life. I don't think that's what we're really seeking. I think that what we're seeking is an experience of being alive, so that our life experiences on the purely physical plane will have resonances within our own innermost being and reality, so that we actually feel the rapture of being alive.[14]

Campbell has pointed to the fact that we humans seek elation and create a constant dialogue between the outside world of physical experiences and our inner world of spirit and meaning. This is the sense of being alive. Mythology has been providing this for us since humanity began the process of understanding the world and experiencing being alive. We are in a process which Campbell has termed the 'inner journey', a re-creation of a mythology, in which we reconnect with the world in order to continue our journey on Earth. We are in a classic moment of inflection, a transformation into something new. In the words of Campbell: 'The black moment is the moment when the real message of transformation is going to come. At the darkest moment comes the light'.[15] We are at this crucial point, which may represent a threat to everything we know, and yet may also be an opportunity to develop something new and more suitable for the path of personal and collective happiness.

Endnotes

Chapter 1

1. Figures for Q4 2011 show Apple's smartphone division generated $24.4 billion of revenue compared to the whole of Microsoft which generated $20.9 billion. See for example http://parislemon.com/post/16997124721/size-matters.
2. Heinrich Rudolf Hertz (1894) *Die Prinzipien Der Mechanik In Neuem Zusammenhange Dargestellt*. In the original German version, we find the term *holonome Systeme* which is translated nowadays as 'holonomic system'. In the 1899 English translation, *The Principles of Mechanics: Presented in a New Form*, we find the term translated as 'holonomous system' with the word 'holonomic' not yet appearing.
3. Herbert Simon (1962) 'The Architecture of Complexity', *Proceedings of the American Philosophical Society*, Vol. 106, No. 6, pp.467–482.
4. Arthur Koestler, *The Ghost in the Machine* (London: Pan Piper, 1970), p.64.
5. A 'holonic network' is fully described as 'a set of companies that acts integratedly and organically; it is constantly re-configured to manage each business opportunity a customer presents. Each company in the network provides a different process capability and is called a holon'. Patrick McHugh, Giorgio Merli & William Wheeler, *Beyond Business Process Reengineering: Towards the Holonic Enterprise*, (Chichester: Wiley, 1995), p.4.
6. *Ibid.* p.14.
7. IBM, *Capitalizing on Complexity*, May 2010, http://www-935.ibm.com/services/ us/ceo/ceostudy2010/index.html.
8. KPMG International, *Confronting Complexity: Research Findings and Insights*, May 2011, http://www.kpmg.com/ca/en/issuesandinsights/articlespublications/pages/confronting-complexity-research-findings-and-insights.aspx.
9. David Baccarini (1996) 'The concept of project complexity – a review',

International Journal of Project Management, Vol. 14, No. 4, pp.201–204.

10. Dimitris Antoniadis, 'Managing Complexity of Interactions in Projects: A Framework for Decision Making' in *Global Perspectives and the Strategic Agenda to 2025: The Task Force Report*, International Centre for Complex Project Management, September 2011, pp.105–122.

11. Dimitris N. Antoniadis (2009) *Managing Complexity in Project Teams*, (PhD Thesis), Loughborough University, UK.

12. Dimitris Antoniadis, 'Managing Complexity of Interactions in Projects: A Framework for Decision Making', in *Global Perspectives and the Strategic Agenda to 2025: The Task Force Report*, International Centre for Complex Project Management, September 2011, pp.105–122.

13. Venkat Ramaswamy & Francis Gouillart, *The Power of Co-Creation: Build It with Them to Boost Growth, Productivity, and Profits*, (New York: Free Press, 2010), pp.46–50.

14. Peter Senge, *The Fifth Discipline: The Art and Practice of the Learning Organization* (Second Edition), (London: Random House, 2006), p.68.

15. *Ibid.* p.8.

16. Victor Turner, *The Ritual Process: Structure and Anti-Structure (Foundations of Human Behavior)*, (Piscataway, NJ: AldineTransaction, 1995).

17. This section on the transition to holonomic thinking has, in part, been inspired by the teachings on holistic science and complexity by Philip Franses at Schumacher College. Complexity can be approached from three different perspectives: (i) Systems theory, where the 'whole remains as an isolated system; rearranged mechanisation with limited reference to context', (ii) Complexity, where the 'whole appears as long term order underlying the connective structure' and (iii) Fundamental, where 'whole meaning is beheld in the context of its transformational potential'. Holistic science 'explores the world to seek renewal through its innate wholeness' and therefore demands a re-conceptualisation of the concept of wholeness (Lectures in Transition Science, Philip Franses, Schumacher College, November 2009).

Chapter 2

1. C. Otto Scharmer, *Theory U: Leading from the Future as It Emerges*, (San Francisco: Berrett Koehler, 2009), p.283.

2. *Ibid.* p.61.

3. 'Atomic Education Urged by Einstein', *New York Times*, May 25th, 1946.

4. Watson, J.B. (1913) 'Psychology as the Behaviorist Views it', *Psychological Review*, 20, pp.158–177, quoted in Arthur Koestler, *The Ghost in the Machine* (London: Pan Piper, 1970), p.19.

5. Arthur Koestler (1970) *The Ghost in the Machine*, Pan Piper, p.36.

6. C. Otto Scharmer, *Theory U: Leading from the Future as It Emerges*, (San Francisco: Berrett Koehler, 2009), p.63.

7. Stephan Harding, *Animate Earth: Science, Intuition and Gaia*, (Totnes: Green Books, 2006), p.30.

8. Jacques Hadamard, *The Psychology of Invention in the Mathematical Field*, (Princeton: Princeton University Press, 1954), pp.147–148.

9. Peter Senge, *The Fifth Discipline: The Art and Practice of the Learning Organization* (Second Edition), (London: Random House, 2006), p.165.

10. Walter Isaacson, 'The Genius of Jobs', *New York Times*, October 29th, 2011.

11. Fritjof Capra, *The Web of Life: A New Synthesis of Mind and Matter*, (London: Flamingo, 1997), pp.5–6.

12. Henri Bortoft, *Taking Appearance Seriously: The Dynamic Way of Seeing in Goethe and European Thought*, (Edinburgh: Floris Books, 2012), p.33.

13. *Ibid.* p.82.

14. Plato, *Parmenides*, translated by Benjamin Jowett, (New York: C. Scribner's Sons, 1871).

15. Jan Smuts, *Holism and Evolution*, (London: The Macmillan Company, 1926), p.86.

16. Peder Anker, *Imperial Ecology: Environmental Order in the British Empire, 1895–1945*, (Cambridge, MA: Harvard University Press, 2002), p.178.

17. Iain McGilchrist, *The Master and his Emissary: The Divided Brain and the Making of the Modern World*, (New Haven: Yale University Press, 2010).

18. The RSA, *RSA Animate – The Divided Brain*, youtu.be/dFs9WO2B8uI.

19. Iain McGilchrist, *The Master and his Emissary: The Divided Brain and the Making of the Modern World*, (New Haven: Yale University Press, 2010), p.237.

20. Michael C. Jackson, *Systems Thinking: Creative Holism for Managers*, (Chichester: Wiley and Sons, 2003).

21. *Ibid.* preface xv.

22. Maurice Merleau-Ponty, *Phenomenology of Perception*, trans. Donald A. Landes, (Abingdon: Routledge, 2012).

23. C. Otto Scharmer, *Theory U: Leading from the Future as It Emerges*, (San Francisco: Berrett Koehler, 2009), p.22.

24. Henri Bortoft, *Goethe's Scientific Consciousness*, (Tunbridge Wells: The Institute for Cultural Research, 1986).

25. Henri Bortoft, *The Wholeness of Nature: Goethe's Way of Science*, (Edinburgh: Floris Books, 1996).

26. Henri Bortoft, *Taking Appearance Seriously: The Dynamic Way of Seeing in Goethe and European Thought*, (Edinburgh: Floris Books, 2012).

27. Ingrid Leman Stefanovic, *Safeguarding our Common Future: Rethinking Sustainable Development*, (Albany, NY: State University of New York Press, 2000).

28. See for example David Seamon, 'Seeing and Animating the City: A Phenomenological Ecology of Natural and Built Worlds', in *The Natural City: Re-envisioning the Built Environment*, eds. Ingrid Leman Stefanovic & Stephen Bede Scharper, (Toronto: University of Toronto Press, 2012).

29. Henri Bortoft, *Goethe's Scientific Consciousness*, (Tunbridge Wells: The Institute for Cultural Research, 1986), pp.29–34.

Chapter 3

1. Quoted in Arthur Zajonc, *Catching the Light: The Entwined History of Light and Mind,* (Oxford: Oxford University Press, 1995), p.1.

2. *Ibid.* p.6.

3. John Barnes, 'Participatory Science as the Basis for a Healing Culture', in Rudolf Steiner, *Nature's Open Secret: Introductions to Goethe's Scientific Writings,* (Herndon, VA: Anthroposophic Press, 2000), p.246.

4. Vicki Bruce, Patrick R. Green & Mark A. Georgeson, *Visual Perception: Physiology, Psychology and Ecology*, (Hove: Psychology Press, 2003), p.25.

5. *Ibid.* p.77.

6. Henri Bortoft, *Taking Appearance Seriously: The Dynamic Way of Seeing in Goethe and European Thought*, (Edinburgh: Floris Books, 2012).

7. Gene Weingarten, 'Pearls Before Breakfast', *Washington Post*, April 8th, 2007.

8. *Ibid.*

9. Ilya Prigogine & Isabelle Stengers, *Order Out of Chaos: Man's New Dialogue with Nature*, (Toronto: Bantam New Age Books, 1984), p.77.

10. Henri Bortoft, *Taking Appearance Seriously: The Dynamic Way of Seeing in Goethe and European Thought*, (Edinburgh: Floris Books, 2012), p.17.

11. Figure 3.2 is 'The Hidden Giraffe' (Henri Bortoft, *The Wholeness of Nature: Goethe's Way of Science,* Floris Books, 1996, p.50). For a discussion see *Ibid.* pp.50–57.

12. Henri Bortoft, Schumacher College lectures, October 2009.

13. Prescott, A.E. & Mitchelmore, M. (2005) 'Student misconceptions about projectile motion', in eds. P. Clarkson, A. Downton, D. Gronn, M. Horne, A. McDonough, R. Pierce & A. Roche, *Building Connections: Research, Theory and Practice*, Proceedings of the 28th annual conference of the Mathematics Education Research Group of Australasia,

Melbourne, MERGA, Sydney, 2005, pp.633–640.

14. For a more detailed account see Henri Bortoft (1996), Chapter 3, 'The Organizing Idea in Scientific Knowledge', pp.138–190.

15. Galileo, 'The Starry Messenger', in *Discoveries and Opinions of Galileo*, Galileo, trans. and ed. Stillman Drake, (Garden City, NY: Anchor, 1957), p.31.

16. M.L. Johnson Abercrombie, *The Anatomy of Judgement*, (London: Free Association Books, 1989).

17. *Ibid.* p.28.

18. *Ibid.* p.27.

19. *Ibid.* p.130.

20. *Ibid.* p.111.

21. *Ibid.* pp.111–12.

22. Jerome S. Bruner & Leo Postman (1949) 'On the Perception of Incongruity: A Paradigm', *Journal of Personality*, 18, pp.206–223.

23. Georg Maier, Ronald Brady, & Stephen Edelglass, *Being on Earth: Practice In Tending the Appearances*, (Saratoga Springs, NY: SENSRI, 2006), p.117.

24. M.L. Johnson Abercrombie, *The Anatomy of Judgement*, (London: Free Association Books, 1989), p.131.

25. *Ibid.* p.131.

26. *Ibid.* p.134.

Chapter 4

1. Goethe, *Dichtung und Wahrheit* (pt 2, bk 6) in *Samtliche Werke*, 16: 271. Quoted in Robert J. Richards, *The Romantic Conception of Life: Science and Philosophy in the Age of Goethe*, (University of Chicago Press, Chicago, 2002), p.334.

2. Arthur Zajonc, 'Goethe and the Science of his Time', in *Goethe's Way of Science: A Phenomenology of Nature*, eds. David Seamon and Arthur Zajonc, (Albany NY: State University of New York Press, 1998), p.21.

3. The full quote 'For philosophy in the proper sense I had no organ' comes from 'Influence of the New Philosophy', *Goethe's Botanical Writings*, trans. Bertha Muller, (Honolulu: University of Hawaii Press, 1952), p.228, cited by Arthur Zajonc, 'Goethe and the Science of his Time' in *Goethe's Way of Science: A Phenomenology of Nature*, eds. David Seamon & Arthur Zajonc (New York: State University of New York Press, 1998), p.18.

4. See for example Rudolf Steiner, *Nature's Open Secret: Introductions to Goethe's Scientific Writings*, trans. John Barnes & Mado Spiegler, (Herndon, VA: Anthroposophic Press, 2000).

5. Rudolf Steiner, *Nature's Open Secret: Introductions to Goethe's Scientific Writings*, trans.   John Barnes & Mado Spiegler, (Herndon, VA: Anthroposophic Press, 2000), p.54.

6. *Ibid.* p.66.

7. *Ibid.* p.17.

8. H. Thomas Johnson & Anders Bröms, *Profit Beyond Measure: Extraordinary Results through Attention to Work and People*, (New York: Free Press, 2000), p.69.

9. *Ibid.* p.191.

10. Mike Rother, *Toyota Kata: Managing People for Improvement, Adaptiveness and Superior Results*, (New York: McGraw-Hill Professional, 2009), p.5.

11. Henri Bortoft, *Taking Appearance Seriously: The Dynamic Way of Seeing in Goethe and European Thought*, (Edinburgh: Floris Books, 2012).

12. Oliver Sacks, *The Man Who Mistook His Wife For A Hat and Other Clinical Tales*, (London: Pan Books, 1986), p.89.

13. Iain McGilchrist, *The Master and his Emissary: The Divided Brain and the Making of the Modern World*, (New Haven: Yale University Press, 2009), p.133.

14. Oliver Sacks, *The Man Who Mistook his Wife for a Hat and Other Clinical Tales*, (London: Pan Books, 1986), p.99.

15. Johann Wolfgang von Goethe, *Theory of Colours*, (London: John Murray, 1840).

16. If you do not have access to a prism, a good on-line article with many photographs of the phenomena we discuss can be found in the article *The Tao of Colours* by Doug Marsh, http://southerncrossreview.org/74/tao-colors-1.html.

17. Dennis L. Sepper, *Goethe contra Newton: Polemics and the Project for a New Science of Color*, (Cambridge: Cambridge University Press, 1988), p.162.

18. Edwin H. Land (1959) 'Experiments in Color Vision', *Scientific American*, Vol. 200, No. 5, pp.84–99.

19. Dennis L. Sepper, *Goethe contra Newton: Polemics and the Project for a New Science of Color*, (Cambridge: Cambridge University Press, 1988), p.24.

20. William Thomson (1883) 'Electrical Units of Measurement', *Popular Lectures and Addresses*, Vol. 1, 3rd May.

21. David Hume, *A Treatise on Human Nature, Book One*, (Glasgow: Fontana/Collins, 1982), quoted in Henri Bortoft, *Goethe's Scientific Consciousness*, (Tunbridge Wells: The Institute for Cultural Research, 1986), p.62.

22. See the section 'The Necessary Connection' from Henri Bortoft, *Goethe's Scientific Consciousness*, (Tunbridge Wells: The Institute for Cultural Research, 1986), pp.59–65.

23. Gregory Bateson, *A Sacred Unity: Further Steps to an Ecology of Mind*, (New York: HarperCollins, 1991).

24. Henri Bortoft, *The Wholeness of Nature: Goethe's Way of Science*, (Edinburgh: Floris Books, 1996), p.158.

25. Johann Wolfgang von Goethe, *The Metamorphosis of Plants*, (Cambridge: MIT Press, 2009), paragraph 3.

26. See for example Günter Theißen and Heinz Saedler (2001) Floral quartets. *Nature*, Vol.409, pp.469–471, and Mark F. Riegner (in press) 'Ancestor of the new archetypal biology: Goethe's dynamic typology as a model for contemporary evolutionary developmental biology.' *Studies in History and Philosophy of Biological and Biomedical Sciences*, http://dx.doi.org/10.1016/j.shpsc.2013.05.019.

27. Henri Bortoft, *Taking Appearance Seriously: The Dynamic Way of Seeing in Goethe and European Thought*, (Edinburgh: Floris Books, 2012), p.86.

28. Craig Holdrege, *Thinking Like a Plant: A Living Science for Life*, (Great Barrington, MA: Lindisfarne Books, 2013). Holdrege uses the terms 'object thinking' and 'living thinking' whereas we have used the terms 'mechanistic thinking' and 'holonomic thinking'. 'Living thinking', as Holdrege says, invites us to imagine 'gaining such flexibility of thought that our ideas were no longer rigid, static, and object-like, but grew, transformed, and, when necessary, died away'. *Thinking Like a Plant* provides us with many exercises based on observing, drawing and imagining the living processes of plants, which, if practised, can help us 'hone our capacity to see dynamism, connectedness, and wholeness'.

29. Johann Wolfgang von Goethe, *Goethe's Works, Hamburg Edition, volume 13*, (Munich: Verlag C.H. Beck, 2002), translated by and quoted in Craig Holdrege, *Thinking Like a Plant: A Living Science for Life*, (Great Barrington, MA: Lindisfarne Books, 2013), p.3.

30. Johann Wolfgang von Goethe, *The Metamorphosis of Plants*, (Cambridge: MIT Press, 2009), paragraph 1.

31. Henri Bortoft, *The Wholeness of Nature: Goethe's Way of Science*, (Edinburgh: Floris Books, 1996), p.276.

32. For many visual examples of the ways in which the same plant grows in different contexts see Craig Holdrege (2013), *Thinking Like a Plant: A Living Science for Life*, (Great Barrington, MA: Lindisfarne Books, 2013), pp.100–115.

33. John Seymour, *The Countryside Explained*, (London: Faber and Faber, 1977), p.116, quoted in Henri Bortoft, *Taking Appearance Seriously: The Dynamic Way of Seeing in Goethe and European Thought*, (Edinburgh: Floris Books, 2012), pp.73–74.

34. Henri Bortoft, *Taking Appearance Seriously: The Dynamic Way of Seeing in Goethe and European Thought*, (Edinburgh: Floris Books, 2012), p.71.

35. Craig Holdrege, *Genetics and the Manipulation of Life: The Forgotten*

Factor of Context, (Hudson, NY: Lindisfarne Press, 1996), p.47.

36. Henri Bortoft (2012) uses this phrase a number of times. The source of the quote can be found in Idries Shah, *A Perfumed Scorpion*, (London: Octagon Press, 1978), p.25:

> Goethe was able to recognise that the idea of a spectrum of light was an error of judgement, arising from the fact that 'a complicated phenomenon should have been taken as a basis, and the simpler explained from the complex'. This error of judgement is a consequence of trying to understand the origin of the phenomenon in terms of the finished product. The Afghan poet and philosopher, Jalaluddin Rumi, described this approach in general as 'trying to reach the milk by way of the cheese'. (Henri Bortoft, 1986, pp.18–19).

37. Craig Holdrege, *Genetics and the Manipulation of Life: The Forgotten Factor of Context*, (Hudson, NY: Lindisfarne Press, 1996), p.48.

38. Ronald H. Brady, 'Form and Cause in Goethe's Morphology', in *Goethe and the Sciences: A Reappraisal*, eds. Frederick Amrine, Francis J. Zucker and Harvey Wheeler, (Dordrecht: D. Reidel, 1987), p.287.

39. Henri Bortoft, Schumacher College lectures, October 2009.

40. *Ibid.*

41. The quote from Emma Kidd comes from an introduction she wrote to her dissertation in an article published on the blog *Transition Consciousness* (www.transitionconsciousness.org). Her dissertation – Emma Kidd (2009) *Re-cognition: The re-cognition of our connection to Nature through Goethe's way of seeing*, Schumacher College, Totnes – can be downloaded here: http://wp.me/p11Bag-mX.

42. One of the teachers who taught Goethean science to Simon at Schumacher College was Margaret Colquhoun. For an in-depth description of how to learn to develop both observational skills and the dynamic way of seeing through the study of plants using a Goethean methodology see Margaret Colquhoun & Axel Ewald, *New Eyes for Plants: A Workbook for Observing and Drawing Plants*, (Stroud: Hawthorn Press, 1996).

43. For privacy, names of participants have been changed.

Chapter 5

1. Prime Minister's Press Conference at the European Council, January 31, 2012, www.fco.gov.uk.

2. Arie de Geus, *The Living Company: Growth, Learning and Longevity in Business*, (London: Nicholas Brealey, 1999), p.7.

3. Ellen de Rooij, 'A brief desk research study into the average life expec-

tancy of companies in a number of countries', Stratix Consulting Group, Amsterdam, August 1996.

4. H. Thomas Johnson & Anders Bröms, *Profit Beyond Measure: Extraordinary Results through Attention to Work and People,* (New York: Free Press, 2000), pp.62–68.

5. *Ibid.* pp.54–55.

6. *Ibid.* p.16.

7. Jeremy Naydler, *Goethe on Science: An Anthology of Goethe's Scientific Writings,* (Edinburgh: Floris Books, 1996), p.66.

8. Mark Riegner, 'Horns, Hooves, Spots and Stripes: Form and Pattern in Mammals' in *Goethe's Way of Science: A Phenomenology of Nature,* eds. David Seamon & Arthur Zajonc, (New York: State University of New York Press, 1998).

9. Edward Lorenz (1963) 'Deterministic Nonperiodic Flow,' *Journal of the Atmospheric Sciences,* Vol 20, March, pp.130–141.

10. The following example comes from Philip Franses, Schumacher College lectures on Transition Science, November 2009. We begin with three variables: x (the convective flow), y (the horizontal temperature distribution) and z (the vertical temperature distribution). The equations Lorenz developed can be simplified in the following manner:

$$x. = x + \mathrm{ad}(y - x)$$
$$y. = y + \mathrm{d}(bx - y - zx)$$
$$z. = z + \mathrm{d}(xy - cz)$$

The variables a, b, c and d are the starting conditions, and all remain constant while calculating changes in x, y and z. We can imagine Lorenz plugging in the following values to begin with ($a = 16.29$, $b = 11.426$, $c = 4.669$, $d = 0.058$) and running the equations iteratively. In running these equations on the computer Lorenz had access to, he made a minor mistake in one of the starting conditions, the difference being only one thousandth, i.e. $x=1.001$ instead of 1.000. As he ran his simulation, the system behaved in a very similar way in which it had run with the prior starting values, but as the simulation continued, he discovered that the final states of the two systems were radically different. This is the 'butterfly effect'; a tiny difference in the starting conditions of a system resulting in extremely different end conditions. If you are not used to these types of equations, then it may not be clear what is happening. The first equation has two different versions or values of x (x and $x.$). The first value of x 'x' represents the value of x at time 1, and '$x.$' the new value of x at time 2. The new value '$x.$' is affected by a, d, x and y. Note that the other two equations function in a similar manner. This is an example of feedback, where the value of one variable feeds back into itself. We can now imagine running these equations through 30,000 iterations. If we start with the initial conditions set to $x = 1$, $y = 0.1$, $z = 0.5$, the end result will be $x = -10.03$, $y = -11.33$, $z = 10.58$. But if we vary just x as we did before, so that the starting conditions are $x = 1.001$, $y = 0.1$, $z = 0.5$, the final conditions will be $x = 2.00$, y = 2.66, $z = 2.55$. If we imagine x to measure temperature, we find that in one simulation the value is -10, and in the other +2, a large and significant difference.

11. Tony Blair, Labour Party Conference Speech, 2nd October 2001.

12. Ilya Prigogine & Isabelle Stengers, *Order Out of Chaos: Man's New Dialogue with Nature,* (Toronto: Bantam New Age Books, 1984).

13. John Briggs & F. David Peat, *Turbulent Mirror: An Illustrated Guide to Chaos Theory and the Sciences of Wholeness,* (New York: Perennial Library, 1990), p.136.

14. Ilya Prigogine & Isabelle Stengers, *Order Out of Chaos: Man's New Dialogue with Nature,* (Toronto: Bantam New Age Books, 1984), p.9.

15. *Ibid.* p.12.

16. *Ibid.* pp.104–106.

17. *Ibid.* p.119.

18. *Ibid.* p.142.

19. Andy Aspaas & Levi Stanley (2000) 'The Belousov-Zhabotinski Reaction', http://ed.augie.edu/~awaspaas/inorg/bz.pdf.

20. Brian Goodwin, *How the Leopard Changed Its Spots,* (London: Phoenix, 1997), p.42–54.

21. Ilya Prigogine & Isabelle Stengers, *Order Out of Chaos: Man's New Dialogue with Nature,* (Toronto: Bantam New Age Books, 1984), p.148.

22. Philip Franses, Transition Science lectures, Schumacher College, November 2009.

23. Brian Goodwin, *How the Leopard Changed Its Spots,* (London: Phoenix, 1997), p.44.

24. 'John Bonner's Slime Mold Movies', Princeton University, youtu.be/bkVhLJLG7ug.

25. Brian Goodwin, *How the Leopard Changed Its Spots,* (London: Phoenix, 1997), p.48.

26. *Ibid.* p.49.

27. John Briggs & F. David Peat, *Turbulent Mirror: An Illustrated Guide to Chaos Theory and the Sciences of Wholeness,* (New York: Perennial Library, 1990), pp.53–57.

28. Ilya Prigogine & Isabelle Stengers, *Order Out of Chaos: Man's New Dialogue with Nature,* (Toronto: Bantam New Age Books, 1984), p.310.

29. *Ibid.* pp.160–170.

30. *Ibid.* p.165.

31. *Ibid.* p.299.

32. Henri Bortoft, Schumacher College lectures, October 2009.

33. Adrian Desmond & James Moore, *Darwin*, (London: Michael Joseph, 1991), pp.404–409.

34. Henri Bortoft, *Taking Appearance Seriously: The Dynamic Way of Seeing in Goethe and European Thought*, (Edinburgh: Floris Books, 2012), note 22, p194.

35. For an introduction to Brian's ground-breaking work see David Lambert, Chris Chetland & Craig Millar, *The Intuitive Way of Knowing: A Tribute to Brian Goodwin* (Edinburgh: Floris Books, 2013).

36. Brian Goodwin, *How the Leopard Changed Its Spots*, (London: Phoenix, 1997), p.3.

37. *Ibid.* p.34.

38. Brian Goodwin, *Nature's Due: Healing Our Fragmented Culture*, (Edinburgh: Floris Books, 2007), p.19.

39. Brian Goodwin, *How the Leopard Changed Its Spots*, (London: Phoenix, 1997), pp.56–57.

40. The information on this passage comes from two BBC documentaries by David Attenborough: 'Supersocieties' (episode 5) from the series 'Life in the Undergrowth' and 'Home Making' (episode 6) from the series 'The Trials of Life: A Natural History of Behaviour'.

41. Abigail Doan, 'Green Building in Zimbabwe Modelled After Termite Mounds' http://inhabitat.com/building-modelled-on-termites-eastgate-centre-in-zimbabwe.

42. See www.mickpearce.com/about.

43. Brian Goodwin, *How the Leopard Changed Its Spots*, (London: Phoenix, 1997), p.66.

44. Stuart Kauffman, *At Home in the Universe: The Search for the Laws of Self-Organization and Complexity*, (New York: Oxford University Press, 1995), p.22.

45. Richard Dawkins, *The Blind Watchmaker: Why the Evidence of Evolution Reveals a Universe without Design*, (New York: W. W. Norton & Company, 1986), p.43.

46. Brian Goodwin, *Nature's Due: Healing Our Fragmented Culture*, (Edinburgh: Floris Books, 2007), p.89.

47. *Ibid.* p.90.

48. Stuart Kauffman, *At Home in the Universe: The Search for the Laws of Self-Organization and Complexity*, (New York: Oxford University Press, 1995), p.44.

49. Roger Lewin, *Complexity: Life at the Edge of Chaos*, (Chicago: University of Chicago Press, 1999), p.53.

50. *Ibid.* pp.53–56.

51. Charles Darwin, *The Origin of Species*, (London: John Murray, 1859), p.489.

52. A partial food web for the Scotian Shelf in the Northwest Atlantic off

eastern Canada. Species enclosed in rectangles are also exploited by humans. This food web is incomplete because the feeding habits of all components have not been fully described. Further, all species – including some of the marine mammals – do not spend the entire year in the area. The image is reprinted with permission and comes from David M. Lavigne (2003), 'Marine Mammals and Fisheries: The Role of Science in the Culling Debate', pp.31–47 in: eds. Nick Gales, Mark Hindell & Roger Kirkwood, *Marine Mammals: Fisheries, Tourism and Management Issues,* Collingwood, VIC, Australia: CSIRO Publishing.

53. Peter Meisenheimer (1995) 'Seals, Cod, Ecology and Mythology', *IMMA Technical Briefing,* 95-01.
54. *Ibid.* p.9.
55. James Lovelock, *The Ages of Gaia: A Biography of Our Living Earth,* (Oxford: Oxford University Press, 2000), pp.34–61.
56. James Lovelock, *Gaia: A New Look at Life on Earth,* (Oxford: Oxford University Press, 2000), p.2.
57. Jules Cashford, 'Gaia: From Story of Origin to Universe Story' in Stephan Harding, *Grow Small, Think Beautiful: Ideas for a Sustainable World from Schumacher College,* (Edinburgh: Floris Books, 2011).
58. Stephan Harding, *Animate Earth: Gaia, Science and Intuition,* (Totnes: Green Books, 2006), p.65.
59. *Ibid.* p.66.
60. *Ibid.* p.66.
61. *Ibid.* p.83.
62. Henri Bortoft, Schumacher College lectures, October 2009.
63. Martin Heidegger, Identity and Difference, (New York: Harper Row, 1969). See also Henri Bortoft, *Taking Appearance Seriously: The Dynamic Way of Seeing in Goethe and European Thought,* (Edinburgh: Floris Books, 2012), p.10.
64. Johan Rockström *et. al.* (2009) 'A safe operating space for humanity', Nature, Vol. 461, 24, pp.472–75.
65. Johan Rockström (2010) 'Planetary Boundaries', *New Perspectives Quarterly,* Winter.

Chapter 6

1. See www.investopedia.com/terms/b/business-ecosystem.asp.
2. Lynn Margulis & Dorion Sagan, *What is Life?,* (Berkeley: University of California Press, 1995).
3. 'Lynn Margulis Obituary', *The Telegraph,* December 13, 2011.
4. Lynn Margulis & Dorion Sagan, *What is Life?,* (Berkeley: University of

California Press, 1995), p.9.

5. *Ibid.* p.14.

6. Humberto R. Maturana & Francisco, J. Varela, *Autopoiesis and Cognition: the Realization of the Living,* (Dordrecht: D. Reidel, 1980), pp.78–79.

7. Helen Pearson (2006) 'What is a Gene?' *Nature,* Vol. 441, pp.398–401.

8. *Ibid.*

9. Ruth Potts and Stephan Harding, *Walking through Deep Time along the Thames,* www.schumachercollege.org.uk/blog/walking-through-deep-time-along-the-thames-ruth-potts.

10. *Ibid.*

11. Michael C. Jackson, *Systems Thinking: Creative Holism for Managers,* (Chichester: Wiley and Sons, 2003), p.32.

12. Henri Bortoft, *The Wholeness of Nature: Goethe's Way of Science,* (Edinburgh: Floris Books, 1996), pp.13–16. In order to help us understand what he meant by 'active absence', Henri used the example of reading a sentence:

    We do not take the meaning of a sentence to be a word. The meaning of a sentence is no-word. But evidently this is not the same as nothing, for if it were we could never read! The whole becomes present within parts, but from the standpoint of the awareness which grasps the external parts, the whole is an absence. This absence, however, is not the same as nothing. Rather, it is an *active* absence inasmuch as we do not try to be aware of the whole, as if we could grasp it like a part, but instead let ourselves be open to be moved by the whole (Henri Bortoft, 1996, pp.14–15).

13. Michael C. Jackson, *Systems Thinking: Creative Holism for Managers,* (Chichester: Wiley and Sons, 2003), preface xv.

14. Toshiyuki Nakagaki, Hiroyasu Yamada & Ágota Tóth (2000) 'Maze-solving by an amoeboid organism', *Nature,* Vol. 407, p.470.

15. Danielle Demetriou, 'Intelligent slime able to navigate its way out of maze', *The Telegraph,* December 29, 2011.

16. Candace Pert, *Molecules of Emotion: Why You Feel the Way You Feel,* (New York: Touchstone, 1997).

17. Irun Cohen (2012) 'Biomarkers, Self-Antigens and the Immunological Homunculus', *Holistic Science Journal,* Vol. 1, Issue 4, pp.24–28.

18. Graham Jones (2012) 'Self and Other: Toward an Expanded View of the Immune System in Health and Disease', *Holistic Science Journal,* Vol. 1, Issue 4, pp.29–37.

19. Richard Karban & Kaori Shiojiri (2012) 'Self-recognition affects plant communication and defense', *Ecology Letters,* 12, pp.502–506.

20. Marco Iansiti & Roy Levien (2004) 'Creating Value in Your Business Ecosystem', *Harvard Business Review,* March 8th.

21. *Ibid.*

22. F. David Peat (2011) 'Chaos and Catastrophe: A New Optimism', *Holistic Science Journal*, Vol. 1, Issue 2, pp.12–14.
23. Satish Kumar, 'Nature Crunch', *Resurgence Magazine*, www.resurgence. org/magazine/article2691-nature-crunch.html.
24. Lynn Margulis & Dorion Sagan, *What is Life?*, (Berkeley: University of California Press, 1995), p.199.
25. See for example the article 'Process and Pilgrimage: walking with science – An overview of its aims, objectives and outcomes: 2009 to present day and beyond', www.earthlinksall.com/pp2012/aboutpp.htm and *Satish Kumar and Philip Franses: Process and Pilgrimage*, DartingtonTV, http://youtu.be/Ut0knb5vPK8.
26. Leopold, Aldo, *A Sand County Almanac*, (New York: Ballantine Books, 1949), p.138.
27. Satish Kumar, *Soil Soul Society: A New Trinity for Our Time*, (Lewes: Leaping Hare Press, 2013).
28. *Deep Ecology*, Resurgence video, http://youtu.be/R2gZ6FRhc3w.

Chapter 7

1. Mark Wrathall, *How to Read Heidegger*, (London: W.W. Norton, 2005), p.22.
2. Alexander Osterwalder & Yves Pigneur, *Business Model Generation*, (Hoboken NJ: Wiley, 2010).
3. Sarah O'Connor, 'Amazon Unpacked', *Financial Times*, February 8, 2013.
4. Frederick W. Taylor, *The Principles of Scientific Management*, (New York: Harper and Brothers, 1911).
5. Robert Costanza *et al.* (1997) 'The value of the world's ecosystem services and natural capital'. *Nature,* 387, pp.253–260.
6. Jochen Zeitz, 'The world has changed – business must change too', *The Guardian*, May 16, 2011.
7. Robert S. Kaplan & David P. Norton (1992) The Balanced Scorecard – Measures that Drive Performance. *Harvard Business Review*, January-February, pp.71–79.
8. Darrell Rigby & Barbara Bilodeau (2013) *Management Tools and Trends 2013*, Bain & Company.
9. Comments made at the Strategy Execution Summit, São Paulo, August 7, 2013.
10. *Ibid.*
11. *Ibid.*
12. Robert S. Kaplan and David P. Norton, *Strategy Maps: Converting Intangible Assets into Tangible Outcomes*, (Boston: Harvard Business

Review Press, 2004).

13. Comments made at the Strategy Execution Summit, São Paulo, August 7, 2013.

14. Dee Hock, *One From Many: VISA and the Rise of Chaordic Organization*, (San Francisco: Berrett-Koehler, 2005).

15. *Ibid.* p.110.

16. Dee Hock, *Birth of the Chaordic Age*, (San Francisco: Berrett-Koehler, 2000), p.30.

17. Mitchell Waldrop, 'The Trillion-Dollar Vision of Dee Hock', *Fast Company*, October 31, 1996.

18. Financial results accessed July 30, 2013, http://global.kyocera.com/ir/pdf/rt130425_e.pdf.

19. Management Philosophy, http://global.kyocera.com/philosophy.

20. See for example the various articles on the Amoeba Management System and the philosophy of Dr. Kazuo Inamori on Kyocera's website, www.kyocera.com.

21. See www.gore.com/en_xx/aboutus.

22. Gary Hamel, 'Break Free', *Fortune Magazine*, September 2007.

23. See www.gore.com/en_xx/aboutus/culture/index.html.

24. Jessica Lipnack & Jeffrey Stamps, *The TeamNet Factor: Bringing the Power of Boundary Crossing Into the Heart of Your Business,* (Hoboken, New Jersey: John Wiley & Sons, 1993), p.82.

25. *Ibid.* p.83.

26. H. Thomas Johnson & Anders Bröms, *Profit Beyond Measure: Extraordinary Results through Attention to Work and People*, (New York: Free Press, 2000), foreword ix.

27. Mike Rother, *Toyota Kata: Managing People for Improvement, Adaptiveness and Superior Results*, (New York: McGraw-Hill Professional, 2009), introduction xv.

28. Mike Rother, John Shook, Jim Womack & Dan Jones, *Learning to See: Value Stream Mapping to Add Value and Eliminate MUDA*, (Cambridge, MA: Lean Enterprise Institute, 1999).

29. H. Thomas Johnson & Anders Bröms, *Profit Beyond Measure: Extraordinary Results through Attention to Work and People*, (New York: Free Press, 2000), pp.16–17.

30. *Ibid.* p.69.

31. *Ibid.* p.73.

32. H. Thomas Johnson (2010) 'Toyota's Current Crisis: Focusing on Growth not Quality', *Systems Thinker*, Vol. 21, No. 1, pp.2–6.

33. This table is adapted from H. Thomas Johnson & Anders Bröms, *Profit Beyond Measure: Extraordinary Results through Attention to Work and People*, (New York: Free Press, 2000), box VI-1, pp.225–226, and is reproduced with permission. It summarises the difference

between Management by Results ('Mechanical Systems Thought') and Management by Means ('Natural Life-Systems Thought'). Johnson & Bröms use the term 'natural life-systems thought' for what we refer to as 'holonomic thinking'. Their term is similar to the concept of 'living thinking' of Craig Holdrege (see Chapter 4, Endnote 28).

34. Richard Wachman, 'Toyota recalls 700,000 vehicles in US amid safety fears', *The Guardian*, March 8, 2012.

35. H. Thomas Johnson (2010). 'Toyota's Current Crisis: Focusing on Growth not Quality', *Systems Thinker*, Vol. 21, No. 1, pp.2–6.

36. *Ibid.*

37. John Lippert, Alan Ohnsman & Kae Inoue, 'Toyoda Asks How Many Times Toyota Errs Emulating GM Failures', *Bloomberg*, June 21, 2009.

38. The term 'greenwash' is defined as a form of whitewashing relating to the area of sustainability, and refers to the practice of companies marketing products and services as environmentally friendly which they know are not.

39. 'DPaschoal entra em nova fase', *Prosperare*, February 17, 2011, http://prosperarebrasil.com.br/ blog/?p=454.

Chapter 8

1. Otto Scharmer & Katrin Kaufer, *Leading from the Emerging Future: From Ego-System to Eco-System Economies*, (San Francisco: Berrett-Koehler Publishers, 2013), p.177.

2. *Ibid.* pp.67–68.

3. Sergio has written a book about his business philosophy: *Será Que É Possível?* (Is It Really Possible?), (São Paulo: Integrare, 2012).

4. See www.nextelinternacional.com/sergiochaia.html.

5. This well-known story appears in Craig Schindler & Gary Lapid, *The Great Turning: Personal Peace, Global Victory*, (Rochester, Vermont: Bear & Co., 1989), p.121, although there is no original source quoted for this story.

6. Bhagawan Sri Sathya Sai Baba, *Sai Avatar Volume II*, (Calcutta: C. J. Gandhi Welfare Trust, 1981) and quoted in Joy Thomas, *Life is a Game. Play It!* (Prasanthi Nilayam: Sri Sathya Sai Books, 1999).

7. Sathya Sai Baba, 'Sathya Sai Education in Human Values', from *Discourses Given By Bhagavan Sri Sathya Sai Baba*, (Prasanthi Nilayam: Sri Sathya Sai Books, 1989).

8. Victor Kanu, *Sathya Sai Baba: Short Autobiography of a Devotee*, (Prasanthi Nilayam: Sri Sathya Sai Sadhana Trust, 2011), pp.104–107 and p.150.

9. '1998 Jan. Victor Kanu speaks at the opening of the Sai School in

Newcastle, South Africa', Saicast, http://vimeo.com/56670393.

10. Joseph Campbell & Bill Moyers, *The Power of Myth*, (New York: Anchor, 2011), p.19.

11. *Ibid.* introduction xix.

12. Dasho Karma Ura, President of the Centre for Bhutan studies, 'The Economics of Happiness' lectures, Schumacher College, February 2010.

13. *Being* and *meaning* are explored from a phenomenological perspective by Martin Heidegger in *Being and Time*, (Albany: State University of New York Press, 2010). Philosopher Mark Wrathall articulates Heidegger's stance by saying that 'a true understanding of a world doesn't amount to knowing facts about it, but knowing how to live in it' (*How to Read Heidegger*, London: W.W. Norton, 2005, p.22). Physicist David Bohm also explored the relation of being and meaning in his essay 'Meaning and Information', in which he wrote that 'meaning is an inherent and essential part of our overall reality, and is not merely a purely abstract and ethereal quality having its existence only in the mind. Or to put it differently, in human life, meaning *is* being', (Paavo Pylkkänen, *The Search for Meaning: The New Spirit in Science and Philosophy*, Wellingborough: Crucible, 1989, p.51).

14. Joseph Campbell & Bill Moyers, *The Power of Myth*, (New York: Anchor, 2011), p.4.

15. *Ibid.* p.46.

List of Figures And Credits

Grateful acknowledgement is made for help with the design, drafting and permission to reproduce the following images and tables:

Figures 1.1, 1.2. Reproduced with permission from Dimitris Antoniadis.

Figure 1.3. Based on Jung's Mandala as envisaged by Stephan Harding (2006), *Animate Earth: Science, Intuition and Gaia,* Green Books, p.36.

Figure 1.3. Systems Models, Figure 5.2 in Michael Rogers & Stephen Morris, Experimental Nonlinear Physics Group, University of Toronto.

Figure 1.3. Business Models. Still from the video *Hyphae — growth process diagram in 2D,* Nervous System, n-e-r-v-o-u-s.com.

Figures 1.4, 1.5, 1.6, 1.7, 1.8, 2.1, 4.2, 5.7, 5.9 and 7.1. Based on originals by Simon Robinson and redrawn by Michael Pruett (www.black2colour.com).

Figure 3.1. From BenFrantzDale (Wikipedia Commons).

Figure 3.2. After Henri Bortoft (1996) *The Wholeness of Nature: Goethe's Way of Science,* Floris Books, p.50, reproduced with permission.

Figures 3.3 and 4.1. Drawn by Michael Pruett (www.black2colour.com).

Figure 3.4. This figure known as 'The Hidden Man' first published in Porter, P.B. (1954) *American Journal of Psychology,* vol. 67, p. 550. It was published in Humphrey, N.K. & Keeble, G.R. (1976) 'How monkeys acquire a new way of seeing', *Perception,* vol. 5, pp. 51–56. Reproduced here with permission from Pion Ltd, London (www.envplan.com).

Figure 4.11. From Fungus Guy (Wikipedia Commons).

Figure 5.1. From User D.328, Lorenz attractor, boxed ($[\rho]=28$, $[\sigma] = 10$, $[\beta] = 8/3$), ultrahigh resolution. Source: Wikipedia Commons.

Figure 5.2. Michael Rogers & Stephen Morris, Experimental Nonlinear Physics Group, University of Toronto. Reproduced with permission from Stephen Morris.

Figures 5.3, 5.4, 5.5. Images reproduced from original videos, reproduced with permission from Professor John Bonner.

Bibliography

Abercrombie, M.L. Johnson (1989) *The Anatomy of Judgement*, Free Association Books, London.

Amrine, Frederick, Zucker, Francis J. and Wheeler, Harvey (1987) *Goethe and the Sciences: A Reappraisal (Boston Studies in the Philosophy of Science)*, D. Reidel, Dordrecht.

Anker, Peder (2002) *Imperial Ecology: Environmental Order in the British Empire, 1895-1945*, Harvard University Press, Cambridge, MA.

Bateson, Gregory (1991) *A Sacred Unity: Further Steps to an Ecology of Mind*, HarperCollins, New York.

Bortoft, Henri (1986) *Goethe's Scientific Consciousness*, The Institute for Cultural Research, Tunbridge Wells.

—, (1996) *The Wholeness of Nature: Goethe's Way of Science*, Floris Books, Edinburgh.

—, (2012) *Taking Appearance Seriously: The Dynamic Way of Seeing in Goethe and European Thought*, Floris Books, Edinburgh.

Briggs, John & Peat, F. David (1990) *Turbulent Mirror: An Illustrated Guide to Chaos Theory and the Sciences of Wholeness*, Perennial Library, New York.

Bruce, Vicki, Green, Patrick R. & Georgeson, Mark A. (2003) *Visual Perception: Physiology, Psychology and Ecology*, Psychology Press, Hove.

Brzezinski, Zbigniew (1997) *The Grand Chessboard: American Primacy and Its Geostrategic Imperatives*, Basic Books, New York.

Campbell, Joseph (2008) *The Hero with a Thousand Faces*, New World Library, Novato, California.

—, & Moyers, Bill (1991) *The Power of Myth*, Anchor, New York.

Capra, Fritjof (1997) *The Web of Life: A New Synthesis of Mind and Matter*, Flamingo, London.

Chaia, Sergio (2012) *Será Que É Possível?*, Integrare, São Paulo.

Colquhoun, Margaret & Ewald, Axel (1996) *New Eyes for Plants: A Workbook for Observing and Drawing Plants*, Hawthorn Press, Stroud.

Darwin, Charles (1859) *The Origin of Species*, John Murray, London.

Dawkins, Richard (1986) *The Blind Watchmaker: Why the Evidence of Evolution Reveals a Universe without Design*, W. W. Norton & Company,

New York.

de Geus, Arie (1999) *The Living Company: Growth, Learning and Longevity in Business*, Nicholas Brealey, London.

Desmond, Adrian & Moore, James (1991) *Darwin*, Michael Joseph, London.

Galileo (1957) *Discoveries and Opinions of Galileo*, Anchor, Garden City NY.

Goethe, Johann Wolfgang von (1840) *Theory of Colours*, John Murray, London.

—, (2009) *The Metamorphosis of Plants*, MIT Press, Cambridge MA.

Goodwin, Brian (1997) *How the Leopard Changed Its Spots*, Phoenix, London.

—, (2007) *Nature's Due: Healing Our Fragmented Culture*, Floris Books, Edinburgh.

Hadamard, Jacques (1945) *The Psychology of Invention in the Mathematical Field*, Princeton University Press, Princeton NJ.

Harding, Stephan (2006) *Animate Earth: Science, Intuition and Gaia*, Green Books, Totnes.

—, (2011) *Grow Small, Think Beautiful: Ideas for a Sustainable World from Schumacher College*, Floris Books, Edinburgh.

Heidegger, Martin (1953) *Being and Time*, trans. Joan Stambaugh and Dennis J. Schmidt, State University of New York Press, Albany NY.

Hock, Dee (2000) *Birth of the Chaordic Age*, Berrett-Koehler, San Francisco.

—, (2005) *One From Many: VISA and the Rise of Chaordic Organization*, Berrett-Koehler, San Francisco.

Holdrege, Craig (1996) *Genetics and the Manipulation of Life: The Forgotten Factor of Context*, Lindisfarne Press, Hudson NY.

—, (2013) *Thinking Like a Plant: A Living Science for Life*, Floris Books, Edinburgh.

Jackson, Michael C. (2003) *Systems Thinking: Creative Holism for Managers*, Wiley and Sons, Chichester.

Johnson, H. Thomas & Bröms, Anders (2000) *Profit Beyond Measure: Extraordinary Results through Attention to Work and People*, Free Press, New York.

Kanu, Victor (2011) *Sathya Sai Baba: Short Autobiography of a Devotee*, Sri Sathya Sai Sadhana Trust, Prasanthi Nilayam.

Kaplan, Robert S. & Norton, David P. (2004) *Strategy Maps: Converting Intangible Assets into Tangible Outcomes*, Harvard Business Review Press, Boston.

Kauffman, Stuart (1995) *At Home in the Universe: The Search for the Laws of Self-Organization and Complexity*, Oxford University Press, New York.

Koestler, Arthur (1970) *The Ghost in the Machine*, Pan Piper, London.

Kumar, Satish (2013) *Soil Soul Society: A New Trinity for Our Time*, Leaping Hare Press, Lewes.

Lambert, David, Chetland, Chris & Millar, Craig (2013) *The Intuitive Way of Knowing: A Tribute to Brian Goodwin*, Floris Books, Edinburgh.

Leopold, Aldo (1949) *A Sand County Almanac*, Ballantine Books, New York.

Lewin, Roger (1999) *Complexity: Life at the Edge of Chaos*, Second Edition, University of Chicago Press, Chicago.

Lipnack, Jessica & Stamps, Jeffrey (1993) *The TeamNet Factor: Bringing the Power of Boundary Crossing Into the Heart of Your Business*, J. Wiley & Sons, Hoboken, NJ.

Lovelock, James (2000) *Gaia: A New Look at Life on Earth*, Oxford University Press, Oxford.

—, (2000) *The Ages of Gaia: A Biography of Our Living Earth*, Oxford University Press, Oxford.

Maier, Georg, Brady, Ronald & Edelglass, Stephen (2006) *Being on Earth: Practice In Tending the Appearances*, SENSRI, Saratoga Springs, NY.

Margulis, Lynn & Sagan, Dorion (1995) *What is Life?*, University of California Press, Berkeley.

Maturana, Humberto R. & Varela, Francisco J. (1980) *Autopoiesis and Cognition: the Realization of the Living*, D. Reidel, Dordrecht.

McGilchrist, Iain (2010) *The Master and his Emissary: The Divided Brain and the Making of the Modern World*, Yale University Press, New Haven.

McHugh, Patrick, Merli, Giorgio & Wheeler, William (1995) *Beyond Business Process Reengineering: Towards the Holonic Enterprise*, J. Wiley & Sons, Chichester.

Merleau-Ponty, Maurice (2012) *Phenomenology of Perception*, trans. Donald A. Landes, Routledge, Abingdon.

Naydler, Jeremy (1996) *Goethe on Science: An Anthology of Goethe's Scientific Writings*, Floris Books, Edinburgh.

Osterwalder, Alexander & Pigneur, Yves (2010) *Business Model Generation*, Wiley, Hoboken NJ.

Pert, Candace (1997) *Molecules of Emotion: Why You Feel the Way You Feel*, Touchstone, New York.

Prigogine, Ilya & Stengers, Isabelle (1984) *Order Out of Chaos: Man's New Dialogue with Nature*, Bantam New Age Books, Toronto.

Pylkkänen, Paavo (1989) *The Search for Meaning: The New Spirit in Science and Philosophy*, Crucible, Wellingborough.

Ramaswamy, Venkat & Gouillart, Francis (2010) *The Power of Co-Creation: Build It with Them to Boost Growth, Productivity, and Profits*, Free Press, New York.

Richards, Robert J. (2002) *The Romantic Conception of Life: Science and Philosophy in the Age of Goethe*, University Of Chicago Press, Chicago.

Rother, Mike (2009) *Toyota Kata: Managing People for Improvement, Adaptiveness and Superior Results*, McGraw-Hill Professional, New York.

—, and Shook, John, Womack, Jim & Jones, Dan (1999) *Learning to See: Value Stream Mapping to Add Value and Eliminate MUDA*, Lean Enterprise Institute, Cambridge MA.

Sacks, Oliver (1986) *The Man Who Mistook His Wife For A Hat And Other Clinical Tales*, Pan Books, London.

Sathya Sai Baba (1981) *Sai Avatar Volume II*, C. J. Gandhi Welfare Trust, Calcutta.

—, (1989) *Sathya Sai Education in Human Values Taken from Discourses Given By Bhagavan Sri Sathya Sai Baba*, Sri Sathya Sai Books, Prasanthi Nilayam.

Scharmer, C. Otto (2009) *Theory U: Leading from the Future as It Emerges*, Berrett Koehler, San Francisco.

—, & Kaufer, Katrin (2013) *Leading from the Emerging Future: From Ego-System to Eco-System Economies*, Berrett-Koeler, San Francisco.

Schindler, Craig & Lapid, Gary (1989) *The Great Turning: Personal Peace, Global Victory*, Bear and Co, Rochester, Vermont.

Seamon, David & Zajonc, Arthur (1998) *Goethe's Way of Science: A Phenomenology of Nature*, State University of New York Press, Albany NY.

Senge, Peter (2006) *The Fifth Discipline: The Art and Practice of the Learning Organization* (Second Edition), Random House, London.

—, Scharmer, C. Otto, Jaworkski, Joseph & Flowers, Betty Sue (2004) *Presence: Human Purpose and the Field of the Future*, Society for Organizational Learning, Cambridge, MA.

Sepper, Dennis L. (1988) *Goethe contra Newton: Polemics and the Project for a New Science of Color*, Cambridge University Press, Cambridge.

Seymour, John (1977) *The Countryside Explained*, Faber and Faber, London.

Smuts, Jan (1926) *Holism and Evolution*, The Macmillan Company, London.

Stefanovic, Ingrid Leman (2000) *Safeguarding our Common Future: Rethinking Sustainable Development*, State University of New York Press, Albany NY.

—, & Scharper, Stephen Bede (2012) *The Natural City: Re-envisioning the Built Environment*, University of Toronto Press, Toronto.

Steiner, Rudolf (2000) *Nature's Open Secret: Introductions to Goethe's Scientific Writings*, trans. John Barnes and Mado Spiegler, Anthroposophic Press, Herndon, VA.

Taylor, Frederick W. (1911) *The Principles of Scientific Management*, Harper and Brothers, New York.

Thomas, Joy (1999) *Life is a Game. Play It!*, Sri Sathya Sai Books, Prasanthi Nilayam.

Turner, Victor (1995) *The Ritual Process: Structure and Anti-Structure*, AldineTransaction, Piscataway, NJ.

Wrathall, Mark (2005) *How to Read Heidegger*, W.W. Norton, London.

Zajonc, Arthur (1995) *Catching the Light: The Entwined History of Light and Mind*, Oxford University Press, Oxford.

Index

You may also be interested in

The history of western metaphysics from Plato onwards is dominated by the dualism of being and appearance. What something really is (its true being) is believed to be hidden behind the 'mere appearances' through which it manifests. Twentieth-century European thinkers radically overturned this way of thinking. 'Appearance' began to be taken seriously, with the observer participating in the dynamic event of perception.

In this important book, Henri Bortoft guides us through this dynamic way of seeing, exploring issues including how we distinguish things, how we find meaning, and the relationship between thoughts and words.

Expanding the scope of his previous book, *The Wholeness of Nature*, Bortoft shows how Goethean insights combine with this dynamic way of seeing in continental philosophy, to offer an actively experienced 'life of meaning'.

This book will be of interest to anyone who wants to understand the contribution and wider implications of modern European thought in the world today.

 Also available as an ebook

florisbooks.co.uk